THE COMMON GOOD AND
CHRISTIAN ETHICS

The Common Good and Christian Ethics rethinks the ancient tradition of the common good in a way that addresses contemporary social divisions, both urban and global. David
Hollenbach draws on social analysis, moral philosophy, and
theological ethics to chart new directions in both urban life
and global society. He argues that the division between the
middle class and the poor in major cities and the challenges
of globalization require a new commitment to the common good. Both believers and secular people must move toward new forms of solidarity if they are to live good lives
together. Hollenbach proposes a positive vision of how a
reconstructed understanding of the common good can lead
to better lives for all today, both in cities and globally.

This interdisciplinary study makes both practical and
theoretical contributions to the developing shape of social,
cultural, and religious life today.

DAVID HOLLENBACH, S.J. is the Margaret O'Brien Flatley
Professor of Catholic Theology at Boston College, where
he teaches theological ethics and Christian social ethics. His
books include *Catholicism and Liberalism: Contributions to American
Public Philosophy*, edited with R. Bruce Douglass (Cambridge
University Press, 1994); *Justice, Peace, and Human Rights:
American Catholic Social Ethics in a Pluralistic World* (1988, 1990);
Nuclear Ethics: A Christian Moral Argument (1983); and *Claims in
Conflict: Retrieving and Renewing the Catholic Human Rights Tradition*
(1979). He has also written numerous chapters in books and
articles in journals such as *Theological Studies, Theology Today,
Human Rights Quarterly, The Annual of the Society of Christian Ethics,*
and *America*.

NEW STUDIES IN CHRISTIAN ETHICS 22

General Editor: Robin Gill
Editorial Board: Stephen R. L. Clark, Stanley Hauerwas, Robin W. Lovin

Christian ethics has increasingly assumed a central place within academic theology. At the same time the growing power and ambiguity of modern science and the rising dissatisfaction within the social sciences about claims to value-neutrality have prompted renewed interest in ethics within the secular academic world. There is, therefore, a need for studies in Christian ethics which, as well as being concerned with the relevance of Christian ethics to the present-day secular debate, are well informed about parallel discussions in recent philosophy, science or social science. *New Studies in Christian Ethics* aims to provide books that do this at the highest intellectual level and demonstrate that Christian ethics can make a distinctive contribution to this debate – either in moral substance or in terms of underlying moral justifications.

New Studies in Christian Ethics

Titles published in the series:

THE COMMON GOOD AND CHRISTIAN ETHICS

DAVID HOLLENBACH, S.J.

CAMBRIDGE
UNIVERSITY PRESS

CAMBRIDGE UNIVERSITY PRESS
Cambridge, New York, Melbourne, Madrid, Cape Town, Singapore, São Paulo

Cambridge University Press
The Edinburgh Building, Cambridge CB2 2RU, UK

Published in the United States of America by Cambridge University Press, New York

www.cambridge.org
Information on this title: www.cambridge.org/9780521802055

First published 2002
Reprinted 2003(twice)

A catalogue record for this publication is available from the British Library

ISBN-13 978-0-521-80205-5 hardback
ISBN-10 0-521-80205-9 hardback

ISBN-13 978-0-521-89451-7 paperback
ISBN-10 0-521-89451-4 paperback

Transferred to digital printing 2006

To the faculty, students, and staff of Hekima College,
who taught me much about the reality of solidarity
and the need for the global common good.

Opus justitiae pax.

Contents

General editor's preface

This book is the twenty-second in the series New Studies in Christian Ethics. It is written by the distinguished Jesuit theologian David Hollenbach on the theme of the common good that has been so central to recent Catholic social theology. More than that, Hollenbach himself has been a seminal influence upon the widely discussed social pronouncements of the American Catholic Bishops in recent years.

David Hollenbach shows that he is well aware of the difficulties that a notion of the common good faces in modern democratic societies. There is the long-standing fear engendered by the religious wars of the sixteenth and seventeenth centuries that still find parallels in tensions between Christians and Muslims in various parts of the world and specifically between Hindus and Muslims in India, between Catholics and Protestants in Northern Ireland, and between Jews and Muslims in Israel (I write this the day after the destruction of the World Trade Center). All too often in the past and in the present the "common" good has been imposed by one religious group upon another through coercion rather than mutually agreed through dialogue. There is also the self-evident cultural pluralism of modern democratic societies with sharp differences within and between religious and secular groups. It is hardly surprising that such societies tend to opt for a goal of tolerance rather than any shared common good.

However, David Hollenbach argues that tolerance on its own is simply not adequate to resolve all of the dilemmas of modern democratic societies. He cites at length two areas that particularly demonstrate this inadequacy. The first concerns the enduring poverty and inequality that characterize sizeable minorities

especially within American cities. The second relates to global issues, such as environmental degradation, which affect people across
class and ethnic groups both nationally and internationally. In both
of these areas Hollenbach argues that the notion of the common
good adds dimensions of mutual respect and interrelatedness that
are not present in a notion of tolerance.

A major section of this book then argues that churches have
an important role to play in contributing to the common good
even within pluralistic societies. David Hollenbach emphatically
does not believe that churches and their theologians should address their concerns only to fellow Christians. On the contrary, he
maintains that there is considerable empirical evidence suggesting
that churches have contributed positively to the common good in
a number of modern societies. He also believes that there are good
theological reasons for believing that such activity is a proper func-
tion of churches. In arguing for this position he is well aware that
he is seeking to counter currently popular exclusive theologians as
well as secular philosophers who consider theology to be irrelevant
to the public forum today.

There are many points of mutual concern between this important book and others within the series. Robert Gascoigne's *The
Public Forum and Christian Ethics* takes a very similar inclusive approach to public theology, from a Catholic position, as does David
Fergusson's *Community, Liberalism and Christian Ethics*, from a
Reformed position. Douglas Hicks's *Inequality and Christian Ethics*
explores at length the issue of urban inequality and Michael
Northcott's *The Environment and Christian Ethics* that of environmental degradation. Together they admirably fulfill the two key
aims of the series as a whole – namely to promote monographs in
Christian ethics which engage centrally with the present secular
moral debate at the highest possible intellectual level and, secondly,
to encourage contributors to demonstrate that Christian ethics can
make a distinctive contribution to this debate.

David Hollenbach's book is a very welcome and significant contribution to a crucial debate within Christian ethics today.

ROBIN GILL

Preface

The initial stimulus for this book came in the mid-1980s while I was working with the Catholic Bishops of the United States on the drafting of their pastoral letter on justice in the American economy. Both during the drafting of this document and after it had been published in its final form, I had the opportunity to speak often about the issues it discussed. These talks and papers were presented to church audiences, in secular academic settings, and in circles concerned with public policy. The experience of interaction with the audiences in all these settings led me to the conclusion that a central concept being advanced by the bishops' letter – the common good – was nearly incomprehensible to most of the people the bishops sought to address. This experience launched me into an extended period of reflection on what could be done to revitalize the notion of the common good in a way that could speak to both Christian believers and to citizens at large. Thus most of the ideas in this book arose from a cultural lack I experienced first-hand in trying to analyze and advocate an understanding of economic justice in pluralistic American society. Many of my preliminary efforts to clarify the issues were presented in writings listed in the Bibliography.

A second stimulus came from two academic terms spent teaching at Hekima College in Nairobi, Kenya, in 1996 and again in 2000. My students at Hekima College came from all over sub-Saharan Africa, east, west, and south. Some of them were from peoples who were at war with each other as we tried to work together in the same classroom. Some of them had themselves been refugees. Dialogue with them further deepened my conviction that developing an understanding of the common good that is plausible in a diverse society is one of the greatest intellectual needs of our time. The problems faced by my African friends made it luminously clear that any understanding of the common good that can be meaningful today will be one that challenges cultural, racial, ethnic, and national definitions of who counts as part of the community. Indeed, the many problems faced throughout Africa today make it essential that we move from the brute fact of the world's growing interdependence to a greater sense of moral interdependence and solidarity.

The book's approach to the idea of the common good is in part inductive. Part One presents some aspects of the current social and cultural situation that suggest we need to bring the idea of the common good back into contemporary discourse and make it usable again. The challenges of poverty in central cities and of growing but unequal global interdependence are not the only ones that suggest the need for a revitalized understanding and commitment to the common good. I hope, though, that they show that the project of this book is not guided by a wistful desire to restore the past. The inductive approach of the book, in other words, begins from currently urgent problems that cannot be successfully addressed within the social paradigm that shapes most cultural and political activity today. Part Two then proposes how the notion of the common good that prevailed long ago might be reconstructed in ways that can speak to the contemporary situation. This section is especially concerned with how religious communities, particularly Christianity, can contribute to the common good. The central philosophical and theological aspects of the overall argument are presented in this second part. These theoretical arguments are developed while continuing to pay attention to the social contexts they seek to address. Thus even the more theoretical parts of the book remain close to the ground on which social interaction unfolds today. Finally Part Three uses the theoretical framework to cast some practical light on the problems raised at the outset, namely, urban poverty and globalization. This is not strictly speaking an "application" of the theoretical framework of a reconstructed understanding of the common good to these problems. Rather, it seeks to illuminate both the practical issues and the theory itself by bringing them into interaction with each other. The outcome is an orientation or direction for the future, not a set of detailed prescriptions for decision-making and policy.

This book is dedicated to the many new friends I made at Hekima College. I also want to acknowledge that I have received much help from others along the way while working on it. Those who have contributed are too numerous to mention by name; the work of many of them appears in the bibliography. I want to single out my colleagues in the field of theological ethics here at Boston College, Lisa Sowle Cahill and Stephen Pope, and, at Weston Jesuit School of Theology, Edward Vacek, James Keenan and Thomas Massaro. Toni Ross, Kristin Heyer, and John Hardt have been very helpful in preparing the manuscript for publication. I also want to thank Margaret A. Farley, who has been continually supportive throughout this project as so often in the past, and my fellow members of the Jesuit Community at Boston College. All these people have helped me understand that there are goods that must be there for all of us if these goods are to be there for any of us.

Note on websites

The publisher has used its best endeavours to ensure that the URLs for external websites referred to in this book are correct and active at the time of going to press. However, the publisher has no responsibility for the websites and can make no guarantee that a site will remain live or that the content is or will remain appropriate.

PART I

Situations

CHAPTER ONE

The eclipse of the public

Over two millennia ago, Aristotle set the challenge this book will address. Aristotle's aim was to discern fitting goals for a good human life. At the beginning of the *Nicomachean Ethics* he argued that a human life can be judged good when it is shaped by a relatively consistent pursuit of ends that are themselves good. Thus much of Aristotle's moral reflection was devoted to determining the nature of the good that people should seek. On this basis he wanted to specify what lifestyles can be called genuinely good patterns of living. His entire understanding of morality was built upon this conviction that a good life is one devoted to the pursuit of good purposes or ends.

One of Aristotle's most significant conclusions was that a good life is oriented to goods shared with others – the common good of the larger society of which one is a part. The good life of a single person and the quality of the common life persons share with one another in society are linked. Thus the good of the individual and the common good are inseparable. In fact, the common good of the community should have primacy in setting direction for the lives of individuals, for it is a higher good than the particular goods of private persons. In Aristotle's words,

Even if the good is the same for the individual and the city, the good of the city clearly is the greater and more perfect thing to attain and to safeguard. The attainment of the good for one person alone is, to be sure, a source of satisfaction; yet to secure it for a nation and for cities is nobler and more divine.[1]

---

[1] Aristotle, *Nicomachean Ethics*, 1094b. This is an adaptation of Martin Ostwald's translation (Indianapolis: Bobbs-Merrill, 1962). The Greek *polis* is translated "state" by Ostwald, but "city" has been used here to avoid the impression that Aristotle is speaking of the good of

Aristotle wrote these words in a context of the Greek city-state (the *polis*), a social and political form quite different from the modern nation-state. So it is not immediately evident what the interdependence of the good of the individual and the common good would mean in the contemporary context. It is clear nonetheless that Aristotle envisioned the larger good realized in social relationships as superior to the good that can be achieved in the life of a single person considered apart from the community.

Indeed Aristotle spoke of the common good realized in community not only as nobler but as "more divine" than the good of persons considered one at a time. This religious dimension of the common good has been echoed throughout much of the later history of Christian reflection on morality, politics, and what is called spirituality today. For example, Thomas Aquinas's discussions of Christian morality often cited Aristotle on the primacy of the common good in the moral life. Aquinas's *Summa Contra Gentiles* reaffirmed Aristotle's statement that the good of the community is more "godlike" or "divine" than the good of an individual human being. Aquinas went on to identify the good to be sought by all persons in common with the very reality of God. St. Thomas wrote that "the supreme good, namely God, is the common good, since the good of all things depends on God."[2] Thus the good of each person is linked with the good shared with others in community, and the highest good common to the life of all is God's own self. For Thomas Aquinas, therefore, the pursuit of the common good carries out the Bible's double commandment to love God with all one's heart, mind, and soul, and to love one's neighbor as oneself.

This centrality of the common good in Christian life was echoed by Ignatius Loyola at the dawn of modernity in the sixteenth

the modern nation-state. Identification of the common good with the good of the modern nation-state can have totalitarian implications that any use of Aristotle today must avoid. Also "person" is used where Ostwald uses "man." Both of these departures from Ostwald's translation point to the difficult problems that must be addressed in making a normative argument for the viability of the notion of the common good today. These problems will be addressed throughout this book.

[2] Thomas Aquinas, *Summa contra Gentiles*, III, 17. Again, the translation has been adapted, using "God" rather than "Him," from that contained in *Basic Writings of Saint Thomas Aquinas*, ed. Anton C. Pegis, 2 vols. (New York: Random House, 1945), vol. II, p. 27. Adaptations in the interest of gender inclusiveness will be made as appropriate in citations throughout this book.

century. Ignatius harked back both to Aristotle and to Aquinas when he set forth the spirit that should govern the Jesuit order he was founding. He wrote that all the decisions of his followers should seek the broader, common good, rather than goals that were less comprehensive in scope. In the document that lays out his founding vision of the Jesuit order, Ignatius stated that "the glory of God" is the goal that should energize all of his followers' activities. But he immediately linked God's glory with the terrestrial reality of the common good. Indeed the *Formula of the Institute* of the Jesuit order came close to identifying the two ideas when it said that all of the order's activities should be directed "according to what will seem expedient to the glory of God and the common good."[3] This single phrase sums up much that is central to Ignatius Loyola's religious vision.

For the first Jesuits the pursuit of this vision of service to the common good included obviously religious ministries, such as the defense and propagation of Christian faith, preaching and other ministries of the Word of God, and the administration of the sacraments. But it also included tasks that might appear more secular, such as the education of youth and the illiterate, reconciling the estranged, and compassionate assistance to those in prisons or hospitals.[4] Such pursuits were mentioned by Ignatius simply as examples of ways toward the common good that he identified with manifestations of God's glory on earth. So for Ignatius the pursuit of this-worldly aspects of the common good was an eminent responsibility of Christians and closely linked with their vocation from God.

Ignatius Loyola's vision of the common good was extraordinarily expansive in scope. Indeed he saw it as *universal*, extending well beyond the city-state envisioned by Aristotle, the medieval kingdoms of Aquinas's understanding or the Renaissance republics closer to his own time. Ignatius saw the common good as the good of the

---

[3] This identification can be found in the apostolic letter of Pope Julius III, *Exposcit debitum* (July 21, 1550) that gave papal approval to the "formula of the Institute" of the Society of Jesus. It is contained in the contemporary normative documents of the Jesuit order, *The Constitutions of the Society of Jesus and Their Complementary Norms, A Complete English Translation of the Official Latin Texts* (Saint Louis: Institute of Jesuit Sources, 1996), 1. Formulas of the Institute of the Society of Jesus, Julius III, no. 1, p. 4.

[4] See John W. O'Malley, *The First Jesuits* (Cambridge, MA: Harvard University Press, 1993), pp. 5, 163–192.

whole of humanity, extending to the ends of the earth. The phrase "the more universal good" appears repeatedly in the *Constitutions* of the Jesuit order as the criterion for decisions in the service of God and the church.[5] This vision of the more universal common good made Ignatius's first followers among the first Westerners to travel beyond the boundaries of the Europe familiar to most previous Christian thinkers. It led them to encounters with the cultures of India, China, and the Americas that had been inaccessible and even unknown. In these missions they sought to bring both the gospel and European knowledge to these cultures. In their encounters with these societies they predictably manifested the same prejudices as their European contemporaries. But in some notable instances they rose above these biases with appreciation for the high achievements of these cultures, seeking to learn as well as to teach.[6] This was evident in their work of constructing the first grammars and dictionaries for Europeans of the newly encountered languages and in their often controversial adaptations of Christian doctrine and worship in light of indigenous religions. Thus echoing Aristotle but going well beyond him by stressing the scope of the common good, Ignatius wrote that "the more universal the good is, the more it is divine." Therefore Ignatius's followers were to choose ministries that gave preference "to persons and places which, once benefited themselves, are a cause of extending the good to many others."[7] At its best, this pursuit of the more universal common good was not simply envisioned as the one-directional transfer of the European vision of the good life to non-European societies. It was to be characterized by an exchange among understandings of what truly good lives could look like.

This brief historical sketch indicates that service to the common good was central to the normative vision of the good life through

[5] For example, in *Constitutions of the Society of Jesus*, nos. 618 and 623. See John W. O'Malley, "To Travel to any Part of the World: Jerónimo Nadal and the Jesuit Vocation," *Studies in the Spirituality of Jesuits* 16, no. 2 (1984).

[6] On the exchanges between the early Jesuits and non-European cultures, see Jonathan D. Spence, *The Memory Palace of Matteo Ricci* (New York: Viking, 1984); Andrew C. Ross, *A Vision Betrayed: The Jesuits in Japan and China, 1542–1742* (Maryknoll, NY: Orbis Books, 1994); John W. O'Malley, Gauvin A. Bailey, Steven Harris, T. Frank Kennedy, eds., *The Jesuits, Cultures, Sciences, and the Arts, 1540–1773* (Toronto: University of Toronto Press, 1999).

[7] *Constitutions of the Society of Jesus*, no. 622.

much of Western thought, from classical Greek moral philosophy, to medieval European Christian theology, to a form of early modern Christian spirituality in its initial encounter with the global realities that have become so central in contemporary consciousness. Oddly enough, however, one rarely finds a definition of the common good in these earlier sources, despite the fact that the concept was so central for them. We can, however, give a general description of what the term often meant to them by contrasting it with several terms that are currently in use.[8]

The common good for these earlier authors was clearly different from the largely economic and utilitarian concept of the general welfare. The notion of general welfare, as ordinarily understood today, sums up the economic welfare of the individual members of the society into one aggregate sum. The gross national product, for example, is frequently taken as an indicator of the general welfare in this way. As has often been noted, however, this kind of utilitarian standard pays little or no attention to how this overall sum is distributed among the members of the society. Indeed the GNP could be growing at a rapid pace while some members of society grow poor or fall into destitution. This general welfare thus need not be *common* to all the members of society. This aggregative good can increase while the well-being of some or many of a society's members declines.

The concept of the public interest is often used today as an alternative to this aggregative notion of general welfare. The idea of the public interest builds upon the modern commitment to the fundamental dignity and rights of all persons. Protection of these rights is thus seen as in everyone's interest. Public institutions and policies that will secure these rights for all persons are thus seen as helping realize the interests of everyone. Understood this way, the public interest is a disaggregative concept. It breaks down the public good into the effects it has upon the well-being or rights of

---

[8] I here rely in part on the helpful discussions of the meaning of the common good in Patrick Riordan, *A Politics of the Common Good* (Dublin: Institute of Public Administration, 1996), esp. chap. 10. See also Drew Christiansen, "The Common Good and the Politics of Self-Interest: A Catholic Contribution to the Practice of Citizenship," in Donald Gelpi, ed., *Beyond Individualism: Toward a Retrieval of Moral Discourse in America* (Notre Dame, IN: University of Notre Dame Press, 1989), pp. 54–86.

the individuals who make up society. Thus, it too lacks the richer understanding of the common that is implicit in many of the authors who shaped the premodern tradition of the common good.

The recently revitalized idea of "public goods" is perhaps the closest contemporary analogue to the idea of the common good in more classical sources. A public good can be described as a good that is present for all members of a relevant community if it is there for any of them. More technically, it is "non-rivalrous in consumption." This means that the enjoyment of this good by some people does not mean that it cannot be enjoyed by others. A beautiful sunset or a clean environment does not become unavailable to one person because it is being enjoyed by someone else. Second, a public good is "non-excludible." Its benefits cannot easily be confined to just some people by excluding others from these benefits. The clean air of a healthy environment, for example, is not like bottled oxygen that may be available to some but not others. If it is there for all, it is there for everyone; if it is present for anyone, it is present for all.[9]

The concept of public goods, however, lacks an important element present in earlier conceptions of the common good. These public goods are largely seen as extrinsic or external to the relationships that exist among those who form the community or society in question. This is easiest to see when the community is an intimate one like a family. The goods shared in a family include the house they live in and the income they share. In a family that is functioning well, these goods are non-rivalrous in consumption and non-excludible. But there is more to a good family or friendship than the sharing in such extrinsic goods. The relationships of concern or affection among siblings and friends go deeper than the sharing of such goods. These positive relationships are, in fact, preconditions for such sharing. There are analogies to relationships of this sort in less intimate societies like cities or states, where the relationships are better characterized by the presence or absence of mutual respect. The quality of such relationships among a society's members is itself part of the good that is, or is not,

---

[9] For a concise discussion of public goods, see Inge Kaul, Isabelle Grunberg, and Marc A. Stern, "Defining Global Public Goods," in Kaul, Grunberg, and Stern, eds., *Global Public Goods: International Cooperation in the 21st Century* (New York and Oxford: Oxford University Press, 1999), pp. 2–19.

achieved in it. One of the key elements in the common good of a community or society, therefore, is the good of being a community or society at all. This shared good is immanent within the relationships that bring this community or society into being. Aristotle, for example, understood the *polis* as an assembly of citizens engaged in debate about how they should live together. The relationships of reciprocal interaction among citizens brought this community into being and went beyond the general welfare achieved by their economic exchanges or the public good of the architecture of the forum where they conducted their debates. Similarly, for Thomas Aquinas the common good included the bonds of affection and even love that linked people together in communities. Throughout this book we will be seeking to clarify the relevance of the varied ideas of general welfare, public interest, public goods, and the common good immanent in mutual human relationships to some of the major issues we face in public life today.

THE HISTORICAL ROOTS OF THE ECLIPSE

Today, however, the idea of the common good is in trouble. John Rawls speaks for many observers in the West today when he says that the pluralism of the contemporary landscape makes it impossible to envision a social good on which all can agree. This is the intellectual and theoretical challenge to the common good today: diversity of visions of the good life makes it difficult or even impossible to attain a shared vision of the common good. Such a shared vision cannot survive as an intellectual goal if all ideas of the good are acknowledged to be partial, incomplete, and incompatible. This pluralism also makes it impossible to achieve a strong form of social unity in practice without repression or tyranny. This is the practical challenge: pursuit of a common good as envisioned by Aristotle, Aquinas, and Ignatius must be abandoned as a practical social objective incompatible with modern freedoms. Thus Rawls asserts that the Aristotelian, Thomistic, and Ignatian vision of the common good "is no longer a political possibility for those who accept the constraints of liberty and toleration of democratic institutions."[10]

[10] John Rawls, *Political Liberalism* (New York: Columbia University Press, 1993), p. 201.

Such conclusions are the direct descendants of social and intellectual developments that led to the normative vision that has come to prevail in the West today. The reigning philosophy gives priority to protecting space for private, autonomous choice. It is called liberalism because of its insistence that showing equal respect for all persons means protecting the liberty of individuals to determine their own form of life when they disagree about what form of life is a good one. In Ronald Dworkin's formulation, it is based on the conviction that equal treatment of citizens demands that "political decisions must be, so far as possible, independent of any particular conception of the good life."[11] Such a stand of neutrality toward ideas of the good life is a necessary element in treating people equally because different persons in fact hold divergent understandings of what counts as good. To favor one conception of the good over another is to favor some persons over others and to treat them unequally. Thus respect for the worth of individuals requires tolerance for the different visions of the good life they hold. In this way, affirming the equality of persons is linked with being non-judgmental about what ways of life are good, at least in public and political life. In public life, all encompassing understandings of the common good must be subordinated to the importance of tolerance.[12] A live-and-let-live ethos thus leads to what John Dewey once called an "eclipse of the public."[13] The good that can be achieved in the shared domain of public life is hidden from view as protection of individual, private well-being becomes the center of normative concern.

The sources of this eclipse of the common good by the reality of pluralism run deep in the modern social and intellectual history of the West. The conviction that pursuit of the common good must be subordinate to respect for equality rests in part on judgments that have been formed by major social and political currents in this history. These judgments are historical and contingent, not

---

[11] Ronald Dworkin, *A Matter of Principle* (Cambridge, MA: Harvard University Press, 1985), p. 191.
[12] See Michael J. Sandel, *Democracy's Discontent: America in Search of a Public Philosophy* (Cambridge, MA: Harvard University Press, 1996), p. 4, and Rawls, *Political Liberalism*, p. 157.
[13] John Dewey, *The Public and Its Problems* (Athens, OH: Swallow Press/Ohio University Press, 1994; orig: Henry Holt, 1927), chap. 4, "The Eclipse of the Public."

self-evident or necessary like the conclusions of mathematics and logic. So it will be useful to recall the historical basis for these judgments. This will set the stage for an inquiry into whether the conclusion that the common good remains in conflict with respect for equality remains valid under the social conditions prevailing today.

For Aristotle in ancient Greece, the common good was the goal of the whole of public life. He conceived of the human being as a social or political animal (*zoon politikon*) whose good is essentially bound up with the good of the *polis*.[14] Indeed he maintained that "a *polis* exists for the sake of a good life, and not for life only."[15] Individuals lead good lives when they make contributions to the good of the city-state. Aristotle, of course, developed his understanding of the shared good of the community in the context of the Greek *polis*, a political unit of quite limited size, and he knew that there were limits to the size of a city-state.[16] Further, the Athens of Aristotle's time was not a homogeneous and egalitarian community. It included significant numbers of resident aliens (metics) and slaves who were not entitled to participate in public life as citizens. Women too were excluded from public life. Such limits on extent and inclusiveness are prime reasons for the suspicion that the idea of the common good is irrelevant or dangerous in a large and diverse society that seeks to treat its members equally.

Nevertheless there are grounds for questioning whether this suspicion is the only lasting lesson egalitarians can draw from Greek thought today. Aristotle understood that the free males of Athens could be treated as equal citizens even when they held different understandings of the good life. The public domain of equal citizenship was the place where different understandings of the good life were to be debated and argued about. The public sphere was the forum where a working idea of the common good was to be forged. It was neither the venue where the more powerful imposed their understanding of the good life on those who were weaker, nor a domain of disengagement from those with different views. There was a third alternative to tyranny on the one hand and abandoning

[14] Aristotle, *Nicomachean Ethics*, 1169b.
[15] Aristotle, *Politics* 1280b, 6–7, 1281a, 3–4, trans. Benjamin Jowett, in Richard McKeon, ed., *The Basic Works of Aristotle* (New York: Random House, 1941), pp. 1188–89.
[16] Aristotle, *Nicomachean Ethics*, 1170a.

pursuit of the common good on the other. The active engagement of free citizens in public debate about how they would live together was the mark of their equality. Our modern commitment to the equal dignity of all persons rightly challenges Aristotle's exclusion of women, slaves, and metics from the role of citizen. But it does not follow that, when citizens hold different understandings of the good life, treating them equally requires that the pursuit of the common good is potentially oppressive or illusory. Equal citizens can start from different understandings of the good but go on to participate actively in defining and pursuing the good they share in common.

In light of Aristotle's thought, the question we face today is whether Aristotle's understanding of free citizenship can be extended to all while also maintaining the pursuit of the common good as a realistic social objective. Today we are acutely aware that a nation as vast and diverse as the United States cannot hope to achieve the kind of social unity that might have been possible in the Athenian *polis*. The size and diversity of the United States, and even more of the world as a whole, make attaining common agreement on the human good today a much more formidable problem than Aristotle ever faced. Aristotle, however, also took disagreements about the best way to organize public life very seriously. In fact he began his investigation into the good of the *polis* by conducting a kind of survey of the different political systems that were in place in the known world of his time. Such an inductive approach to identifying the shape of the good society holds much promise, and the argument below will return to it.[17] But Aristotle's goal was to identify a good form of public life for a very modest-sized city-state, not for a vast and pluralistic country like the United States or for an interdependent world-wide community. The change in historical context between Aristotle's Athens and the United States today is one of the chief sources of doubts about whether we can regard the common good as a realistic goal today. Historical context and historical experience, not eternally valid facts, are the source of these doubts.

In a somewhat similar way, Thomas Aquinas thought about the common good in the relatively homogeneous context of medieval

---

[17] Aristotle refers both to "what has been contributed by our predecessors" and to "our collection of constitutions" as the basis of his study of the good of political communities in *Nicomachean Ethics*, 1181b.

Western Christendom. Aquinas was certainly aware of the existence of the Jewish and Arab-Muslim worlds; in fact he was
influenced by some of the great thinkers of these worlds. He
learned much from non-Christians such as Aristotle, from Jews like
Maimonides, and from Muslims such as Ibn Sina (Avicenna) and
Ibn Rusd (Averroes). He had robust confidence that human reason
is capable of grasping the broad outlines of the common good even
in a society that is not religiously unified. Despite this notable intellectual openness, however, Aquinas wrote at a time when Christianity shaped the horizon of European civilization and culture. This
horizon was the formative background for the way he thought of the
common good.[18] Aquinas's awareness of non-Christian traditions
did not raise questions about the possibility of a shared understanding of the good society in the deep way religious pluralism does for
us today. We can no longer presume the relatively homogeneous
cultural background that Aquinas most often took for granted.

Thus it is evident that the size and cultural heterogeneity of society make discussion of the common good a very different task today
than it was for Aristotle or Aquinas. In such a discussion, the issue
we face is whether it is reasonable to hope that adherents of different
religious and cultural traditions can identify aspects of the good life
that are common to the lives of all human beings. If that hope can be
sustained, pursuit of the common good will remain a possibility. But
if experience leads to the abandonment of that hope, tolerance of
irreconcilable differences will be the most we can expect to achieve.

Eclipse of that hope is exactly what has happened due to the
experience of profound religious conflict at the dawn of modernity
in the West. When the Reformation shattered the religious unity
of Europe, a fundamental gap was opened up between ancient
and modern approaches to public life. The sixteenth-century split

---

[18] This is evident in the way Thomas Aquinas assumed that the religious practices of
non-Christians should only be publicly tolerated within Christendom when intolerance
would do greater harm than that caused by the public presence of the non-Christian
rites themselves. See *Summa Theologiae* II-II, q. 10, art. 11. Citations of the *Summa Theologiae*
are from *Summa Theologica*, 5 vols., trans. Fathers of the English Dominican Province
(Allen, TX: Christian Classics, 1948). It should be noted that Aquinas did think that such
toleration was often called for. His reasoning in support of such tolerance, however, is very
different from the liberal defense of tolerance. It is also very different from the Catholic
position officially adopted at the Second Vatican Council.

between Catholics and Protestants, and among different kinds of Protestants as well, led to sharply conflicting conceptions of what a good society should look like. In fact these conflicts led to overt religious war and persecution. The sixteenth- and seventeenth-century wars of religion were caused in significant measure by efforts to promote ideas of the social good narrowly based on particular religious understandings.[19] These religious understandings of the common good were matters with a depth that would admit no compromise by those who held them faithfully. These sixteenth-century religious visions of the good society were the roots of "irreconcilable latent conflict."[20] When these latent conflicts came to the surface, the consequences were very bloody indeed. For example, when the Peace of Westphalia finally ended the Thirty Years War in 1648, 15 to 20 percent of the population of the Holy Roman Empire had perished from war-related causes.[21]

This memory of sixteenth- and seventeenth-century strife has marked Western historical imagination with a deep suspicion toward all proposals to base social life on convictions about the good life. Visions of the full human good, especially religious visions, have come to appear as sources of division, not unity. Political theorists often appeal to the religious wars that followed the Reformation for historical, experience-based evidence of the dangers that lurk in any attempt to base public life on ideas of the common good.[22] They fear that the outcome of pursuing strong ideas of the common good will be war between groups that hold competing ideas of the good life, oppression of those holding minority views of the good by those in the majority, or straightforward

---

[19] It is worth noting that in the sixteenth and seventeenth centuries, as today, conflicts with religious dimensions often have political and economic causes that are at least as important as the religious disagreements that become the rallying points for the participants. This can raise questions about whether religious tolerance will resolve such conflicts or whether other solutions to the economic and social causes must be found. If the latter is the case, such conflicts need to be viewed in a larger context than the liberal commitment to tolerance can provide on its own.

[20] See Rawls, *Political Liberalism*, pp. xxv–xxvi.

[21] Geoffrey Parker, *The Thirty Years' War* (London: Routledge and Kegan Paul, 1984), p. 211.

[22] For example, John Rawls states that "the historical origin of political liberalism, and liberalism more generally, is the Reformation and its aftermath, with the long controversies over religious toleration in the sixteenth and seventeenth centuries." *Political Liberalism*, p. xxiv.

tyranny. In Rawls's words, "A public and workable agreement on a single and general comprehensive conception [of the good] could be maintained only by the oppressive use of state power."[23] Thus a public regime based on a positive moral commitment to tolerance came to be seen as the only reasonable alternative to continued religious war. The memory of post-Reformation religious conflicts remains deep in the Western psyche today and it is reinforced by contemporary conflicts that have explicitly religious dimensions. Because of these historical experiences, the notion of the common good seems very dangerous to many political theorists in the West.

This suspicion is not limited to ideas of the common good that are based on Christian religious convictions. It extends to understandings of the common good found in the Western political tradition known as civic republicanism. This republican tradition is represented by thinkers as religiously different from Thomas Aquinas as were Cicero, Machiavelli, and Rousseau. These thinkers envisioned personal well-being and the well-being of the republic as inseparable. Being a good person required fulfilling one's responsibilities as a citizen for the public good. Indeed personal virtue and good citizenship were often identified in republican thought. This was an appropriation of Aristotle's understanding of the bonds between fellow citizens as the most honorable forms of friendship.[24] And very recently Hannah Arendt sought to retrieve this high estimate of citizenship by identifying genuinely human action with

---

[23] Rawls, "The Idea of an Overlapping Consensus," *Oxford Journal of Legal Studies* 7 (1987), 1–25, at 4. See Rawls's more recent formulation of this idea in his *Political Liberalism*, pp. 36–38. Rawls acknowledges that basing the institutions of society upon a "conception of justice that can be understood as in some way advancing the common good" (usually the common good understood in religious terms) need not lead to religious war and persecution. As he understands the idea of the common good, however, such a society will not treat all its members as free and equal citizens but, at best, as entitled to have their good taken into account and to be consulted in the formation of policies. He sees such a society as based on a "reasonable consultation hierarchy" and distinguishes it from a democratic society as understood in liberal terms. This, however, is not the only way to conceive of the role of the common good in a free society, as I will try to indicate below. See Rawls, *Political Liberalism*, p. 109, and Rawls, *The Law of Peoples* (Cambridge, MA: Harvard University Press, 1999), pp. 62–78.

[24] Aristotle writes that "friendship seems to hold states together" and that "concord is friendship among fellow citizens" in *Nicomachean Ethics*, 1155a and 1167b. "State" is Ostwald's translation of *polis*. Aristotle himself, of course, raised the question of how large a *polis* could be before this kind of unity becomes impossible. See *Nicomachean Ethics*, 1170b–1171a.

the kind of communication and argument about public affairs that takes place among fellow citizens.[25]

This civic republican tradition, however, carries dangers that bring it under the same kind of suspicion as is directed at religious conceptions of the common good today. For Rawls, any comprehensive conception of the good life, whether religious, philosophical, or moral, carries the same dangers as became evident in the wars of religion. So we must abandon the notion that political life can achieve the kind of strong community for which the republican tradition hopes.[26] Pursuit of such communal bonds in political life carries a high danger of conflict. It may also require repression or oppression. This is the "dark underside" of republicanism pointed out by Jean Bethke Elshtain, despite her sympathies for the nobility of its understanding of citizenship. The civic virtue that has often moved people and nations to great actions together has had one glaring problem historically: it has frequently been "armed."[27] From republican Sparta, to Plato's ideal republic at Athens, to Machiavelli's exhortations to Lorenzo de'Medici on the usefulness of fear in governing Florence, to Rousseau's elevation of the general will over that of the individual, there has been a notable tendency to identify the common good with political control and military victory. Civic *virtù* becomes a close relative of military valor. So the same fear that rises from the memory of religious wars is brought to the surface by talk of republican virtue. The same apprehension arises about the high place it grants to the idea of the common good. These fears lead to suspicion that any notion of the common good,

[25] Hannah Arendt, *The Human Condition: A Study of the Central Dilemmas Facing Modern Man* (Garden City, NY: Doubleday Anchor, 1959), esp. pp. 155–185. Arendt writes that the *polis* as the sphere of human action "properly speaking, is not the city-state in its physical location; it is the organization of the people as it arises out of acting and speaking together, and its true space lies between people living together for this purpose, no matter where they happen to be" (177). Thus the question of whether the Greek idea of the *polis* is viable today is a question of the possibility of genuine communication and argument about the public affairs of a nation or a world as large, diverse, and complex as ours.
[26] See Rawls, *Political Liberalism*, p. 146.
[27] Jean Bethke Elshtain, "Citizenship and Armed Civic Virtue: Some Critical Questions on the Commitment to Public Life," in Charles H. Reynolds and Ralph V. Norman, eds., *Community in America: The Challenge of Habits of the Heart* (Berkeley: University of California Press, 1988), pp. 47–55, at 50. Elshtain develops these ideas in an extended feminist meditation on the idea of civic virtue and war in her *Women and War* (New York: Basic Books, 1987).

whether based on religious or secular-philosophical grounds, will lead to trampling upon the freedom and dignity of those who do not share it. Within this historically formed imaginative framework, respect for equal dignity appears possible only by standing on guard against the imposition of values we do not already hold. A certain wariness sets the agenda for how we deal with diversity and pluralism. This wariness is a deep bias imprinted on the contemporary social imagination by some of the major currents in the modern social and political history of Europe. The question this leaves open, however, is whether this imaginative predisposition fits the contours of the history that is unfolding today. We will argue below that it does not.

PLURALISM AND THE COMMON GOOD TODAY

The relevance of these historical considerations is not confined to the role they have played in calling the idea of the common good into question in academic philosophy and political theory. Skepticism about the compatibility of a shared vision of the good life with respect for freedom is widespread in contemporary popular consciousness in the West today, especially in the United States. People today are increasingly aware that they have many different kinds of neighbors, both nearby and far away. And these neighbors have many ideas about what a good life is. The reality of pluralism impinges on people daily as they rub shoulders at their workplace with those who have different religious beliefs and cultural traditions, and whose race or ethnicity is different from their own. They hear languages other than English as they commute to work and do the shopping. This diversity can, of course, be seen as a source of variety that enriches human life both for individuals and in society. But the experience of diversity is also accompanied by regular reports in the media of ethnic and religious conflict.[28] Television also

---

[28] Diana Eck writes that "pluralism is not just another word for diversity. It goes beyond mere plurality or diversity to active engagement with that plurality . . . to the active attempt to understand the other." It will become clear in my discussion of intellectual solidarity in chapter 6 that I fully endorse this goal. Eck also writes, however, this engagement and effort to understand "is not a given but must be created." Whether this is possible is the issue being raised here. See Diana Eck, *A New Religious America: How a "Christian Country" Has Become the World's Most Religiously Diverse Nation* (New York: HarperSanFrancisco, 2001), p. 70.

brings images of urban gang conflict, drive-by shootings, and drug-use into middle-class homes. Under the influence of such reports and images, diversity can seem more a threat than an enrichment. If people who are different from oneself seem at least potentially dangerous, it becomes difficult to see them as neighbors. It becomes hard to imagine that a life that is shared with them in significant ways could also be a good life.

Some years ago the political theorist Michael Sandel stated that "we can know a good in common that we cannot know alone."[29] Sandel was suggesting that a shared social life makes knowledge of the common good possible. His argument also implies that a shared life together makes practical pursuit of this common good a social necessity. This book will argue that Sandel's statement is true. But it is difficult to make a realistic case for this position when society is as aware of its diversity as we have become today. This awareness of diversity is deeply tinged by historical memories of religious wars and by images of ethnic and religious conflict from the contemporary scene. Sandel's statement depends upon a sizeable number of people being able to appreciate and value existing bonds of social connection with each other. This positive experience of social interdependence enables persons to learn from one another, thus giving rise to understandings of the good life that could not be envisioned apart from their connections. But if large numbers of those with whom one rubs shoulders are seen as strangers, positive experiences of social unity are unlikely to arise. It is even less likely when divergences of culture, tradition, and ways of life make them look like threats to each other. When fear of these threats sets the tone, interaction with people who are different is perceived as a danger to be avoided. Serious interaction and mutual vulnerability can seem more like a "common bad" than a good to be shared in common. Defense of one's turf becomes the first requirement of the good life. The common good becomes a will-o'-the-wisp in such an environment. So a positive experience of life together, common knowledge of what a good life is, and the philosophical idea of the common good itself all seem to evanesce together.

[29] Michael Sandel, *Liberalism and the Limits of Justice* (Cambridge: Cambridge University Press, 1982), p. 183.

This is a relatively new situation for the West in general and for the United States in particular. Pluralism and group conflict, of course, have been around for a long time. The novelty today is that consciousness of pluralism has become routine. Cultural and religious differences are taken for granted as a part of the way things are and will remain in the future. In post-Reformation Europe, knowledge of religious differences between Protestants and Catholics was real, but such disagreements were not simply accepted as here to stay. Believers hoped for conversion or victory over their religious adversaries at an unspecified future date. Similarly, in the days of the Cold War before the tumultuous events of 1989, Westerners could map the globe into the free world, the Communist world, and those regions over which the other two blocs contended for influence. Within this framework one could envision the common good as the expansion of Western values throughout the world. Such a shared vision of the good society of the future followed from the principle that freedom is better than tyranny. Alternatively, Marxists in the Eastern bloc could project the common good as the international victory of socialism. The end of the Cold War has destroyed these simplifications and made the picture much more complex.

Several years ago Francis Fukuyama predicted that the end of the ideological conflict of the Cold War would lead to the "end of history," with Western liberal democracy spreading across the globe and making future politics peaceful but boring.[30] This now seems naive to say the least. The rise of ethnic and religious conflict on the international stage has uncovered latent differences among peoples that seem to go at least as deep as the formerly contending Western and Marxist ideologies. For example, awareness of the presence of Islam as a major political force in the world has grown rapidly in the West, thanks to the visibility of the Ayatollah Khomeini, Muamar Khadaffy, Saddam Hussein, and most especially in light of the terrorist attacks on the World Trade Center in New York that led the United States and its allies into full-scale war in Afghanistan. In the face of this Islamic resurgence, the France

[30] Francis Fukuyama, "The End of History," *The National Interest* 16 (Summer, 1989) 4, 18. Fukuyama has developed this article at book length in *The End of History and the Last Man* (New York: Free Press, 1992).

20 *The common good and Christian ethics*

that gave the West the revolutionary principles of liberty, equality, and fraternity has been unsure whether Muslim girls should be permitted to wear religiously prescribed head-coverings in French schools. Agonizing conflicts in Northern Ireland, the former Yugoslavia, and Central Africa have also raised new questions about the possibility of harmony among people with different traditions about the meaning of the good life.

One does not have to look very hard to find similar divisions among communities within the United States. The country faces divisive questions about the meaning of religious freedom today. Do First Amendment protections of religious freedom extend to permitting Native Americans to use peyote in their religious rites, to Caribbean immigrants practicing Santaria rituals involving animal sacrifice, and to those citizens who want to send their children to religiously affiliated schools with the financial support that vouchers would provide? Court rulings on such cases have stimulated efforts to pass a "Religious Freedom Restoration Act," implying that the first American freedom has been undermined and needs to be restored. The emergence of new religious movements, "cults" and even militias in the United States show that at least some Americans believe that the traditional religious and social institutions of the country cannot be relied on to help them live good lives. On the basis of memories of slavery, lynchings, ethnic exclusion, and newly awakened awareness of historical patterns of abuse and discrimination, advocacy groups argue forcefully against trusting the traditional ways of doing things. These traditional ways and institutions do not protect their well-being or give them a fair chance to live good lives. Others see these advocates as threats to the republic and respond in kind. Thus debates about remedies for the effects of racial discrimination, for example, have been deeply divided on whether equal protection of fundamental rights should be color-blind and opposed to affirmative action, or color-conscious and supportive of affirmative action.[31] In Martin Marty's words

During the final quarter of the twentieth century many groups of citizens have come to accuse others of having wounded them by attempting to

---

[31] See for example, K. Anthony Appiah and Amy Gutmann, *Color Conscious: The Political Morality of Race* (Princeton: Princeton University Press, 1996), and Stephen Thernstrom and Abigail Thernstrom, *America in Black and White: One Nation, Indivisible* (New York: Simon and Schuster, 1997).

impose a single national identity and culture on all. [An] other set, in turn, has accused its newly militant adversaries of tearing the republic apart. They do this, it is said, by insisting on their separate identities and by promoting their own mutually exclusive subcultures at the expense of the common weal. Taken together, these contrasting motions produce a shock to the civil body, a trauma in the cultural system, and a paralysis in the neural web of social interactions.[32]

In this way, the injustices of the past haunt the present in the United States today and threaten new conflicts.

Awareness of diversity is thus a prominent fact in daily experience today. When difference generates conflict, fear grows. And such fear makes further conflict more likely. This raises the spectre that we have fallen into a downward spiral in which awareness of differences leads to conflict, which in turn leads to fear, more conflict, more defensive boundaries, and onward to deepened perceptions of difference. At least this much can be said: in the face of these tensions we cannot simply presume that there is a good shared in common by people who are more or less the same, nor is it obvious that this shared good can be readily identified. Indeed quite a few social commentators think the hope that we can identify and pursue the common good is utopian today. Perhaps it is a nostalgic hangover from time past, when people lived side-by-side in close-knit neighborhoods and in countries where those who were significantly different could be kept at a safe distance. We may be inclined to say: "Once upon a time there was a common life where what was good for one was good for all. In those days we could hold town meetings and elect representatives to decide how to achieve the shared good that benefits all of us. But today, the best we can hope for is tolerance toward all that makes us different from one another, and at worst we have to be ready to fight." Thus when people disagree about the good life and take it for granted that this disagreement is here to stay, the hope that they can "know a good in common that they cannot know alone" seems a rather thin one.

[32] Martin E. Marty, *The One and the Many: America's Struggle for the Common Good* (Cambridge, MA: Harvard University Press, 1997), p. 3. Marty uses the term "trauma" to characterize this set of conflicts over the past several decades throughout this book. See the book's index under "trauma."

Pluralism, by definition, means disagreement about what is finally true and good. A pluralist society is one where people do not
share an understanding of the full breadth and depth of the good
life. Thus almost by definition pluralism seems to make conceiving
of a common good an impossible task. More strongly, it suggests
that we should abandon efforts to encourage people to live in a
way that realizes a common vision lest these efforts perpetuate past
injustices, deepen conflicts, or even precipitate war. Where there is
no shared vision of the good life does it make sense to speak of a
community at all? When people who hold different understandings
of what makes for a good life regard each other warily and with
suspicion, it would be more accurate to speak of a tense juxtapo-
sition of human beings than of a community. Perhaps that is the
best we can hope for. Perhaps the pursuit of a vision of the good life
to be lived in common by all is a dangerous prelude to oppression
and even tyranny.

PUBLIC OPINION: THOU SHALT NOT JUDGE

Some recent social-scientific investigations have concluded that
failure to recognize this situation is precipitating a deep cultural
rift in the United States today. This *Kulturkampf* is putatively not
restricted to disagreements on single issues such as abortion or affirmative action, though such disagreements certainly exist. Rather,
authors such as James Davison Hunter, Christopher Lasch, and
Gertrude Himmelfarb have suggested that a fundamental conflict
of world-views has developed that is splitting American citizens
into opposed camps. In Hunter's analysis these splits are pitting
orthodox or traditional wings of the middle class against those who
regard themselves as progressive. In Lasch's reading, it sets the
middle-class working people against upper middle-class managerial elites.[33] In both cases the battle lines of this supposed culture
war are located *within* the middle class itself. In Himmelfarb's view,
the division cuts through class lines and through lines of religion,
race, ethnicity, and gender as well. It is an "ethics gap," with "moral

---

[33] See James Davison Hunter, *Culture Wars: The Struggle to Define America* (New York: Basic
Books, 1991), and Christopher Lasch, *The Revolt of the Elites and the Betrayal of Democracy*
(New York: W. W. Norton, 1995).

disarray on the one hand and religious-cum-moral revival on the other."[34]

If this picture of culture war is true, the consequences for the United States as a whole could be ominous. Aristotle and many after him have long argued that societies with a large middle class are less subject to internal conflict than those polarized between rich and poor. Middle economic status supposedly makes people politically moderate, strengthening the stability of society. In Aristotle's words, "it is manifest that the best political community is formed by citizens of the middle class, and that those states are likely to be well administered in which the middle class is large . . . Where the middle class is large, there are least likely to be factions and dissensions."[35] Following this line of reasoning, a polarization of the middle class would threaten social and political stability. Weakening of middle-class consensus about what constitutes the good life would act as a solvent on the glue that holds the whole society together. Thus Alan Wolfe states that "if even a part of this story about middle-class decline and fracturing is true, the implications could not be greater. The issue is simple to state: an angry, inward-looking, and hopelessly divided middle class is not a middle class at all." Thus the hypothesis that there is a culture war underway in the United States raises "the prospect that the democratic stability that has kept the country together since the Civil War will no longer be attainable."[36] One might add that middle-class instability and internal conflict in the United States would also have very great implications for the world as a whole.

For this reason the contention that the United States is not only pluralistic but culturally at war with itself over a broad range of moral values calls for careful scrutiny. Wolfe believes that the facts do not support the culture-war hypothesis and he is relieved to be able to say so. Nevertheless, the data that lead Wolfe to this conclusion are not reassuring from the point of view of concern for the common good. A number of empirical studies, including

[34] Gertrude Himmelfarb, *One Nation, Two Cultures* (New York: Alfred A. Knopf, 1999), chap. 6, esp. pp. 116–117.

[35] Aristotle, *Politics* 1295b, 35–38, 1296a, 8–9.

[36] Alan Wolfe, *One Nation After All: What Middle-Class Americans Really Think: About God, Country, Family, Racism, Welfare, Immigration, Homosexuality, Work, the Right, the Left, and Each Other* (New York: Viking, 1998), pp.14–15.

Wolfe's own, suggest that conflict is being avoided precisely by abandoning the pursuit of the common good. This abandonment appears to many to be a key to a more humane society. Tolerance for difference rather than pursuit of a common good seems the safest path. It seems the path least likely to perpetuate past harms or provoke new violence, and the route most compatible with the freedom so highly valued in modern Western cultures. Or so, it seems, many Americans have concluded.

There are many indications in the United States today that tolerance of diversity occupies the place held by the common good in the thought of Aristotle, Thomas Aquinas, and Ignatius Loyola. Tolerance of difference, not the common good, has become the highest social aspiration in American culture. And the range of matters to which tolerance is extended has been broadening. Historically the need for tolerance has been associated in the West with the fact of religious disagreement. Religious freedom became the "first freedom" in the minds of Americans and religious co-ercion the "first oppression." Today, however, the fear of conflict focuses not only on religious disagreement as a source of social strife but on many other types of disagreement about the good life as well. The wars of religion led many in the past to argue that religion must become a private matter if social peace is to be possi-ble. Today it is argued that *all* fully articulated visions of the good life should similarly be viewed as private or "non-public." Again John Rawls is representative of this trend in political theory. He maintains that today there is a need to extend tolerance beyond the religious sphere to all comprehensive "conceptions of what is of value in human life, and ideals of personal character, as well as ideals of friendship and of familial and associational relationships, and much else that is to inform our conduct, and in the limit to our life as a whole." Thus Rawls asserts that avoiding conflicts like the religious wars of the past means we should today "simply apply the principle of toleration to philosophy itself," that is, to all fully developed understandings or visions of the good life.[37]

This appeal for a broadening of the scope of tolerance is not an esoteric invention of political theory. It is clearly a strong force

37 Rawls, *Political Liberalism*, pp. 10, 13.

Table 1.1. *"Morality is a personal matter and society
should not force everyone to follow one standard"*

Agree strongly	469
Agree somewhat	575
Disagree somewhat	259
Disagree strongly	113
Don't know	57
No answer	8

Source: General Social Survey, question 374 D Codebook variable: PERMORAL[38]

in the climate of American public opinion today. For example, the *General Social Survey* of American beliefs and attitudes reveals the high place given to tolerance by the American public. Table 1.1 indicates that most Americans think of morality, not just religion, as a personal matter rather than as a set of standards that should be enforced in society at large. 67 percent of Americans agreed, either "strongly" or "somewhat," that morality is "personal." One could interpret this as meaning that judgments about right and wrong are simply private matters having little or nothing to do with the well-being of the larger society. Such an interpretation would imply that many Americans think morality is not concerned with the common good of the larger community. If this is correct, the common good is a dead issue in the minds of most Americans. Before reaching this conclusion, however, we should note that this question in the *General Social Survey* is two-pronged, for its second clause raises the issue of whether morality should be enforced by unspecified coercive means. Agreement with the statement could be explained by the respondents' aversion to political coercion and the dangers of excessive state power, not by their conviction that morality does not extend to the public good.

Another question in the *General Social Survey* suggests that viewing morality as personal is related to many Americans' belief that morality, both public and private, is a domain of ambiguity.

---

[38] Data from the *General Social Survey* have been downloaded from the Inter-University Consortium for Political and Social Research world-wide web homepage: http://www.icpsr.umich.edu/gss/.

Table 1.2. *"Right and wrong are not usually a simple matter of black and white; there are many shades of gray"*

Agree strongly	589
Agree somewhat	624
Disagree somewhat	115
Disagree strongly	102
Don't know	43

Source: General Social Survey, question 374 B Codebook variable: BLKWHITE

Table 1.2 indicates that over 82 percent agreed either "strongly" or "somewhat" that the answers to moral questions are "gray" rather than "black and white." This grayness is a likely source of the desire to keep moral decisions within the zone of personal discretion. Few people want to surrender close-call moral decisions to anyone who might use coercive power to settle such matters for them. Suspicion of state coercion, of course, is compatible with the belief that we have moral obligations to promote the common good and that there is such a thing as a public morality. This reading of the responses would imply that the common good should be pursued by citizens through their voluntary, uncoerced activity. Such voluntary activity for the common good could even be regarded as morally required. Those who see morality in shades of gray may simply be saying they do not want bureaucrats or police making such judgments for them.

Other attitudes uncovered by the *General Social Survey*, however, imply that the conviction that morality is "personal" has a deeper root than fear of coercion.[39] A third question suggests that when Americans say morality is "personal" they in fact mean it is "private." Table 1.3 shows that 57 percent either strongly agree or agree that "we make our own fate." These responses highlight the individualistic view of human existence that has long been evident

---

[39] Alan Wolfe, in his most recent book, *Moral Freedom: The Search for Virtue in a World of Choice* (New York: W. W. Norton, 2001), seems at times to suggest that Americans view "moral freedom" as not being coerced or directed by some authority. At other times he seems to imply that "moral freedom" means there are no preexisting moral standards whether coercively enforced or not. It is not entirely clear to me which meaning of moral freedom Wolfe finds present in American culture, though on p. 224 he states it is the former rather than the latter.

Table 1.3. *"We each make our own fate"*

Strongly agree	200
Agree	510
Neither agree nor disagree	237
Disagree	149
Strongly disagree	79
Can't choose	44
No answer	65

Source: General Social Survey, question 673 G Codebook variable: OWNFATE; responses from the year 1998

in American culture. A clear majority of Americans believe they are in charge of their own destinies. The widespread presence of such belief is further confirmed by "The Way We Live Now Poll" conducted for the *New York Times Magazine*. In this poll, 85 percent of a random sample of Americans agreed with the statement "I believe it is possible in America to pretty much be who you want to be," while only 14 percent disagreed. This positive response varied very little by income, with 82 percent of those earning less than $30,000 per year and 90 percent of those earning more than $75,000 agreeing with the statement. [40] Such beliefs imply that living a good life is not dependent on the conditions of public life, whether these are economic, political, or cultural. If a good life is "self-made" there is little reason to be concerned about the quality of public life; morality becomes a matter of the private rather than the public good.

Taken at face value, the statement that we make our own fate implies that we are not ultimately vulnerable to contingencies of social and natural circumstances. Circumstances of birth, family relationships, economic conditions, sexual, racial or ethnic identity, environmental conditions, international war and peace, and a host of other factors can be ignored as unimportant to what one's life ultimately amounts to. Whatever others may do, people still have the freedom to shape their lives in accord with the values they

[40] Results of "The Way We Live Now Poll" were published in *The New York Times Magazine* (May 7, 2000). The data for the question cited here can be found on p. 66 of this issue of the Magazine.

hold. This suggests that social and natural conditions are not very important in living a good life. It is not a big leap from this pre-supposition to the conclusion that the idea of the common good is irrelevant to living well. The good life, and morality with it, is seen as a private matter both in its source and its scope.

This privatized view of the good life depends on a very selective reading of the forces actually at work in shaping lives. It is so se-lective that it cannot be taken literally. Rather, agreement with the statements that "we make our own fate" and "you can pretty much be who you want to be" must be more an indication of what people think is most important than of their realistic description of how human lives actually unfold. It suggests that those aspects of life under the power of personal freedom are more important to most Americans than those determined by social contexts or historical contingencies. Thus affirming that fate is self-made is as much an indication of an individualistic value system as is it a description of fact. It puts the quality of public life low on the scale of goods and directs attention away from goods that can only be realized in the shared life of the larger society. Thus it devalues the common good and directs attention away from the common conditions of public life.[41]

It would be risky, of course, to base large generalizations about American culture on a few survey questions such as these. Indeed the interpretation just suggested is at best hypothetical. There is further evidence, however, of the fragility of the common good in American culture today. Ironically it is most evident in the work of a social scientist who has strongly rejected the culture-war hypoth-esis. Alan Wolfe's study, *One Nation After All*, is based on empirical research that goes deeper than the inevitably hypothetical inter-pretations of correlations among responses uncovered by survey research. Wolfe interviewed approximately two hundred middle-class Americans in depth, pursuing open-ended, oral questioning on key issues of public morality. His goal was to discover, with more subtlety than is possible with survey instruments alone, what a

---

[41] For an interpretation of these questions of the *General Social Survey* that support the ar-gument presented here, see Daniel Rigney and Michael Kearl, "A Nation of Gray In-dividualists: Moral Relativism in the United States," *Journal of Social Philosophy* 25, no. 1 (Spring, 1994), 20–45.

representative group of middle-class Americans really think on matters of public morality.[42]

Wolfe rejects the culture-war scenario and argues that the beliefs and values of the American middle class are still largely homogeneous. In fact he finds something close to consensus on what is valued most highly by the middle class in the United States today. This consensus on the *summum bonum* can be summed up in a single word: *tolerance*. The high value placed on tolerance is evident in the attitudes toward religious belief Wolfe found in the middle class. But tolerance is central not just in attitudes toward religion; it is also evident in middle-class attitudes on a large number of other questions with important consequences for the quality of public life. These include the structure of family life, gender roles, immigration, multiculturalism, and race. By actually talking to people in some depth and asking them what they really mean when they express their opinions, Wolfe concludes that America is not coming apart at the seams in a culture war. If there is a culture war going on in the United States it is largely being fought by intellectuals rather than ordinary middle-class people. Wolfe's hopeful conclusion is that the tolerance of the American middle class is not reflected in high-visibility wars of words conducted in the academy and the mass media. In fact, the American middle class today is a restraining force on academic and political elites, as Aristotle would have predicted. Average Americans are too non-judgmental to get sucked into battles that might tear the country apart. From this Wolfe takes a certain modest comfort.[43]

For example, his interviews indicate that the United States is not about to enter a period of war between traditionalist religious believers and progressive secularists. Neither a war with guns nor a war of words based on religious disagreement seems imminent

---

[42] Those interviewed by Wolfe were selected for their geographical, racial, cultural, ethnic, and job-related representativeness of the suburban middle class. Within this representative framework, Wolfe tilted the sample somewhat toward the conservative end of the cultural spectrum, to assure that the "progressive," "new-class," and managerial "elites" held by other theorists to be the originators of the culture war did not dominate the interviews. Wolfe's research method and sample make his conclusions more ominous for the viability of the idea of the common good than if they could be seen as biased toward the "liberal" end of the culture. See Wolfe, *One Nation After All*, pp. 19–35 for a description of the sample on which Wolfe's study is based.

[43] *Ibid.*, p. 309.

among the people. It is true that Americans are more likely to be religious believers than are citizens of any of the other advanced industrial nations of the North Atlantic. But the American religious style is a "quiet faith" that is strongly averse to religious conflict. Indeed Wolfe suggests that most middle-class Americans have added an eleventh commandment to the biblical decalogue: "Thou shalt not judge."[44] In light of the terrible bloodshed of past and present religious wars, this is encouraging. The faith of middle-class Americans has been tempered by their almost absolute aversion to strife and conflict about religious beliefs. In Wolfe's words, "Religious tolerance in America bears a distinct resemblance to laissez-faire economics: you can do what you want so long as you let me do what I want."[45]

Wolfe also finds that this tolerance is not restricted to matters of religion. It extends to matters of race, ethnicity, family structure, and many other matters of public morality, with the notable exception of homosexuality. He calls this tolerant stance on a broad spectrum of issues "capacious individualism." The ethic that informs it he calls "morality writ small." This is an ethic that aspires to "modest virtues" and "ordinary duties," such as kindness and honesty rather than larger goals of social justice and social equality. These modest virtues are surely important; their lively presence among ordinary Americans is surely preferable to the anger and resentment that the practitioners of group conflict promote. A culture war in the United States would be a very bad thing. The American Civil War has already shown this vividly, and the recent abominations in the former Yugoslavia and in Rwanda have confirmed it afresh. So Wolfe breathes a sigh of relief to find tolerance alive and well in the United States.

It remains an open question, however, whether generous and tolerant individualism is up to dealing with the problems we face today. Despite Wolfe's relief that cultural war does not seem imminent in the United States, he has nagging doubts about whether non-judgmentalism can provide what we need as we face the future. Shortly after the appearance of *One Nation After All*, Wolfe confessed that his research left him "somewhat depressed." The

---

[44] *Ibid.*, p. 54. [45] *Ibid.*, p. 63.

principal reason for this is that morality writ small lacks "a shared sense of national purpose." The ethic of tolerance shows the right instincts, but it "lacks a vision of how to put them to constructive use." Americans may value personal responsibility highly, but they also have a distinct lack of enthusiasm for meeting the responsibilities of national citizenship. "They seemed to want the benefits of being American without the obligations of paying taxes or paying attention." They are also distinctly unenthusiastic about the international responsibilities that go along with being an American in the emerging global context. Wolfe conjectures that this narrowness of vision is a by-product of the prosperity of the middle class. In the comfortable world of the middle class, morality writ small translates into "couch-potato politics," an unwillingness or inability to articulate common purposes and act to secure them.[46]

In other words, middle-class Americans lack a vision of the common good, both in their approach to national life and in their understanding of the role of the United States internationally. This lack raises fundamental questions. Will a culture in which tolerance is the prime virtue generate a society good enough to sustain its citizens' loyalty over the long haul? Does avoiding judgments lead to an attenuated vision of what is possible by telling us never to say anything in public that others do not already agree with? If tolerance becomes a card that trumps all strong proposals on how we should live together, will it stifle the imagination needed to address pressing public problems? The next chapter will suggest that creative response to some of the pressing social problems emerging today will require a considerably stronger commitment to the common good than we now have.

[46] Alan Wolfe, "Couch Potato Politics," *New York Times* (Sunday, March 15, 1998), sec. 4, p. 17.

CHAPTER TWO

Problems tolerance cannot handle

The prevailing values of tolerance and non-judgmentalism emerged in the social and intellectual history of the modern West as expressions of a developing commitment to the equal dignity of all persons. This commitment is a huge achievement that must not be forgotten or negated. This history, however, has engrained in the modern Western imagination not only a positive commitment to equality but also the suspicion that pursuing stronger notions of shared goods will lead to oppression and violence. It will be argued here that, in the context of several of the major social developments of our time, commitment to equality and pursuit of the common good can become allies rather than adversaries.

Judith Shklar has proposed an interpretation of our inherited social vision that makes explicit its linkage of commitment to equality with suspicion of the dangers of the common good. She calls her interpretation the "liberalism of fear." It begins from the presupposition that the political pursuit of the *summum bonum*, however this highest good is defined, is almost guaranteed to lead to cruelty and violence. When people with convictions about what a good society should look like also have the power to act on these convictions, everyone else is in danger. Those who lack the power to define and enforce their own definition of the highest good must be on guard. A liberal democracy seeks to assure the equal dignity of all by protecting the weak against the strong. It does this by protecting people against the threat that anyone's understanding of full human good will be coercively imposed on all. The ancient pursuit of the common good is in this way replaced by the effort to avoid the worst evil, understood as the infliction of cruelty by those in power on those who are different and too weak to change their status. According to this interpretation, the tolerance we have learned from historical experience does not reject classical virtue in favor of self-indulgence. Rather it guards against "cruel military and moral repression and violence." From history we have learned to choose "a self-restraining tolerance that fences in the powerful to protect the freedom and safety of every citizen, old or young, male or female, black or white."[1]

Shklar calls this a liberalism of fear, but a liberalism of wariness seems a more accurate description of the form it takes in public opinion today. People are wary concerning whose ideas about what makes life worth living will set the terms under which they live together. They are wary of people who hold conceptions of the good life that differ from their own. These concerns help shape both the questions that get asked and the provisional answers that are taken for granted concerning how to live together. Who will decide? Whose vision of how to live will prevail? The questions that do not get asked are also significant. Could real engagement with those who hold different visions of the good life teach us something important? Could deliberation about how we should live together be mutually enriching and lead to a better public life for all? Such questions do not arise when wariness sets the agenda. Respect for equal dignity of all people appears possible only by standing on guard against the imposition of values we do not already hold.

The role played by this wariness as a guiding presupposition of social life was an innovation in response to the historical circumstances that arose with modernity several centuries ago in the West. Suspicion toward all ideas of the common good is not an eternal requirement of reasonableness or of respect for the equal dignity of all persons. Such suspicion is justified if advocacy of an idea of the common good is identified with its coercive imposition on those who do not share it. Such linkage of the notion of the common good with oppression and coercion has strong warrants. But these warrants are historical, not eternal, truths. If the historical conditions that led to modern Western suspicions about ideas of

---

[1] Judith N. Shklar, *Ordinary Vices* (Cambridge, MA: Harvard University Press, 1984), p. 5. For a concise presentation of Shklar's understanding of these ideas see her "The Liberalism of Fear," in Nancy Rosenblum, ed., *Liberalism and the Moral Life* (Cambridge, MA: Harvard University Press, 1989), pp. 21–38.

the common good have changed, the presuppositions that will be appropriate guides for public life today may also need to be revised. Indeed, seeing received social presuppositions as the products of historical circumstances may help us recognize a new relevance for the common good. Avoidance of conflict is crucial, to be sure, but there are major social and political questions today that call for more vision than tolerance can generate on its own. Among these are the struggles of poor African Americans in US central cities and the confusion that prevails in public opinion regarding the international responsibilities of the United States in the post-Cold-War world. Let us consider these two questions as illustrations of the limits of what tolerance can produce.

RACE, POVERTY, AND SOCIAL ISOLATION IN CENTRAL CITIES

The reality of urban poverty illustrates the fact that tolerance, taken by itself, is not a sufficient resource for addressing the urgent problems confronting American public life today. Economic deprivation, unemployment, single parenthood, homelessness, and frightening drug-related violence mark the quality of life in American cities. The populations of the inner cores of many large American cities are heavily African American and they are largely poor. The linked realities of urban poverty and race continue to be among the most urgent problems facing the country today. Periodic irruptions of civil unrest remind citizens of how much remains to be done if they are to address the continuing plight of the urban poor. But the short-lived attention to urban problems stimulated by this unrest suggests that the nation is unprepared to make efforts to address these problems that are commensurate with their seriousness. One of the most important factors impeding an adequate response is the preeminence of the virtue of tolerance over commitment to the common good in the United States today. A case for this claim takes the following form.

First, most middle-class Americans live in neighborhoods that isolate them from people of significantly different social-economic backgrounds. This isolation is due, on one level, to the apparently impersonal forces of the real estate market. These market dynamics, however, are sustained by zoning laws and other boundaries that are the result of political choice rather than geography. Anthony Downs has argued that the social-economic hierarchy of neighborhoods is founded on two moral principles accepted by most Americans. Americans appear to believe, first, that every household has the right to live in a neighborhood populated largely by other households approximately like itself. Second, they hold that each neighborhood has the right to protect the quality of its life, its environment, and its property values by excluding groups of people that would significantly diminish these.[2] Downs states that these principles of homogeneity and self-protective exclusion do not extend to the legitimation of racial discrimination. Nevertheless there can be little doubt that other criteria for the desired form of homogeneity have the obvious direct effect of economic and class stratification and indirect racial consequences as well. In Downs's view, these criteria ought to be challenged despite the fact that they appear to be accepted as morally legitimate by the majority of Americans. Such a challenge can arise only within a moral framework that expands the understanding of community beyond that of homogeneous groups of the like-minded or those who are similarly situated economically. Such a challenge will be dependent on the development of an understanding of the common good that reaches beyond the boundaries of existing groups.

Second, pursuit of community by middle-class Americans today takes forms that deepen the crisis of the inner cities. In the face of numerous problems that bedevil our complex social world, the need for a stronger sense of community is very much alive among those with the education and leisure to contemplate the realities of the larger society around them. But the problems seem so huge that the quest for community is directed into relatively manageable realms such as networks of friends and others who are enough like oneself for commonalities to be established comparatively easily. This point has been made in a book that has been central in discussions of American culture and morality in recent years: *Habits of the Heart* by Robert Bellah and four co-authors. It argues that many Americans recognize today that they cannot go it alone

---

[2] See Downs's remarks in "Cities, Suburbs, and the Common Good," *A Woodstock Occasional Paper* (Washington, D.C.: Woodstock Theological Center, 1991). Background for this analysis is developed more fully in Downs, *Neighborhoods and Urban Development* (Washington, D.C.: Brookings Institution, 1981).

in the face of the complexities of contemporary life. They need some sense of connection with others if they are to find meaning and a sense of both direction and control in their lives. But *Habits of the Heart* also describes an unfortunate and arguably pathological result of some of the efforts to find community today. The quest for community among suburbanites often leads to the development of "lifestyle enclaves." People in such enclaves find and express their identities through linkages with other persons with "shared patterns of appearance, consumption, or leisure activities . . . " Their relationships are based on some feature of private rather than public life. They "do not act together politically" as citizens of a polis and they "do not share a history."[3] Rather, they act as friends together in a kind of club. So they are not likely to translate their need for community into ways of thinking and acting that are capable of addressing issues such as the divisions between core cities and suburbs. In fact the need for community, when expressed in lifestyle enclaves, can have exactly the opposite effect. It can lead to the construction of walls and moats, in the form of bigger and better malls and tougher zoning ordinances that are designed to strengthen the locks that protect the privileged from those who are different.

Third, increased racial tolerance among white suburbanites is not a single key that will unlock the doors that keep the poor of the inner city from sharing in the national well-being. It is not even the most important key. Class differences between suburb and inner city have become more important in sustaining these boundaries than are negative racial attitudes and prejudices. Racial prejudice continues to be an operative force in American life to be sure. On the basis of a variety of studies, Orlando Patterson estimates that one in four Americans of European background "harbor mildly racist feelings toward Afro-Americans" and that one in five is a "hard-core racist."[4] Nevertheless it is also clear that the presence of racist attitudes has notably declined over recent decades. This

[3] Robert Bellah, Richard Madsen, William M. Sullivan, Ann Swidler, and Steven M. Tipton, *Habits of the Heart: Individualism and Commitment in American Life* (Berkeley, CA: University of California Press, 1985), p. 335.

[4] Orlando Patterson, *The Ordeal of Integration: Progress and Resentment in America's "Racial" Crisis* (Washington, D.C.: Civitas Counterpoint, 1997), p. 61.

change has not been accompanied by an improvement in the situation of blacks who live in the inner city. This suggests that something other than racial intolerance or prejudice is at the root of the problem of urban poverty.

In fact, the well-being of a sizable part of the African American population in the United States has notably improved over the second half of this century. The status achieved by black middle-class Americans is significantly improved today compared to the time of the Supreme Court's 1954 *Brown* v. *Board of Education* decision calling for racial integration in public schools. This improvement, both in absolute terms and relative to Americans from European backgrounds, can be measured on a number of scales: level of educational attainment, income, the holding of high political offices, and executive responsibility in business firms. These changes have led Patterson to conclude that "In almost all areas of life, progress – sometimes quite dramatic – has been made in surmounting the ingrained and institutional evils of racism and oppression . . . [T]here is no gainsaying the clear trend lines of progress in changing ethnic attitudes and in the improved condition of the vast majority of Afro-Americans."[5]

Patterson sees this progress of the black middle class as linked to the high level of tolerance in the United States today, a level that is much higher than that in other nations. It is noteworthy that, in a 1991 comparative poll, only 13 percent of Americans reported that they disliked members of the African American minority in the United States, while 42 percent of the French reported their dislike of the North Africans in France, 45 percent of Germans were ill-disposed to Turkish immigrants, 49 percent of Czechoslovakians disliked the Hungarians among them, and 21 percent of the English were negatively disposed to the Irish. In this international perspective the United States can claim to have achieved a remarkable level of openness to ethnic and racial minorities. Patterson calls it "truly amazing."[6]

[5] *Ibid.*, p. 1. See all of chap. 1 of this book for the data and analysis on which Patterson bases his statement.

[6] *Ibid.*, p. 18. Patterson cites the comparative data on ethnic tolerance from the Times Mirror Center for People and the Press, *The Pulse of Europe: A Survey of Political and Social Values and Attitudes* (Washington, D.C.: Times Mirror Center, 1991).

Wolfe echoes this positive picture of the improving conditions of black middle-class life and of declining racism. On the basis of his interviews, he concludes that white middle-class Americans do not choose to live in largely white suburbs because of racial hostility.[7] Rather they prefer to live in the suburbs simply because the suburbs are the place where they can live better lives by insuring good schools for their children, owning their own homes, and living in safe neighborhoods. Wolfe draws this conclusion not only because his white respondents told him these were their motives but also because African Americans themselves prefer to live in the suburbs for the same reasons if they can. The movement of blacks from the inner city to the suburbs is a reality today, for middle-class African Americans want to participate in the American dream too. The tearing down of some of the barriers to such movement by the black middle class is surely an improvement in the American racial situation. It can be attributed to greater tolerance for ethnic and racial diversity and applauded as such.

Nevertheless there are serious reasons to question whether racial tolerance is a sufficient basis for addressing the continuing and even deepening crisis of America's cities. Despite Patterson's positive assessment of the improving lot of the African American middle-class, he first points out that black median incomes are still only 60.8 percent of the incomes of European Americans. This is only a 1.6 percent improvement in the ratio over the past twenty years.[8] More starkly, African Americans at the lower end of the economic spectrum continue to live in dire straits. Nearly 10 million African Americans live in poverty. This is close to 25 percent of the black population in the United States. Blacks are 2.6 times more likely to be poor than are European Americans, and their families are more than three times more vulnerable to poverty than their white counterparts. Hardest hit are black children.[9] In other words, a large portion of blacks in the United States – those who have not made it into the middle class – have not benefited from increased racial tolerance.

[7] Wolfe, *One Nation After All*, pp.180–195.   [8] Patterson, *The Ordeal of Integration*, p. 25.
[9] *Ibid.*, pp. 28–29.

So a credible case can be made that the disparity between the quality of life in suburbs and in core cities is based less on racial intolerance than on class differences, though race continues to play a subordinate role.[10] The division between classes is economic in nature of course – money matters here as almost everywhere. Urban/suburban differences, however, are also manifest in the quality of schools, rates of labor force participation and unemployment, levels of drug use, incidence of crime, and levels of single parenthood. The choice to live in the suburbs can be explained largely by people's desire to benefit from the advantages of the suburbs and to avoid the disadvantages of the cities in these areas. Racial intolerance need not be invoked as a primary cause of the division between suburb and inner city. This is also evident from the fact that many of the poor in the United States are white. In Wolfe's words:

At least with respect to decisions about where to live, class may well be replacing race as the significant motivating force. If true, that does not make for a just society; an unequal distribution of such goods as safety, education, and opportunities for children raises questions about justice whatever the criteria used to differentiate those who get more from those who get less. But it does make for a different story. Suburbanites in America may be withdrawing from something, but whatever it is, it is no longer just about race.[11]

[10] The Public Broadcasting System television news magazine, *Frontline*, produced an overview of the emerging class divisions among African Americans, titled "The Two Nations of Black America," originally aired on February 10, 1998. It features interviews with a number of members of the Harvard University Afro-American Studies program, among others. The "Synopsis" of the show summarizes its argument as follows:

In this *Frontline* report, correspondent Henry Louis Gates, Jr., a Harvard scholar, explores the gaping chasm between the upper and lower classes of black America and probes why it has happened: 'How have we reached this point where we have both the largest black middle class and the largest black underclass in our history?' His personal essay draws a picture of growing black success along with deepening black despair and argues that black upper classes now have more in common with their white colleagues and peers than with those they have left behind in the inner cities. Reviewing the thirty years that have passed since the death of Martin Luther King, Jr., Gates shows that while many blacks reaped the reward of the civil rights movement and affirmative action and gained middle class status, just as many were left behind in an expanding underclass of poverty.

This Synopsis and other materials relevant to the class divisions among African Americans are available on the Internet at: http://www.pbs.org/wgbh/pages/frontline/shows/race/ (downloaded August 1, 2001).

[11] Wolfe, *One Nation After All*, p. 188.

So even if disadvantages based on race have declined, the problems of American cities are not on the verge of solution. Serious class-based disparities between cities and suburbs remain very real, and those who are on the bottom side of these disparities lack the basic conditions that make good lives attainable.

If racial prejudice is not the primary cause of the problems besetting the inner-city poor, increased racial tolerance is not an adequate remedy for these problems. Deprivation caused by economic inequality and class divisions will not be addressed directly or adequately by increasing the level of racial tolerance in society. Acceptance of racial differences within a commitment to our common humanity must surely be pursued in its own right. Nothing said here should be taken to suggest otherwise. But the virtue of tolerance, by itself, is not now a sufficient moral resource for addressing the problems of the poor in America's core cities. Toleration alone will not overcome class divisions and the despair they engender among the poor. Addressing these problems in a serious way will require reflection on the barriers that isolate the inner-city poor from both the white and the black middle class in the suburbs. It will also mean concerted efforts to overcome these class barriers. Tolerance means *acceptance* of difference, perhaps even a kind of *acquiescence* in such differences.[12] When such acceptance of differences leads to inclusion of those who have been excluded by a long history of racist attitudes and actions, tolerance makes very important contributions to the creation of community. But when barriers are the result of economic inequalities that are deeply ingrained and institutionalized in the class structures of society, more than an attitude of tolerance is needed. Tolerance as acceptance of differences is a psychological stance entirely inadequate for the development of a creative response to urban poverty today.

This means the dominant middle-class morality writ small, with its preference for the quiet virtues, is an inadequate cultural resource for addressing the plight of American cities. Wolfe knows this, for he writes that "The conditions of life for the poorest black Americans have approached levels of desperation and hopelessness

---

[12] See Nicholas Rescher, *Pluralism: Against the Demand for Consensus* (Oxford: Clarendon Press, 1993), pp. 5, 80, 90, 93, cited by Marty, *The One and the Many*, pp. 96–98.

that no civilized society ought to accept."[13] Patterson knows it too, for he sees the race picture in the United States today as marked by a paradox: it is the best of times for the black middle class but among the worst of times for poor blacks in America's central cities. He writes that "What is unjust ... and what should excite far greater outrage, is the systematic exclusion of certain groups from the social and cultural capital essential for success in this society."[14] Acceptance or tolerance of difference will certainly not knit up the tears in the flesh of the American body politic today. When acceptance of difference becomes acquiescence in deep social disparities and human misery it becomes part of the problem, not part of the solution. The belief that "we make our own fate" will continue to deepen the isolation and reinforce the despair of the inner-city poor. It will also raise the fences and strengthen the locks that protect many suburbanites from a common life with the neighbors who appear on their TV screens. The only alternative to a country sharply divided into enclaves and ghettos is greater solidarity across existing class divisions, linking the middle-class suburbanites and the poor in the cities in politically and economically effective ways. Only a stronger human interconnectedness can overcome the nihilism and meaninglessness that plague poor ghettos. Only a sense of such connectedness can lead the middle class to look beyond the gates that protect them and their like-minded neighbors. We need a stronger understanding that pursuit of the good life is only possible when we seek some goods in common. We will only be ready to address the realities of urban poverty when, in Cornel West's words, we "focus our attention on the public square – the common good that undergirds our national and global destinies."[15]

This requires a kind of community that is both deeper and wider than a suburban enclave or an isolated inner-city ghetto. Bellah *et al.* contrast the suburban enclave with the community described by Aristotle as the *polis* and by Cicero as the *res publica* – the "commonwealth" or the "commonweal." This stronger community can come to be only when we recognize that divisions between city and

[13] Wolfe, *One Nation After All*, p. 223. [14] Patterson, *The Ordeal of Integration* p. 10.
[15] Cornel West, *Race Matters* (Boston: Beacon Press, 1993), p. 6.

suburb affect all who live in the larger metropolitan region, not only those in the ghettoes. For this urban – suburban division is a "common bad" that reduces the quality of life for all it affects. It also impedes the attainment of the shared good of a metropolitan community that is livable, safe, and prosperous for all. Thus Cornel West argues that the urban – suburban rift paradoxically shows that "our common destiny is more pronounced and emperiled precisely when our divisions are deeper."[16] A good community is a place where people are genuinely interdependent on each other through their participation in, discussion concerning, and decision-making about their common purposes. It is a place where people make decisions together about the kind of society they want to live in together. It is a community that goes beyond tolerance to the pursuit of the common good. Addressing the problems of American cities will be impossible if we cannot more closely approximate the ideal of such a community in the United States today. We will return to how a vision of the common good points the way toward such a community in chapter 7.

HOW BIG A WORLD?

A second challenge to the primacy of a live-and-let live ethos is the growing global web of interaction that links people together across the national boundaries that have traditionally separated them. Trade, finance, mass communications, the interaction of cultures, protection of the environment, the AIDS crisis, and the reality of poverty are all matters that have increasingly global dimensions. Today, economic, cultural, and political affairs occur within networks of human interaction that stretch across national borders. An ethos whose primary values are independence and autonomy is not adequate to address this new interdependence. Such an ethos systematically avoids attending to the impact of human interconnections on the quality of life by focusing on the freedom and choices of individuals one at a time. When the possibility of attaining good lives and freedom itself are becoming more dependent on new interconnections, however, much more attention must be given to the way the well-being of individuals is shaped by institutional

[16] *Ibid.*, pp. 3–4.

connections with others. Globalization is thus challenging the received tradition of public values that has prevailed in the West for the past several centuries.

The term "globalization" is used in a variety of ways with both negative and positive normative overtones. In the United States, for example, third-party presidential candidate Ralph Nader identifies it with the dominant power of large, transnational corporations: "The global corporate model is premised on the concentration of power over markets, governments, mass media . . . critical drugs and seeds, the workplace and corporate culture. All these . . . homogenize the globe and undermine democratic processes and their benefits."[17] In the developing world, the term "globalization" often carries even more negative connotations. K. N. Panikhar sees it as "ensuring the necessary climate for domination and hegemonization [of developing countries] by the consortium of the world capitalist countries."[18] On the other hand, President George W. Bush sees these new global linkages as opportunities for positive economic change that will improve the lives of the poor through the expansion of markets and trade. In his words, "Vast regions and nations from Chile to Thailand are escaping the bonds of poverty and oppression by embracing markets and trade and new technologies. What some call globalization is, in fact, the triumph of human liberty stretching across national borders. And it holds the promise of delivering billions of the world's citizens from disease and hunger and want."[19] Others who hope that global interconnections can open up new, positive forms of cross-cultural understanding also express positive expectations. As Martha Nussbaum has put it, "the imagination can cross cultural boundaries" and can lead to "the acknowledgement of certain common needs and goals amid the many local differences

[17] Ralph Nader, "In the Public Interest" newspaper column (December 7, 1999). Cited on the website of Issues 2000. Internet source:
http://www.issues2000.org/Ralph_Nader_Free_Trade.htm (downloaded June 20, 2001).
[18] K. N. Panikhar, "Globalization and Culture," *Voices from the Third World* 20, no. 1 (1997), 50.
[19] George W. Bush, "Remarks by the President to the World Bank," July 17, 2001, available on the White House website at
http://www.whitehouse.gov/news/releases/2001/07/20010717-1.html (downloaded December 16, 2001).

that divide us."[20] In this view, growing global communication and interaction can deepen mutual understanding where ignorance or hostility formerly reigned, increasing the possibilities of a more just and peaceful world.[21]

Which of these responses to globalization is right? To answer this question we must put the connections among people back at the center of social and moral inquiry. What kinds of interaction will enhance the quality of people's lives? What is the scope of the political, economic, and cultural communities that will be most supportive of good lives for their members? How big a world can we live in while aspiring to live well? In other words, emerging patterns of interaction and interdependence call for reflection on the scope of the communities and the reach of human relationships that will make good lives possible. An ethos that does not acknowledge that many of the goods and bads in human lives arise within different forms of human interconnection, therefore, has no way to address the new and unavoidable questions raised by globalization. To address these questions we need a form of moral inquiry that explores how human interconnections are central to attaining or failing to attain the good life. The idea of common goods and common bads, therefore, must play central roles in a normative framework adequate to guide response to new forms of global connection. It is certainly true that a philosophy of independence and autonomy can critique the negative aspects of global connectedness. But it can also lead to uncritical judgments that human connections in any form are threats to human well-being and to similarly negative verdicts about the possibilities of globalization. If we are to discern the difference between the negative and positive aspects of globalization we need a more discriminating stance than an autonomy-based, live-and-let-live normative framework can provide.

The lack of a coherent framework that takes account of the global dimensions of the common good is evident in the confused and conflicting currents of public opinion on a variety of cross-border

---

[20] Martha C. Nussbaum, *Cultivating Humanity: A Classical Defense of Reform in Liberal Education* (Cambridge, MA: Harvard University Press, 1997), p. 83; see also chaps. 2, 4, and Conclusion.

[21] See examples of these hopes in, for example, Pierre Teilhard de Chardin, *The Phenomenon of Man* (New York: Harper and Row, 1965), esp. Book Four, chaps. 1 and 2.

issues today. American attitudes toward the overall phenomenon of globalization are slightly more positive than negative. Sixty-one percent of Americans think that the government should "actively promote" globalization or "allow it to continue," while only 26 percent think government should try to "slow it down" or to "stop or reverse it." Of those advocating governmental resistance to globalization, however, just under half thought such resistance could succeed. When asked to rate the general effects of globalization with 0 as completely negative and 10 as completely positive, the average American response was 6.04. This was slightly more positive than the evaluation found in most European countries.[22]

The stance of most Americans toward global or international affairs can be characterized as one of "guarded engagement" and "tempered internationalism." It is internationalist rather than isolationist, for Americans recognize that the United States cannot pull up the drawbridge to the rest of the world. In 1998, 61 percent of Americans thought "it would be best for the future of the country if we take an active part in world affairs" while only 28 percent thought it would be best "if we stay out of world affairs."[23] But this internationalism is tempered by a desire to be "realistic" about the terms of engagement with the larger world. For example, though most Americans believe that they have a moral obligation to aid poor countries and especially to provide assistance to people who are hungry, approximately half of Americans think present levels of aid should be reduced. This is a notably more favorable public attitude to foreign aid than in the recent past. But when compared to citizens of other developed countries, a relatively

[22] See Program on International Policy Attitudes, *Americans on Globalization: A Study of US Public Attitudes*, March 28, 2000, section 1, "Globalization in General." PIPA is a joint program of the Center on Policy Attitudes (COPA) and the Center for International and Security Studies at Maryland (CISSM), School of Public Affairs, University of Maryland. This report available on the Internet at http://www.pipa.org/OnlineReports/Globalization/contents.html (downloaded June 19, 2001).

[23] Chicago Council on Foreign Relations, "American Public Opinion and US Foreign Policy 1999," ed. John E. Reiley (Chicago: Chicago Council on Foreign Relations, 1999), 4. For a provocative study of the differences between American public opinion on the wisdom of international engagement and the beliefs of policymakers about what the public actually believes, see Steven Kull and I. M. Destler, *Misreading the Public: The Myth of a New Isolationism* (Washington, D.C.: Brookings Institution, 1999).

large number of Americans think their country gives too much to poor countries. This negative attitude seems to be due to very high overestimates by Americans of the amount of aid actually being provided by the United States as well as to their concerns about both the effectiveness of aid and about corruption among recipient governments.[24]

American opinion about engagement with the larger world is marked by a combination of ethical values and factual understandings of what is actually happening that can only be called confused. This confusion is evident when we probe behind the general attitudes toward international engagement to more specific aspects of such engagement. The generally positive descriptive phrases "tempered internationalism" and "guarded engagement" obscure the fact that the concrete global issues about which decisions must be made evoke quite different kinds of response. Active involvement in world affairs can take very different forms. These range from policies aimed at protection of the global environment, to protection of American jobs in the global market, to prevention of genocide by military means, to maintenance of low oil prices. Calling positive public opinion toward engagement with these issues "internationalism" veils the important factual and normative differences among the different kinds of global connection these issues involve. Thus Alvin Richman has pointed out that "internationalist" and "isolationist" are not at opposite ends of a single scale on which all attitudes toward the larger world can be measured. Different issues evoke quite different attitudes, and we must pay attention to what is actually at stake in the responses of public opinion to these issues. Richman has distinguished four different dimensions of public opinion that can help clarify the present state of thinking about how the good life in a highly developed country like the United States is connected with the well-being of people in other parts of the world.[25]

---

[24] Program on International Policy Attitudes, *Americans on Foreign Aid and World Hunger: A Study of US Public Attitudes*, February 2, 2001, Executive Summary. Available on the Internet at http://www.pipa.org/OnlineReports/BFW/toc.html (downloaded June 19, 2001).

[25] Alvin Richman, "American Support for International Involvement: General and Specific Components of Post-Cold War Changes," *Public Opinion Quarterly* 60 (Summer, 1996), 305–321. Richman's analysis is based on the Chicago Council on Foreign Relations 1995 quadrennial survey, "American Public Opinion and US Foreign

Drawing on 1995 data, Richman points out that Americans' highest level of global concern is in areas where activities occurring outside the United States or across US borders have an impact on the quality of life within the US itself. For example, 85 percent of Americans in 1995 thought it "very important" to stop the flow of illegal drugs from abroad into the US, 72 percent thought reducing illegal immigration very important and 62 percent favored decreasing all forms of immigration (up from 49 percent in 1986). The same high level of concern with activities abroad that have negative effects within the US is clear from the fact that 83 percent thought that "protecting the jobs of American workers" is very important. For each of these matters the high level of interest stems from a concern for the well-being of individual Americans and of the national community as a whole. Such interest clearly does not provide evidence that growing global interdependence is making Americans more cosmopolitan in their value system, though these interests all count as indicating a concern with international affairs. In fact one could draw the opposite conclusion: interdependence is leading to more defensive stances and Americans want to protect their own good more vigorously than was necessary when the world was less interdependent.[26]

These survey results may suggest that the "realist" model of international relations most adequately reflects the beliefs actually held by Americans. This theory holds that in international politics we should pursue the national interest; we should seek outcomes that enhance the well-being of American citizens. According to this realist model, it would be a mistake to conceive of foreign policy as an altruistic activity whose purpose is to relieve the suffering or overcome the oppression of people in other countries.[27] But a second

Policy 1995." More recent data is available in Chicago Council on Foreign Relations, "American Public Opinion and U.S. Foreign Policy 1999," available on the Internet at http://www.ccfr.org/publications/opinion/AmPuOp99.pdf (downloaded June 25, 2001)

[26] This conclusion is explicitly drawn in the Chicago Council on Foreign Relations 1999 survey of American attitudes on foreign policy: "The ranking of goals, particularly among the general public, shows a strong emphasis on self-interest, with the highest goals addressing concerns about the economic and social wellbeing and the physical safety of Americans." Chicago Council on Foreign Relations, "American Public Opinion and US Foreign Policy 1999," 17.

[27] This phrase is from a recent statement of the case for "realism" under current global conditions: Michael Mandelbaum, "Foreign Policy as Social Work," *Foreign Affairs* 75, no. 1

dimension of public opinion toward international involvement raises questions about whether Americans can be flatly categorized as foreign policy realists. Richman calls this the dimension of "US global interests." It highlights concerns about realities that have common effects on the whole human community and become US interests precisely because the US is part of the global whole. Examples of public concern for goods that are simultaneously important to the United States and to the whole world include the facts that many Americans think it "very important" to prevent the spread of nuclear weapons (82 percent), to secure adequate energy supplies (64 percent), and to improve the global environment (53 percent).[28] In the same vein, 62 percent agreed in 1995 that "the United States should cooperate fully with the United Nations."[29] In each of these areas the concept of the national interest or the common good of the country cannot be defined over against the good of the larger world. An issue such as the protection of the global environment points to ways that the good of one country and the good of the larger world are intertwined or, in the long run, even identical. It calls for a wider horizon for thinking about the national interest than the realist paradigm of international affairs has traditionally envisioned. This widening is necessary because the scope of the national interest as understood in traditional realism does not correspond to the way genuine goods and harms cut across national boundaries in the new era of globalization. Clearly, it is not excessively idealistic or unrealistic to include the depletion of the ozone layer or the spread of nuclear weapons as matters that touch the national interest. Looking beyond national borders to goods and evils with global effects is a requirement of a more enlightened realism when nuclear proliferation or environmental protection is at issue. Such an enlightened realism calls for an expansion of the scope of the community that must be considered when the national interest is being defined. The American people seem to sense this, at least incipiently, in certain areas of their national life.

(January/February, 1996), 17. For a parallel view, see Stephen John Stedman, "The New Interventionists," *Foreign Affairs* 72, no. 1 (1992–1993), 1–17.

[28] The data have been updated from those used by Richman in light of Chicago Council on Foreign Relations, "American Public Opinion and US Foreign Policy 1999," 16, though the more recent data lead to the same conclusion.

[29] Richman, "American Support for International Involvement," 316–317.

However, a third dimension of global interdependence raises the question of just where US interests are closely linked with the larger world. The "military security" dimension of public opinion deals with the link between US interests and those of strategic allies and the public's willingness to send US troops abroad. The trends during the post-Cold War period indicate a slight decline in the importance given to US defense of the security of allies, including Western Europe and South Korea but not including Israel, and a decreased support for commitment to NATO. Richman interprets these findings as an indication that public opinion has swung toward a less Euro-centered focus rather than as a decline of public support for security interests as such.[30] Commitment to the security of non-European countries, however, is also relatively low, for only 32 percent believe that it is very important for the United States to protect weaker nations against foreign aggression.[31]

Richman's fourth dimension of international concerns also suggests that there is not likely to be strong support for placing American interests at risk, especially the lives of American soldiers, for strictly humanitarian purposes. He calls this dimension "global altruism." With the exception of concern for combating world hunger, which is judged "very important" by 62 percent of Americans, measures of altruistic motivations for international involvement are the lowest of those uncovered by the surveys. In 1999, 39 percent of Americans said it was very important that US foreign policy promote and defend human rights in other countries, 29 percent said this of helping to bring democracy to other nations, and 29 percent of helping to improve the living standards of less developed countries.[32] All of these measures were at a twenty-year low in 1994. Americans therefore are unlikely to favor international engagement to promote the well-being of people in other countries when this is not immediately linked with domestic well-being. This seems especially true if the engagement being contemplated is military and it is just what the realist international relations paradigm

[30] *Ibid.*, 310, 319 321.
[31] Chicago Council on Foreign Relations, "American Public Opinion and US Foreign Policy 1999," 16.
[32] The data are for 1999 are in *ibid.*, 16. For Richman's interpretation of the 1994 poll data, see his "American Support for International Involvement," 313 314.

would predict. It supports Michael Mandelbaum's critique of the early promises and actual attempts by the Clinton administration to promote the well-being and human rights of people in Bosnia, Somalia, and Haiti. In Mandelbaum's view, Clinton's initial policies failed because they did not have public support.[33] It took a while for the Clinton administration to recognize this, but when it did so its policies became more rational because more realistic, for example, by granting priority to trade with the People's Republic of China over support for human rights in that country. The cost of this supposedly more "rational" policy, however, became tragically evident when the United States' earlier experience in Somalia led the Clinton administration's refusal to take action to prevent the 1994 genocide in Rwanda. The upshot of this "realistic" decision was the death of nearly one million people.[34]

These polls suggest, therefore, that Americans see a link between their own good as a nation and the good of people in other countries where this link is direct and obvious. An example of this kind of direct linkage is the need for environmental protection, a good that is indivisible in the long term because all countries are mutually dependent on the biophysical environment that knows no boundaries. The cutting of trees in the rain forests of Brazil affects CO_2 levels world-wide and the emissions from both developed and developing countries have an impact on the ozone layer on which the whole biosphere depends. Americans also see value in strengthening international institutions such as the United Nations because such institutions, if effective, can bring benefits to all nations. In areas such as these it is relatively easy to perceive the existence of a transnational or global common good that reaches beyond narrow definitions of the national interest. From a pragmatic point of view, it is clear that such issues cannot be addressed at all if self-interest

---

[33] Mandelbaum, "Foreign Policy as Social Work," 16.

[34] See the poignant and passionate statement of the failure of the international community in the face of the Rwanda genocide by the Canadian commander of UN forces in Rwanda, Romeo A. Dallaire, "The End of Innocence: Rwanda, 1994," in Jonathan Moore, ed., *Hard Choices: Moral Dilemmas in Humanitarian Intervention* (Lanham, MD: Rowman and Littlefield, 1998), pp. 71–86. President Clinton made an apology of sorts for US failure to act during his brief visit to Rwanda on March 25, 1998. Clinton's speech is available on the Internet at: http://usinfo.state.gov/regional/af/prestrip/w980325a.htm (downloaded June 28, 2001).

is defined in an exclusivist or nationalist way. On questions such as protecting American jobs, however, the traditional definition of the national interest as a narrowly construed protection of the country's citizens seems to be operative in public opinion. The same is true in the low levels of support for promotion of human rights abroad and assistance to poor countries.

Globalization, therefore, is deepening public concern about the shared goods that can be achieved in transnational relationships. But this concern is growing in some domains though not in others. It is relatively easy to make a pragmatic case for environmental protection, adequate energy supplies, non-proliferation of nuclear weapons, and support for collective security through the UN as goods that are both commonly shared and that help secure the well-being of individual US citizens. Thus these shared goods have come to be positively valued by the public. But this seems to have occurred without significantly challenging the underlying stance that grants primacy to the good of individuals within the boundaries of their country. Transnational issues that go beyond obvious interests of individual citizens, such as protection of human rights in other countries and assistance to poor nations, still receive low public support.

The awareness that some common goods converge with individual well-being, of course, could be the initial premise for an argument that transnational common goods should play a larger part in the public philosophy than a live-and-let-live ethos will support. This is indeed the case. The problem, however, is this convergence is less recognized than it needs to be in a world where global interdependence increasingly touches many aspects of human well-being and where public opinion is still inclined to grant normative priority to independence. This bias in public opinion should not be surprising given the continuing strong influence of a public philosophy that sees autonomy as its highest and almost exclusive value. This bias, however, obscures many of the less immediately evident ways that interdependence either threatens or supports personal well-being today. The value orientations present in public opinion, therefore, easily blind us to many ways that individual and shared well-being are interconnected.

This is evident from the ways that real-world events that evoke the four different strands of American public opinion distinguished by Richman are in fact practically intertwined with each other. We cannot draw sharp distinctions among international concerns that are intrinsically global, such as the environment, those that are focused around domestic well-being, such as the impact of trade on American jobs, and those that seem entirely dependent on altruism, such as protection of human rights and aid for the poor in other countries. These different threads of the growing web of interdependence are tangled together. This leads to confusion about when and where pursuit of realistic self-interest can promote the good life today and when and where a more cosmopolitan perspective on globally shared goods is needed. Because of this confusion, public opinion is increasingly prone to support actions whose outcomes are at odds with each other. Xabier Gorostiaga says these confusions reflect the "contradictions of globalization."[35] As examples, consider a few of the tensions evident today.

First, environmental issues and poverty in developing countries are connected with each other. The struggle for survival in developing countries is one of the most significant threats to the flora, fauna, and atmosphere of the world, for it drives the desperately poor to exploit whatever resources are available, regardless of the long-term environmental impact.[36] When the rich press poor countries to adopt environmentally sensitive policies, this can hamper development, which in turn can have further harmful environmental effects. The value the American public places on environmental protection is thus in tension or even conflict with the low value it places on working to overcome poverty in less developed countries. As representatives of developing countries often point out at international conferences, developed countries already consume disproportionate percentages of the world's natural resources. Policies that fail to support development in poor countries can also be expected to keep population growth high in those countries, which will also have negative environmental effects. Conversely, the reduction of poverty has historically led to population decline, which in turn has positive benefits for environmental quality. Positive public

---

[35] See Xabier Gorostiaga, "Geocultural Development," paper presented to the conference on "Desafíos éticos para el siglo XXI." Santiago, Chile, 1995. Gorostiaga uses this term with a somewhat different connotation than it has here.

[36] See Thomas M. Landy, "Connecting Poverty and Sustainability," *Boston College Environmental Affairs Law Review* 21 (Winter, 1994), 277–289.

attitudes toward environmental protection and the apparently low value placed by the public on aid to developing countries thus give contradictory directions to US international policies. Similarly, protection of human rights and the promotion of democracy are linked with economic development and thus with population and environmental concerns, but the valuations operative in public opinion do not reflect this linkage.

A second contradiction is directly economic. It has often been pointed out that maintaining American jobs in a global marketplace requires strong demand for American goods in other parts of the world. Thus fulfilling the desire to protect the jobs of Americans requires economic strength and growth elsewhere, including enhanced development in poor countries. Through the 1970s and 1980s, the US government as well as international financial institutions such as the International Monetary Fund viewed the free market as the engine that would bring further growth to potential trading partners in already advanced countries and new demand for US goods in developing countries. The so-called "Washington consensus" on development policy saw free trade and free markets abroad as the principal ways both to stimulate development in poor countries and simultaneously to protect American jobs and prosperity.[37] This set of policies called for fewer restrictions on trade and the movement of capital, and for less government intervention in the market more generally. In more recent years, however, questions have arisen about the adequacy of this model. American labor unions have taken increasingly strong stands against trade arrangements such as the North American Free Trade Agreement. The United Auto Workers, for example, has argued that expansion of NAFTA to the Americas as a whole

---

[37] See John Williamson, "What Washington Means by Policy Reform," in Williamson, ed., *Latin American Adjustment: How Much Has Happened?* (Washington, D.C.: Institute for International Economics, 1990); Williamson, "What Should the Bank Think about the Washington Consensus?" paper prepared as a background to the World Bank's World Development Report 2000 in July 1999, available on the Internet at http://www.iie.com/papers/williamson0799.htm (downloaded July 16, 2001). For proposed revisions in this consensus, see Moisés Naím, "Washington Consensus or Washington Confusion?" *Foreign Policy* 118 (Spring, 2000), 87–103; Jeffrey Sachs, "A New Global Consensus on Helping the Poorest of the Poor," keynote address at the World Bank's Annual Bank Conference on Development Economics, April 18, 2000, available on the Internet at http://orion.forumone.com/ABCDE/files.fcgi/210_Sachs.pdf (downloaded July 16, 2001).

would be a "huge mistake." In the UAW's view, such an expansion of free trade without sanctions for poor labor and environmental conditions in other countries "would trigger a race to the bottom as countries compete with each other for investment on the basis of who has the lowest labor and environmental standards. It would also raise the specter of massive surges of imports in the agricultural and manufacturing sectors that could threaten the livelihoods of thousands of Americans."[38] At the same time, the World Bank has qualified its faith in the market as a sure route to advancement of the poorest in less developed countries. The World Bank's 2001 *World Development Report* stresses that the vulnerability and powerlessness of the world's poorest people means that development policy should address their needs directly if development is to reach them.[39] Free markets and a smaller role for government will not do the job alone. The provision of basic social services and protection of the most vulnerable members of society are among the most fundamental roles of the state and are essential to broad-based development.[40] Virtually no one doubts that markets are here to stay and are essential to a dynamic economy that promotes human well-being. But there are rising tensions and even contradictions between the commitment to the market as the means to increased well-being and the actual effects of the market on the poorest members of society. Also, the significant efforts to restrict immigration into developing countries show that the commitment to freedom of movement of economic resources across borders applies to capital and products but not to labor. Thus it is far from evident how the public philosophy of autonomy that shapes American public opinion today can effectively address the crisscrossing of the economic issues raised by globalization and the tensions among them.

A third contradiction of globalization might be called the paradox of growing limitations on state sovereignty. Growing global interdependence is putting pressure on the independence and

---

[38] United Auto Workers Action Alert, "No Fast Track for Bush Administration," June 4, 2001, available on the Internet at: http://www.uaw.org/action/060401fasttrack.html (downloaded July 16, 2001).

[39] World Bank, *World Development Report 2000/2001* (Oxford and New York: Oxford University Press, 2000), esp. pp. 31–41.

[40] See World Bank, *World Development Report 1997: The State in a Changing World* (Oxford and New York: Oxford University Press, 1997), chap. 3.

sovereignty of states from a number of directions. Pressures on national governments are being exerted from "above" by international organizations such as the UN, from intergovernmental bodies like the European Union and the World Trade Organization, and from transnational political regimes governing matters such as human rights and the environment. These pressures can make national governments less immediately responsive to the self-identified needs of their citizens. At the same time, there is pressure on national governments from "below" by regional and ethnic communities whose experience of globalization has led to a reassertion of their distinctive cultural identities. Pressures for the devolution of power from national to regional levels or even secession in Québec, Scotland, Wales, Euskal Herria (the Basque Country) and Catalunya (Catalonia) are examples of this phenomenon in the developed world. It is even more widespread in the developing world, where civil strife has been an all-too-frequent result. Finally, national governments experience pressure from the "side" by the growing cadre of non-governmental organizations that increasingly influence governments through their well-organized transnational activities. The influence of these non-governmental bodies has increased dramatically due to the enhanced communication made possible by the internet and other global communications systems.[41]

Democrats have long sought to keep government responsive to those it governs by limiting the power of the state. So declining governmental power may sound good from a democratic point of view. But the matter is not so simple. These pressures make it more difficult than in the past for national governments to formulate coherent policies. This in turn can make governments less able to respond to the expressed needs of their citizens. At the same time, the governments of nation-states remain very significant forces in the lives of their citizens. The policies of these states are one of the most important ways people can get a "grip" on the complexities of the globalization process.[42] The paradox, therefore, is

---

[41] See Jessica T. Mathews, "Power Shift," *Foreign Affairs* 76, no. 1 (January/February, 1997), 50–66.

[42] Robert O. Keohane, "Hobbes's Dilemma and Institutional Change in World Politics: Sovereignty in International Society," in Hans-Henrik Holm and Georg Sørensen, eds.,

that globalization connects people with each other in new ways politically while it also leads them to look to older political structures to help them deal with the impact of these new connections.

In short, a social vision that does not regard human connection as central to the attainment of well-being lacks the conceptual tools needed to think through these new issues raised by globalization. Human beings are increasingly embedded in a complex, transnational framework of interdependence. Their well-being is increasingly dependent on the connections among them, on levels including the environmental, economic, cultural, and political. A value system that gives primacy of place to non-interference and non-judgmentalism lacks the criteria needed to address these connections in a critical manner. Such a critical approach calls for a different starting point; it requires a framework that can assess the relative merits of different modes of living *together*. It calls for new thinking about how the common good might play a more central role in world affairs.

THE NEED FOR SHARED GOODS

New thinking about issues such as urban poverty and emerging patterns of world-wide interdependence will require some basic changes in presuppositions about public life today. We need to rethink the attitudes and ideas that shape the way we live together. Taken together as a more or less coherent body of beliefs, these attitudes and ideas can be called our public philosophy. Michael Sandel has defined such a public philosophy as "the political theory implicit in our practice, the assumptions about citizenship and freedom that inform our public life."[43] This theory is most often tacit in the patterns of public life, but it is operative even when only partially recognized. It is the set of taken-for-granted understandings of how

Whose World Order? Uneven Globalization and the End of the Cold War (Boulder, CO: Westview Press, 1995), p. 177. For other, complementary interpretations of these pressures on the nation-state from above, below, and the side, see Michael Mann, "Has Globalization Ended the Rise and Rise of the Nation-State?" *Review of International Political Economy* 4, no. 3 (Autumn, 1997), 472–496, and James N. Rosenau, "Governance and Democracy in a Globalizing World," in Daniele Archibugi, David Held, and Martin Köhler, eds. *Re-imagining Political Community: Studies in Cosmopolitan Democracy* (Stanford, CA: Stanford University Press, 1998), pp. 28–57.

[43] Michael Sandel, *Democracy's Discontent*, p. 4.

we should interact with one another. It is also the source of the questions we ask when faced with novel social situations requiring innovative responses. If these presuppositions prove incapable of providing satisfactory responses to pressing practical questions, the public philosophy needs to be rethought and revised.[44] The issues of urban poverty and global interdependence challenge the adequacy of a public philosophy shaped by the attitude of wariness and the values of tolerance and non-judgmentalism. We need to develop a public philosophy in which social connections and the goods that can only be achieved through these connections play more central roles. This will be a public philosophy that combines commitment to the common good with respect for the equality and freedom of all members of the relevant communities.

The prevailing public philosophy of tolerance presupposes that people are safest when no one can interfere with their pursuit of their own understandings of the good. It does not go so far as to suggest that people are better off when they are alone. That would be absurd. But it does regard communal interaction with suspicion. But we face problems of a very different kind from those that made tolerance such a deeply held value. The situation of today's cities and growing global interdependence suggest that finding stronger shared vision is required. Building a public philosophy on wariness toward the dangers of the idea of the common good leads in the wrong direction. Contemporary urban poverty and global interdependence both reveal strong social currents that isolate individuals and threaten them through social fragmentation. Such threats will be misinterpreted if they are forced into an intellectual Procrustean bed that was constructed in the sixteenth and seventeenth centuries. Where domination of one group by another is the problem, building defensive barriers against the surrounding social ambiance can appear a reasonable response. But if isolation and fragmentation are among the principal dangers, strategies designed solely to keep people from interfering with one another will be misdirected. Inappropriately directed fear of tyranny can slide

---

[44] There is an evident parallel between this description of the way the public philosophy comes to be revised and Thomas A. Kuhn's well-known model of innovation in the sciences. See his *The Structure of Scientific Revolutions*, second edition, enlarged (Chicago: University of Chicago Press, 1970).

into fear of any form of social connectedness or interdependence of persons in society. It can lead to responses that actually deepen isolation and social fragmentation. What is needed is to discover a better way to live together.

The problems raised by urban poverty and global interdependence are admittedly not the whole story of contemporary social life in the United States and the West more generally. But there are other important matters that raise similar questions about the adequacy of a public philosophy of wariness and tolerance. Among these is the issue of how to provide adequate health care to *all* people when technological innovation is relentlessly opening up new treatment options and driving up costs.[45] Equally significant is the fact that citizenship has itself become a problematic concept in our time. One author has named this problem the "eclipse of citizenship."[46] The low percentage of Americans who exercise their right to vote is only the most visible evidence for this eclipse. A strong case can be made, therefore, that the issues raised here are representative of significant currents in contemporary social life. They provide evidence that the liberalism of wariness and tolerance, taken neat, is a way of avoiding rather than addressing many of the problems we face today. "I won't bother you if you don't bother me" implies that everyone would be better off if people would just leave each other alone.[47] This is not an adequate stance toward key problems in social life today.

[45] Daniel Callahan has been arguing the need for a revitalized conception of the common good in health care ethics for many years. See, for example, his *What Kind of Life: The Limits of Medical Progress* (New York: Simon and Schuster, 1990), "Bioethics: Private Choice and the Common Good," *Hastings Center Report* (May/June, 1994), 28–31, and *False Hopes: Why America's Quest for Perfect Health is a Recipe for Failure* (New York: Simon and Schuster, 1998).

[46] Robert J. Pranger, *The Eclipse of Citizenship: Power and Participation in Contemporary Politics* (New York: Holt, Rinehart and Winston, 1968). See also Michael Walzer, "The Problem of Citizenship," in *Obligations: Essays on Disobedience, War, and Citizenship* (Cambridge, MA: Harvard University Press, 1970), pp. 203–228.

[47] Richard Rorty says this is his and Dewey's view of the matter: "He [Dewey] assumed that no good achieved by earlier societies would be worth recapturing if the price were a diminution in our ability to leave people alone, to let them try out their private visions of perfection in peace." See Rorty, "The Priority of Democracy to Philosophy," in Merrill D. Peterson and Robert Vaughan, eds., *The Virginia Statute for Religious Freedom: Its Evolution and Consequences in American History* (Cambridge/New York: Cambridge University Press, 1988), p. 273. This, however, is only one aspect of Rorty's (and Dewey's) public philosophies, for they both have strong commitments to human solidarity in the context of democracy. This tension raises central issues that will be discussed below.

The growing *de facto* interdependence in both national and international life requires a stronger vision of the goods we share in common. It calls for exploration of how the well-being of individual people might be advanced by seeking goods we must share in common if we are to have them at all. For the suburban middle class, "lifestyle enclaves" often seem to be the only form of communal connection that is realistically available, with a consequent devaluation of larger forms of public life. But the social divisions that make enclaves necessary can be addressed only by a renewed commitment to a larger public good. Addressing these divisions also calls for the discovery of ways to draw African American male youth out of the detached stance that Orlando Patterson calls the "cool-pose street culture."[48] Cornel West puts this more positively as the challenge of repoliticizing of black working poor and underclass, along with increasing the involvement of the black middle class in such politics.[49] In both the cities and suburbs, therefore, public life needs to emerge from its eclipse. This will depend on revitalizing a sense of being a citizen linked to others in a common world. A similar and even more daunting task arises as we contemplate how to govern a more interconnected, globalizing world in ways that respect democratic commitments to equality and self-governance.

There is considerable irony in the present situation. The same social conditions that set people on guard against too-close connection with each other are the very conditions of a qualitatively new form of objective, structured interconnection among persons. Technology, bureaucracy, mobility, and rapid communication make the public world seem alien and impersonal. At the same time these factors heighten the impact that the structures of the public world have on the dignity and meaning of individual lives. This increased *de facto* "socialization" of many domains of human living was identified as one of the principal "signs of the times" by both Pope John XXIII and the Second Vatican Council.[50] In such circumstances,

[48] Patterson, *The Ordeal of Integration*, pp. 171–203. Patterson sees this culture as continuous with broader American values but as an extreme expression of its worst aspects. Patterson's interpretation should be carefully distinguished from the one presented by those Patterson calls "professional racists such as Charles Murray" (p. 178).

[49] Cornel West, *Keeping Faith: Philosophy and Race in America* (New York: Routledge, 1993), pp. 288–89.

[50] See Pope John XXIII, *Christianity and Social Progress (Mater et Magistra)*, no. 59, in David J. O' Brien and Thomas A. Shannon, eds., *Catholic Social Thought: The Documentary Heritage*

the eclipse of citizenship threatens to allow the institutions of social life to slip from the control of human freedom or to fall under the direction of powerful elites. Thus at the very time that it has become increasingly difficult to sustain a vision of the common good, it is more urgently important that we find a way to do so.

The question we face is this: can commitment to the common good be revitalized without simultaneously encouraging conflicts like the religious wars that generated the liberalism of fear in the early days of the modern West? Alternatively put, can commitment to the common good become a moral force in contemporary life without legitimating or, worse, intensifying the conflicts between groups holding different ideas of what is truly good? William Galston answers these questions in the affirmative: "[T]he fact that liberalism was born in fear does not mean that it must necessarily remain there."[51] The increased interdependence of our emerging historical context provides opportunities to reconsider ways that classical conceptions of the common good can reshape presuppositions about how we might live together. The new context in fact demands the discovery of alternatives to the public philosophy of tolerance we have inherited from the past few centuries. This does not mean, of course, that romantic appeals to "the good old days" of ancient conceptions of the common good will address our problems. What has been called the "terminal wistfulness" of some recent appeals to premodern ways is not very helpful.[52] We cannot simply invoke Aristotle or Aquinas for solutions to our problems. Their world was vastly different from ours and one hopes we have actually learned something from the intervening centuries. But entirely

(Maryknoll, NY: Orbis Books, 1992), p. 93; Vatican Council II, *Pastoral Constitution on the Church in the Modern World (Gaudium et Spes)*, no. 25, in O'Brien and Shannon, eds., *Catholic Social Thought*, p. 181.

[51] William A. Galston, *Liberal Purposes: Goods, Virtues, and Diversity in a Liberal State* (Cambridge: Cambridge University Press, 1991), p. 12. Galston adopts a somewhat less ambitious approach to answering these questions affirmatively than will be developed here and in the subsequent chapters of this book.

[52] The phrase "terminal wistfulness" is Richard Rorty's, "The Priority of Democracy to Philosophy," p. 272. Though I share Rorty's rejection of this nostalgia, it will be clear below that I do not endorse Rorty's alternative to it. Ideas of community and the common good need to be *critically reconstructed*, not simply retrieved. See also Jeffrey Stout, *Ethics After Babel: The Languages of Morals and Their Discontents* (Boston: Beacon Press, 1988), chap. 10, "Liberal Apologetics and Terminal Wistfulness."

to dismiss such ancient conceptions of the common good may fore-
close possibilities we cannot afford to ignore.

This book does not aspire to provide detailed answers or policy
recommendations for the numerous problems in the areas of urban poverty and international politics in an interdependent world.
These issues are discussed here as illustrations of the way urgent
practical matters are pressing our society to develop a different normative and moral framework for conducting its affairs. The goal
here is a relatively modest one: to shed some new light on these
complex matters by drawing upon aspects of the tradition of reflection on the common good that are too often overlooked today.
Part Two will propose some theoretical orientations that can help
develop such a framework.

PART II

Frameworks

CHAPTER THREE

Recovering the commonweal

A long time ago, Cicero expressed concerns like those we have been outlining about the likely effect of the waning of a vision of the public good on the future of the prosperous Roman Empire of his day. Fifty years before the birth of Christ, Cicero had concluded that the citizens of Rome no longer possessed the common vision required if they were to be a people at all. They had lost the moral consciousness needed to sustain their common life together. Cicero used the Latin phrase *res publica* to describe this common life. Literally this means "the public thing." It can more aptly be translated as civil affairs, the commonweal, the common good, a commonwealth, or simply a republic. Cicero defined the commonweal this way:

Res publica, res populi, populus autem non omnis hominum coetus quoquo modo congregatus, sed coetus multitudinis iuris consensu et utilitatis communione sociatus.

A commonwealth is a thing of the people. But a people is not any collection [*coetus*] of human beings brought together [*congregatus*] in any sort of way, but an assemblage [*coetus*] of people in large numbers associated [*sociatus*] in agreement [*consensu*] with respect to justice [right, *juris*] and a partnership for the common good [*utilitatis communione*].[1]

Cicero's use of the Latin words *coetus, congregatus, consensu,* and *communione* points directly to the social union he presupposes must exist in a republic. Persons are envisioned as bound together by strong connections. They have come together in a *coetus* – the Latin word

---

[1] Cicero, *De Re Publica*, I, xxv, 39, trans. C. W. Keyes, Loeb Classical Library, vol. CCXIII (Cambridge, MA: Harvard University Press, 1966), pp. 64–65. I have translated *res populi* literally as "a thing of the people" rather than following Keyes's translation ("property of the people") because of the Lockean connotations of the English word "property."

is cognate to *coitus*, sexual union. Their good is shared in a *communio* or communion. The links among them are formed by their common consent, their *consensus*, about what is just, right, and good. Understood this way, a republic requires a notable degree of social unity, perhaps a considerably higher level than the experience of the past several centuries leads us to expect today.

In 1787, when Benjamin Franklin was asked what kind of government the American founders had provided for the new nation of the United States, he replied: "A republic if you can keep it."[2] Have we "kept it," or has the social unity required to be a republic been lost? Before dismissing hope for such unity as romantic and even dangerous, we should remember that Cicero's definition of a republic was not formulated for a small, relatively homogeneous city-state. He was envisioning what was required in the "public affairs" of a Roman regime that extended well beyond the middle of the Italian peninsula to much of the world known to his readers. Cicero's context was in some ways more like that of the contemporary United States than like the Athens of Pericles or Aristotle. He knew that this close social unity had in fact evanesced in the Rome of his day. But he saw that as the source of Rome's problems, not as an inevitable consequence of its size. This lack of the bonds of common life was particularly problematic precisely because the demands of Rome's public life had grown in proportion to its extent. Cicero had concluded that, without a common vision and commitment among the citizens, no governmental structure would be "sufficient to found or to preserve . . . a commonwealth whose dominion extends so far and wide."[3] The lack of a shared sense of the good meant Rome was no longer prepared to address the problems of its complex social life. So it could no longer be called a republic in any meaningful sense: "It is through our own faults, not by any accident, that we retain only the form of the commonwealth, but have long since lost its substance."[4] In Cicero's view, Rome was already well advanced in the process of its decline and fall.

This sort of Ciceronian diagnosis has been applied to the United States by some recent political and philosophical thinkers. For

[2] Franklin's words are recorded in the diary of James McHenry, published in *The American Historical Review* 9 (1906), 618. Cited in John Bartlett, *Familiar Quotations*, revised and enlarged edition, ed. Emily Morrison Beck (Boston: Little, Brown, 1980), p. 348.
[3] Cicero, *De Re Publica*, v, i, 1.   [4] *Ibid.*, v, i, 2.

example, Alasdair MacIntyre has argued that Western societies, including the United States, possess but "simulacra of morality." We have "lost our comprehension, both theoretical and practical" of central aspects of morality, namely of the virtues needed to sustain the common good.[5] In some of his writings, MacIntyre regrettably yields to the wistfulness that is often found among such critics. According to MacIntyre's diagnosis, we need a shared vision of the good but lack it. But he has nothing to say about how we might address the problem so defined. We also lack the resources needed to regain such a vision. So the prognosis is grim. Like Rome, we are already well down the path of decline.

This is not a helpful response. We have been tracing some of the reasons to worry that there is a lack of shared national purpose in America today and that this is having serious negative consequences. The questions that now need to be addressed concern what needs to be done to remedy this lack and what can be done. Fortunately there are both traditional and more recent resources that lead in more constructive directions than are contained in MacIntyre's lament. The stakes here are high, so we cannot afford simply to deplore the present circumstances. A generation ago, the distinguished theologian John Courtney Murray stated the alternatives this way: "whether we like it or not, we are living in a religiously pluralistic society at a time of spiritual crisis; and the alternatives are the discovery of social unity or destruction."[6] Despite Murray's uncharacteristically apocalyptic tone, he was convinced that a stronger basis for social unity could be found than is provided by the philosophy of wariness. He was also convinced that the needed social unity can be combined with the great modern discovery of equal respect for the freedom of all.

FROM WARINESS TO SOLIDARITY IN FREEDOM

Reflection on how we might go about recovering the common good in a way that respects freedom can begin with some further considerations concerning tolerance. The high value placed on

[5] Alasdair MacIntyre, *After Virtue: A Study in Moral Theory* (Notre Dame, IN: University of Notre Dame Press, 1981), p. 2.
[6] John Courtney Murray, "Intercreedal Co-operation: Its Theory and Its Organization," *Theological Studies* 4 (1943), 257–286, at 274.

tolerance today can be rethought as expressing an aspiration for a good society of a certain kind. The hope placed in tolerance can be seen as a desire for a social good, not simply for the private well-being of individuals considered one at a time. Considered from such a social point of view, tolerance is important because we do not want society to be riven by religious or cultural war. Both the past several centuries in the West and the painful experiences of the Yugoslavias and Rwandas of the world today show that such conflicts have very high costs. These costs are born by individuals to be sure. But a large part of the cost to individuals is a direct result of the painful social losses that occur when common life disintegrates into the chaos of warring factions. Preventing these social losses requires respect for diverse religious faiths or other comprehensive understandings of the good life. But respect for this diversity does not mean total abandonment of the pursuit of a good shared in common. Rather it is a challenge to develop an understanding of the common good of a pluralist society – an understanding of the goods that we can and must pursue together even though we do not agree about what is good in every aspect of life.

A democratic republic is a social good, not simply a summation of the goods of its individual citizens considered one at a time. From this social standpoint, tyrannies and authoritarian governments undermine the common good itself. It is obvious, of course, that tyranny harms the individuals who are oppressed by it. But Aristotle and Thomas Aquinas pointed out that a tyrant is a ruler who uses governmental power for the ruler's own private good or for the good of some faction, rather than for the good of all the members of the community being governed.[7] Tyranny, like war, makes it impossible for many to share in the life of society in a way that actualizes their potential both as persons and as contributing members of the community. A tyrannical regime treats those it oppresses as if they did not really belong to the society. The tyrant or tyrannical in-group claims the social good as its own fiefdom. An authoritarian regime may claim to be serving the good of the people, but dachas on the Black Sea and Swiss bank accounts rarely

---

[7] Aristotle, *Nichomachean Ethics*, 1160b; *Politics*, 1279b; Thomas Aquinas, *Summa Theologiae* II–II, q. 42, art. 2, ad 3.

seem to be available to all when such regimes are in power. To be common, the common good must be the good of the people understood inclusively. In other words, an authoritarian regime is one whose understanding of who should share in the social good is too narrow. A tyranny's vision of the good is not a vision of a commonweal or of a good that is genuinely common.

In light of this kind of social evil, an appeal for tolerance can be heard as a demand that the social good be accessible to all. It makes a claim that people should not be excluded from sharing in the life of the commonwealth because of their religion, their race, their ethnicity, their gender, or other characteristics judged irrelevant to their status as citizens. Such considerations highlight that tolerance aims to secure a kind of society where basic respect is forthcoming for all people no matter where they have been born or live on the social and cultural map. Thus one can reenvision the aspiration for tolerance as an aspiration for a social good – the good that is realized when all persons share in the political, social, and cultural life of the communities whose activities affect their well-being. Seen in this light, tolerance is an instrumental rather than an ultimate value; its purpose is to assure that the common good is truly common, i.e., shared in by all.

It can be asked, of course, whether this does not finally amount to protecting the well-being of individuals considered one at a time. Respect for the dignity and well-being of persons, to be sure, implies that persons are not mere parts of the social whole, like cogs in a large machine. The good of an individual person is not simply a part or a mathematical fraction of the good of the larger society. But neither is the social good simply the mathematical sum of individual goods. The relation between the good of persons and the common good is more complex than the mathematical operations of division or summation can represent. For this reason individualistic arguments that conceive of tolerance as leaving individuals alone miss the important social and public dimensions of respect for persons. People who live alone have no occasion to be either tolerant or intolerant; the concept simply does not apply to them.

Seeing tolerance as a call to leave each other alone would suggest that in a maximally tolerant society there would be a minimum of human interaction. Following this line of thinking, the best way to be fully tolerant of others would be never to speak and never to do anything that actually affects other people. For all speech that is not simply a repetition of what someone else has already said must either add to or disagree with what the other has voiced. Meaningful speech very often suggests that the person addressed should develop or change what he or she presently thinks and has already expressed. Tolerance understood as leaving each other alone would avoid making such suggestions; it would simply accept what the other has said and leave the matter at that. No new ideas would ever be proposed in public, for their very newness could be seen as some sort of challenge to those who do not already agree with them. In the same way, any form of genuine human action adds to or tries to change the direction of what is happening. Simply drifting along in the current of already unfolding events is not human action at all. Innovative action does not simply tolerate the direction of events but seeks to reorient it – sometimes incrementally, sometimes in fundamental ways. Tolerance understood as never challenging opinions that sustain the *status quo* would therefore reduce us to silence and inactivity. It would lock us into our own solitude in a state of suspended animation.

There is something fundamentally wrong with formulating the aspiration for mutual respect among persons in terms that lead to such absurd consequences. It is obvious, of course, that a public philosophy built around tolerance does not aim to get people to stop talking and acting. But this *reductio ad absurdum* suggests that something important is missing when we formulate the ideal of respect by only focusing on its importance for individuals regarded one at a time.

There is an alternative, however, that sees the commitment to tolerance as expressing a desire that no one be excluded from those goods they can only have together. This alternative comes into view when we recognize that mutual respect is a social reality. Respect for the worth of persons is embodied in the relationships of social interaction and in the societal structures that make genuine interaction possible. From such a perspective, mutual respect means interacting in ways that enhance the good of all who are involved in the social give-and-take. Mutual respect, therefore, is a shared or common good. It is a good that is realized when the members of society share in creating their life together. This good is truly common only when all members of society jointly create a common life together. It will be a common good only if all members also benefit from the good that has been created. Looked at from this perspective, the values sought in the name of tolerance are aspects of a good that is fundamentally social. Such a common good-based approach provides a theoretically more coherent way to understand the values tolerance seeks to protect. It provides a more efficacious way to secure these values in practice. It can also energize more helpful ways of responding to the growing *de facto* interdependence of the world today than can conceptions of tolerance that are part of a hangover from the excesses of the seventeenth century.

Charles Taylor has developed a line of argument that shows the plausibility and even the necessity of such a common good-based conception of mutual respect. It harks back to ancient understandings of the social nature of human existence while also showing how these ancient ideas can be retrieved in ways that are supportive of the freedoms valued so highly in our time. It will be useful to consider his argument here.

First, Taylor maintains that the modern notion that all persons have an equal claim to freedom is an idea that has been socially generated. It is the outcome of the social and cultural history of modern Western society. It is evident that self-determination and freedom to choose one's own way of life have not been valued as highly in all past cultures as they are in the West today. Very few societies, including contemporary non-Western ones, rank these values as high as we do. How do we explain this fact? Taylor argues that the idea that all persons ought to be treated as free, self-determining agents worthy of the respect called for by tolerance is a distinctively modern creation. The aspiration for universal self-determination had a social matrix. Its emergence was dependent on the social crises of the early modern West, and it is sustained today by social practices and institutions that were developed in response to these past social struggles. Contemporary Western men and women did not, all by themselves, come to demand respect as self-determining agents. They learned to value self-determination through interaction with the larger society in its social, religious, and political history.

They also learned that fulfilling this aspiration can only take place in social interaction with others. Self-determination is not isolated self-sufficiency. If literal self-sufficiency were possible it would be a kind of imprisonment in solitary confinement. Rather, placing a high value on self-determination goes together with a judgment about the inherent goodness of social practices and political institutions that sustain active participation by all in public life. The high value of self-determination is therefore linked with a judgment about a good that is shared in common. A society is a good society when it sustains freedom from tyranny, oppression, and war through the mutual respect its members show one another in their interactions and relationships. Further, sustaining this kind of society requires sustaining the social practices and public institutions that make it possible. The good of the individual as an equal, self-determining agent and the good of these practices and institutions are mutually implicating.

Taylor describes the internal connections between these social practices and our self-understanding as free persons worthy of equal respect this way:

[T]he free individual with his own goals and aspirations . . . is himself only possible within a certain kind of civilization . . . it took a long development of certain institutions and practices, of the rule of law, of rules of equal respect, of habits of common deliberation, of common association, of cultural self-development, and so on, to produce the modern individual; and . . . without these the very sense of oneself as an individual would atrophy.[8]

In other words, without the institutions and practices developed by modern democratic societies we could not sustain the value of mutual respect we affirm in the name of tolerance. The seemingly

---

[8] Charles Taylor, "The Nature and Scope of Distributive Justice," in *Philosophy and the Human Sciences*, Philosophical Papers 2 (Cambridge: Cambridge University Press, 1985), p. 309. He also puts it this way in another place:

[W]e live in a world in which there is such a thing as public debate about moral and political questions and other basic issues. We constantly forget how remarkable that is, how it did not have to be so, and may one day no longer be so. What would happen to our capacity to be free agents if this debate should die away, or if more specialized debate among intellectuals who attempt to define and clarify the alternatives facing us should also cease, or if the attempts to bring the culture of the past to life again as well as the drives to cultural innovation were to fall off? What would there be left to choose between? And if the atrophy went beyond a certain point, could we speak of choice at all? How long would we go on understanding what autonomous choice was? ("Atomism," in *Philosophy and the Human Sciences*, p. 205.)

individualistic value of tolerance, therefore, is sustained by implicit judgments about a good that is necessarily social and public. This good cannot even be conceived unless we think about the quality of relationships that connect persons together.

Taylor concludes that "the free individual or autonomous agent can only achieve and maintain his identity in a certain type of culture."[9] This kind of culture is one in which all persons have a voice in deliberation about public action. Its social practices and institutions provide the matrix out of which the freedom of modern self-determination is born.[10] These practices *protect* the freedom of individuals to be sure, as the ethic of tolerance would insist. But the practices and institutions of democracy are not merely instrumental means for the protection of a freedom that already exists for individuals considered as separate from society. In a way that the ethic of tolerance fails to take into account, these practices also *generate and sustain* the sense of being an agent in society, of having the power to make a difference by speaking and acting in a life shared with others.[11] They are therefore constitutive of the good of the self-determining personality. Being a self-determining person is internally linked with the social practices and institutions of a democratic polity – with the practices that make a republic possible in a pluralist society.

Taylor further develops this argument for the link between self-determination and the common good through an analogy with the way language works. The distinction drawn by Ferdinand de Saussure between a given language (*langue*) such as English or French, and a particular act of speaking (*parole)* is the basis of this analogy. A language such as English is a shared reality, a cultural system of communication that an individual learns from society. A child does not invent this language but is taught and receives it as a social given. After learning to speak the language one then uses it in all one's speaking. A particular act of speaking would be impossible without already having learned a given language like English. Every act of speaking, of course, communicates a specific message with a particular meaning. Cultures do not speak; people do. And

[9] *Ibid.*   [10] *Ibid.*, p. 209.
[11] Taylor, "The Nature and Scope of Distributive Justice," p. 310.

when people speak, they do not communicate whole languages but specific meanings. But actually communicating any meaning at all would be impossible unless both the speaker and the hearer already shared knowledge of a common language. The communication of a specific meaning by the speaker depends both on shared knowledge of a common language (*langue*) and on the particular insights the speaker expresses in speech (*parole*). The social reality of the shared language, therefore, is *in* the speaker, just as the specific meaning of the speaker is communicated *in* the shared language. The shared good of a language is not merely an instrument that individuals use to communicate; it is constitutive of speech itself. If speech is to be meaningful at all, it cannot be "decomposed" into the actions of entirely separate individuals who use the language as an external tool.[12] The social good of the language and the individual good of speaking are internally connected. They are aspects or dimensions of each other. What is common and what is individual are both required in any successful communication. The common and the individual mutually interpenetrate and mutually determine each other. This suggests, more generally, how the common good and the good of an individual person can be mutually determining in a similar way.

The same is true of the way learning and innovating are interconnected in speech communication. What a person says on a given occasion is often a commonplace that is already well known to many, perhaps even to the person being addressed. If so, the speaker is simply passing on or repeating something received from others in the culture. On the other hand, what is said can be innovative and boldly creative, communicating meaning that no one but the speaker has ever thought of before. Communicating such innovations, however, depends on already sharing a language with those

---

[12] Taylor, "Irreducibly Social Goods," in *Philosophical Arguments* (Cambridge, MA: Harvard University Press, 1995), pp. 134–135. As the basis of this analysis Taylor cites Ferdinand de Saussure, *Cours de linguistique générale* (Paris: Payot, 1979), chap. 4. He also cites Ludwig Wittgenstein's arguments against the possibility of a private language from *Philosophical Investigations* (Oxford: Basil Blackwell, 1953), paras. 258ff. On the more general question of how culture and social institutions are *in* the consciousness of individual persons while persons express themselves and act only *in* culture and society, see Peter Berger, *An Invitation to Sociology: A Humanistic Perspective* (New York: Doubleday Anchor, 1963), chaps. 4 and 5; Peter Berger and Thomas Luckmann, *The Social Construction of Reality: A Treatise in the Sociology of Knowledge* (New York: Doubleday Anchor, 1967).

to whom one speaks. Even the most innovative acts of communication, such as great poetry or major intellectual achievements in the sciences, cannot be totally innovative. Entirely innovative speech would be possible only in a language that nobody else knew, which is a self-contradictory idea. A language must be shared if it is to be a language at all. Unless some meaning is already shared no one could understand any of the speaker's utterances. These utterances would not be meaningful speech but gibberish. If they were recorded and played back at a later time not even the original speaker could understand them. The ability of individual persons to communicate innovative or idiosyncratic ideas, therefore, is inextricably connected with already sharing a language with others in society.

More generally, this suggests that one can be self-determining in an innovative way only by having received the capacity to innovate from a culture and by being part of a shared history that nurtures such self-determination. Being dependent on the community for these capacities and being a self-determining agent are reciprocally connected. You cannot have one without the other. You cannot have the good of "autonomy" without the kind of good society that makes it possible. This interpenetration of the good of personal freedom and the good of a certain kind of community suggests that our reigning public philosophy has been seriously misled by the way the term "autonomy" connotes a capacity present in the lives of individuals as long as no one else interferes with it or restricts it.

This linguistic analogy can therefore shed some light on more general interconnections between the good of individual persons and the common good. It suggests that individual freedom and the maintenance of the common good need not be opposed alternatives but can be complementary. Just as specific acts of speaking depend on sharing a language with others, the freedom of individual persons is actualized in a shared social context that makes choice possible. Self-determination is not a solo activity but has social preconditions. Moreover, these social preconditions are not external to the person who makes the free choices; they are internally constitutive of the capacity for freedom itself. For example, in a society that accepts slavery or tyranny as legitimate institutions, those who are enslaved or oppressed will very often simply accept the lack of freedom as their fate. The acceptance of such a fate undercuts the very freedom needed to alter existing social patterns of dominance. Conversely, a culture that holds that freedom and mutual respect are due to all persons will sustain people's desire to be free from domination and will enable them to resist actively if necessary. A culture that values equal freedom for all supports individual efforts to live in freedom, while a culture that legitimates domination undercuts such efforts. Since cultures are shared, social realities, the good of a culture that supports freedom is a shared good. The freedom that results in such a culture is a shared good as well.

It is true, of course, that individual persons can and do challenge the prevailing practices and values of their culture, just as speakers of English can introduce changes in English vocabulary and usage. English speakers can also use their familiar language to communicate genuinely novel ideas and to write great poems that no one else could create. There is a parallel in the way individuals can both freely create their own lives and stimulate social change. For example, the experience of the seventeenth century brought the innovative practices and institutions of religious freedom to Western Europe. Some one person, of course, must have been the first European to say that the good life is one where religious freedom is respected. This was a new insight about both the personal and the social good. But this innovative idea arose in response to unfolding social conflicts. The idea that religious freedom is a good thing did not simply pop from nowhere into the head of this innovator; it was stimulated by the social context and was proposed as a revision of existing social practices and institutions. It also had historical roots. The personal and social good of religious freedom was not created *ex nihilo*, but was a reworking of long-standing traditions and ideas about the good life in light of new historical circumstances.

So as Taylor puts it, the freedom to be self-determining is always "situated freedom."[13] It is the freedom of a situated self – a self that lives, moves, and has its being in community, in a social setting of interaction with other persons. To possess this freedom is not simply to be left alone. Rather it comes into being when a

---

[13] Taylor presents his extended historical argument for the possibility of "situated freedom" and the reasons it is often occluded in our culture in *Sources of the Self: The Making of the Modern Identity* (Cambridge, MA: Harvard University Press, 1989). See esp. pp. 513–515.

person participates in interactive life with other persons, sometimes receiving from them quite passively, sometimes contributing gentle innovations in the interactive process, sometimes challenging them strongly or even rebelling against them. Whichever of these forms it takes, human freedom is never a solitary possession. Securing and sustaining this freedom demands more than keeping disconnected individuals from interfering with each other. To eliminate interaction entirely would not protect personality but dissolve it. Rather, self-determination is participation in communal give-and-take – sometimes giving, sometimes taking, but always responding to and interacting with others.

We have learned from experience that the practices and institutions of democratic society are essential to securing such participation for all persons. These practices are essential to making this participation possible not just for free males, or for Catholics, Lutherans, or Calvinists, or for Christians or theists, but for all. These practices are social goods. When these goods are realized at all, they are present in the interactions and relationships that connect people together in a community of mutual respect. When they are not realized, either some people end up dominating others or there is no interaction at all. In either of these alternatives, the good of some individuals is harmed and the common good of mutual relationship is diminished. In a society like ours today the many threads of social interdependence are becoming more tightly woven. Thus we face a choice between pursuing the good of social participation for all or accepting the evil that occurs when the strong dominate the weak or the privileged try to wall themselves off from the vulnerable. In an increasingly interdependent world there is nowhere to hide, nowhere simply to be left alone. In such a world, the internal connection between self-determination and democratic social practice means we face the choice of discovering how to achieve good lives together or accepting the fact that some people (likely very many) will not have good lives at all.

Without the kind of relationships that sustain social participation, individuals are unlikely to be able even to imagine that they have options among which to choose. Social relationships that enable and support active engagement with other persons, therefore, are constitutive of self-determination. A person is not free alone, but only in

a community of freedom – a community in which freedom is shared
with others. To invoke the linguistic analogy again, a person who
does not share a language with others cannot say anything novel,
for without a language nothing at all can be said. In the same way
a person whose freedom is not socially sustained will be unable to
imagine that there are real options for choice. More precisely, the
options envisioned by a person who is isolated or unable to participate in social interaction will be either trivial or so grandiose as to
be illusory. Choices among options that can enhance the genuine
good of the self are choices among options conceived by the individual in interaction with others. They lead, in turn, to actions by
which the individual influences the environing community of other
persons.

We can say, therefore, that self-determination exists *between* persons in the relations that make them who they are. Martin Buber's
meditation on the relation between an *I* and a *thou* evokes the
centrality of relationship in the direct, one-to-one interpersonal
encounters between persons. Relation is prior to and constitutive
of the self. This is obviously the case in the way infants and children
become who they are through their relations with their parents. But
Buber sees it as true in an even more significant way in the way interpersonal relations make persons who they are throughout adult
life. The good of relationship with others is an *a priori* condition of
the good of the self.[14] This insight, however, need not be restricted
to the direct interactions between two persons who directly encounter each other one-on-one. It is also descriptive of the role of
interrelationship in broader domains of social life. Hannah Arendt
pointed to this societal importance of relationship in her efforts to
revive the republican ethos. The action and speech of public life are
inter-action, inter-communication. Using the same term as Buber,
she wrote that the location of public life is "between" persons. To
be sure, action and speech reveal the interests of individuals. But
they are just as certainly directed toward other persons. Arendt
noted that the "interest" of an individual is literally *inter-est*, something which is *(est)* between or among *(inter)* persons. The realm of
human affairs, therefore, is "the web of human relationships" that
exists where people live actively together. Speech and action have

---

[14] Martin Buber, *I and Thou*, second edition (New York: Charles Scribner's Sons, 1958),
pp. 14–15, p. 27.

privileged roles in bringing this web into being. But since speech and action rise from and are directed into the already existing web, there is no such thing as the speech or action of a solitary person but only of a person in inter-action with other people.[15]

Any good of a person that is a real good, therefore, is embedded in the good of the community. Conversely, any common good that is a real good is simultaneously the good of persons. The good shared with others is constitutive of the good of persons regarded one at a time; the good of persons regarded one at a time cannot exist without some measure of sharing in the common good. The "good" of an isolated self, therefore, cannot be a *bonum honestum*, a genuine good. It is illusion or surrealist fantasy, for the individual cannot be self-sufficient in any literal sense.[16] There are, of course, certainly occasions when the fun of fantasy and the iconoclasm of Dada are needed to keep life genuinely alive. Play is an essential dimension of social creativity. The same is true of genuine solitude, contemplation, and mysticism. But none of these can occur without the sustaining relationships that make them possible and none of these activities ever leave the human community entirely behind. The community that makes these activities possible is not a mere means. It is constitutive of these activities and always present within them.

HUMAN RELATIONSHIPS AS VALUABLE IN THEMSELVES

Two thinkers from a generation ago help clarify how social relationships are good in themselves, not simply as means to the good of individuals. Jacques Maritain and Yves Simon both argued that relationships with others are intrinsically valuable.[17] Such relationships

---

[15] Hannah Arendt, *The Human Condition*, pp. 162–63.

[16] As Iris Murdoch puts it:

One might start from the assertion that morality, goodness, is a form of realism. The idea of a really good man living in a private dream world seems unacceptable. Of course a good man may be infinitely eccentric, but he must know certain things about his surroundings, most obviously the existence of other people and their claims. The chief enemy of excellence in morality (and also in art) is personal fantasy: the tissue of self-aggrandizing and consoling wishes and dreams which prevents one from seeing what is outside one. *The Sovereignty of Good* (New York: Schocken Books, 1971), p. 59.

[17] The distinction between that which is enjoyed as good in itself and that which is useful as a means to another good is classically discussed by Aristotle in *Nicomachean Ethics*, 1096b–1097a. Aristotle applies this distinction in distinguishing friendships that are useful or

can, of course, be necessary means to the attainment of goods that are valued in themselves. Some human relationships, such as those in the workplace, can be means to the meeting of basic material needs. They are necessary means to human flourishing and even survival. But human relationships also have non-instrumental value. We seek such relationships for their own sake, not because, once obtained, they enable us to satisfy other desires in solitude. We want these human relationships not as means only but as ends in themselves.[18]

Maritain argued for this intrinsic value by observing that social relationships arise not only from the experience of need or deficiency but also from the "very perfections" of human beings. When a good that simply fulfills deficiency has been obtained, the desire for it ceases. For example, human beings need food like all other living things. They depend on nurturance from beyond themselves, and this nurturance is a means to their individual well-being. But communication with other persons is not simply a means like food, which is no longer needed once hunger has been satisfied. The good of a relationship with another person does not exist "inside" an individual in the way food fills an empty stomach. Rather the good of relationships with others is realized in the interactive activities of communication and love that are distinct capacities of persons. Human beings have a positive capacity for such relationships with each other, and realizing this capacity brings something new into being that continues to be valued for its own sake.[19] Human beings can form relationships with others for the sake of the relationships themselves. These relationships are valuable for their own

---

pleasant from friendships that are valued for themselves in *Nicomachean Ethics*, 1155b–1157b. It is also discussed by Augustine in *De Doctrina Christiana (On Christian Doctrine)*, trans. D. W. Robertson (Indianapolis, IN: Bobbs-Merrill, 1958), bk. 1, sec. 3–5, pp. 9–11. For Aristotle, political activity is good in itself; for Augustine political activity must be subordinated to a proper relation to God, though this subordination is not strictly that of means to end. The relation of the political to the religious in Augustine's thought will be discussed in chapter 5 below.

[18] The parallel between this way of putting the importance of interhuman relationships and Kant's third formulation of the categorical imperative is evident. See *The Foundations of the Metaphysics of Morals*, trans. Lewis White Beck (Indianapolis, IN: Bobbs-Merrill, 1959), p. 47. It reinforces the link between personal self-determination and the common good argued for above.

[19] Jacques Maritain, *The Person and the Common Good*, trans. John J. Fitzgerald (Notre Dame, IN: University of Notre Dame Press, 1966, originally published in 1946), p. 47.

sake. They arise from "our accomplishments, our fulfillment, our plenitude, from the abundance and superabundance of successful life."[20] Friendship and love, then, are not simply means to personal fulfillment. If they are regarded only as means to the good of the individual, they cease to be friendship or love in any genuine sense. A friend, of course, may do many things that help meet the needs of the other partner in the friendship. True friendship, however, is not *egoïsme à deux* – it is not a good that simply meets the private needs of the friends considered apart from each other. There can of course be partnerships of this kind, but they are not friendships in the full sense. The good of friendship must be a shared good that is valued for itself if it is to exist at all.

In the same way the common good of public life is a realization of the human capacity for intrinsically valuable relationships, not only a fulfillment of the needs and deficiencies of individuals. It is true, of course, that social life is necessary to meet a person's needs for food, shelter, familial nurturance in childhood, basic education, the protection of public safety, etc. From one point of view, therefore, these dimensions of the common good are instrumental to the good of the individual. Human beings are vulnerable and needy. But it is also true that eating with others, sharing a home with others, and benefiting from education, intellectual exchange, and friendship are all aspects of a life of positive social interaction and communication with others. They are not merely extrinsic means to human flourishing but are aspects of flourishing itself. This shared life of communication and interaction with others, in all its aspects, is good in itself. This helps explain why the common good of social life cannot be disaggregated without remainder into the private goods of the people who are members of the society. For such disaggregation dissolves the bonds of relationship that constitute an important part of good lives. If we overlook these bonds of relationship, the goods of the relationships themselves will not be part of the picture of the common good. The good of community itself will be ignored. The common good, therefore, is not simply a means for attaining the private good of individuals; it is a value

[20] Yves R. Simon, *The Tradition of Natural Law: A Philosopher's Reflections*, ed. Vukan Kuic (New York: Fordham University Press, 1967), p. 90.

to be pursued for its own sake. This suggests that a key aspect of the common good can be described as *the good of being a community at all* – the good realized in the mutual relationships in and through which human beings achieve their well-being.

In a republic, this intrinsic good is realized in the shared speech and cooperative action of citizens determining how they will live together. Such communication and shared action happens in communities of different sorts and sizes, ranging from families to nation-states and, in our time, to the larger world community. It is also realized in the political sphere when people govern themselves together in freedom as fellow citizens. Of course, participation in this shared public life depends on antecedently meeting certain elemental needs of the individual. In this sense there is an instrumental dimension to the common good. For example, a person needs to learn a language from society if he or she is to participate in the public speech and argument of a self-governing community. In the same way, a person who lacks food, housing, or freedom from the constant fear of crime will be unable to share in the active self-governance of a democratic republic. The education through which one learns a language is in this sense an instrumental good. But these goods are also constitutive parts of intrinsically valuable interaction and communication with other persons. A shared language is not only a means that makes speaking with others possible; it is internal to and constitutive of the act of communication itself. Language is not merely a tool that allows individuals to mumble words in solitude.

Further, social communication in a democratic polity is itself a constitutive dimension of the shared public life of free, self-governing citizens. It is valuable in itself as well as an instrument to the private ends of individuals. In a similar way, food, housing, and public safety are intrinsic parts of a shared life together, not simply means to the well-being of individuals. By sharing in these goods, people share a common life that no hungry, homeless, or crime-threatened individual can know. Non-human animals can be hungry; only a person can feel the lack of social connectedness that is the most serious deprivation faced by the poor and homeless in our society. Non-human animals can be sick; only a human being can know the loss of being left out of the advanced health care system of the United States today. Non-human animals cannot speak; only a human being can know the humiliation of not being listened to. These human deprivations are so serious because they deprive people of the distinctively human capacity for lives lived in mutual relationship with others and of genuine participation in the good of social life itself.

In other words, the common good of a republic fulfills needs that individuals cannot fulfill on their own and simultaneously realizes non-instrumental values that can only be attained in our life together. These non-instrumental values include the relationships that come into existence in public speech, joint action, and shared self-governance. These are all dimensions of a kind of freedom that can exist only in a community linked together by bonds of reciprocal solidarity. They are goods that, by their very nature, cannot be enjoyed privately. They exist in the relationships between people talking and acting together, and they evanesce when people fall silent or disperse.[21] The freedom they bring is the power that arises when men and women are free together. This is the power of a community of freedom, a community of people acting together in reciprocal respect for one another's dignity. This kind of freedom cannot exist for isolated individuals no matter how autonomous they imagine themselves to be.

The power of this shared freedom is evident in the way tyrants seek the isolation of their subjects. Divide and conquer is the first principle of tyrannical, authoritarian, or colonial rule.[22] When citizens are isolated from each other, through restrictions on their speech and association together, they are no longer citizens but are transformed into subjects of the power of another. With isolation comes powerlessness in the face of the material, economic, and political forces that inevitably shape people's lives. If citizens refuse to accept this isolation and seek the shared freedom of common speech and action, a tyrant can repress them only by violence. Authoritarian rule offends against the common good of shared

---

[21] Arendt, *The Human Condition*, p. 179.

[22] *Ibid.*, p. 181. For a stimulating analysis of how the colonial strategies of European powers in Africa exemplified this principle and led to some of the deep problems of Africa today, see Mahmood Mamdani, *Citizen and Subject: Contemporary Africa and the Legacy of Late Colonialism* (Princeton, NJ: Princeton University Press, 1996), esp. Part 1.

freedom most obviously when it resorts to force to prevent citizens from speaking and acting with each other openly. When this happens true tyranny is the result. If citizens retreat into privacy on their own, whether because of fatigue or because they have lost a vision of the good of shared freedom, they make an apparently non-violent authoritarianism possible. Such "velvet tyranny" remains a form of domination nonetheless; all but the rulers have no say about the conditions that shape large parts of their lives and little effective voice about the tenor of their lives as a whole. Conversely, when citizens insist upon speaking freely about their lives together, and when they set out to act together in light of this speech, the good of democratic self-rule begins to come into existence. This is the power of shared freedom. It does not depend on guns, on holding political office, or even on money. It is the shared freedom that made the velvet revolutions that brought down the Berlin Wall in the face of a nuclear-armed Communist *apparat*.[23] It is just as surely needed to keep power in the hands of a self-governing people in the West. For today in the West, the market and a politics of the image driven by money and media threaten to reduce citizens to political consumers rather than self-governing agents. An ethic of tolerance whose highest value is protection of the right to be different in private abandons the hope that more than this can be expected. The common good of a commonweal, the shared freedom of a republic, and the good of persons (including the good of personal freedom) rise or fall together.

This intrinsic good of shared self-rule can, of course, be achieved to greater or lesser degrees in different societies. For this reason, some have argued that seeking the good of such a life in common is a form of "perfectionism" and that it is in any case unattainable in a complex and diverse society like ours.[24] It is claimed that pursuing the common good understood in this way runs the danger of letting the best become the enemy of the good. The solidarity of shared self-rule, however, is not an all-or-nothing affair. We do not

---

[23] For the very influential and eloquent statement of the power of shared speech in resisting tyranny, see Václav Havel, "The Power of the Powerless," and "A Word About Words," in *Open Letters: Selected Writings 1965–1990*, ed. Paul Wilson (New York: Vintage, 1992), pp. 125–214, pp. 377–389.

[24] See Rawls, *Political Liberalism*, pp. 194–195.

have to choose between a utopian republic, with total and constant participation by all, and an ethic based on wariness and the pursuit of privacy. It is possible to realize the solidarity of a commonweal to greater or lesser degrees. We can use the scale of solidarity in a self-governing community of freedom as a measure of a society's relative goodness. Using this scale to orient our choices can help us discern the route that leads to a better society.[25] It can suggest ways of defining human rights in terms of the minimum levels of social participation required by mutual respect for human freedom and dignity (which will be discussed below in chapter 6). Such a scale will, therefore, enable us to think creatively about problems that tolerance cannot solve, like urban poverty and the challenges of global interdependence. The good of shared self-determination marks a course for addressing these challenges, rather than invoking "the fact of pluralism" to trump substantive proposals for political and cultural change.

The solidarity of shared freedom is an essentially dynamic standard. It sets us on a transformative path rather than leading to an all-or-nothing call for utopia. This is because it is a normative standard that takes history seriously; it presumes that the internal link between the good of persons and the common good is itself historical and dynamic. Invoking the norm of solidarity in shared freedom therefore means starting from where we are and seeking to move toward a common life in which more people are free and active participants. But it is also true that a decision to accept such a standard is already an act that will make a major difference in the lives of citizens. To adopt such a criterion for the direction we should be moving is itself the first step out of self-protective wariness toward the solidarity necessary for a morally interdependent community. This first step would be a kind of breakthrough, for it would set us on a path very different from that suggested by an ethic that seeks the good life primarily in the domain of privacy or in lifestyle enclaves. This first step can only be taken by citizens committed to the solidarity of shared speech and action. So to begin the recovery of the shared good of a commonweal is already to have moved well down the road that leads to its fuller achievement.

---

[25] Taylor, "The Nature and Scope of Distributive Justice," p. 302.

We live, here and now, in an increasingly interdependent web of relationships with many other persons and with the natural environment. A public philosophy that acknowledges this *de facto* reality is both necessary and possible. It is required by what human beings have become at the beginning of the twenty-first century. The human good, including the good of freedom and self-determination, is a "public thing" – a *res publica*. Achieving this good calls for a common life in which freedom is more fully shared, for a society in which all people more fully participate in the common goods that can be achieved in their social, political, and economic activity together. Response to this *de facto* context calls for a public philosophy whose normative understandings of the good also take common life seriously. Human beings are indeed capable, perhaps especially in our own day, of shared speech and action. Such capacities are essential characteristics of human beings, and we have not ceased being human. The actualization of these capabilities is no doubt a daunting challenge in a world that is as culturally complex and politically confusing as ours is today. But to decline the challenge would be to abandon the quest for freedom that has been the mark of modernity. If we reconceive freedom as a shared reality perhaps it will not seem a quest that is too much for us today. The normative standards of a public philosophy of freedom in community are both a reflection of what human beings are and a projection of what they can become when they live good lives in a commonwealth. The rest of this book will elaborate some of the implications of pursuing such a recovery of the commonweal. It will suggest what the lives we share together could look like if shared freedom became a guiding value in our public philosophy.

CHAPTER FOUR

Religion in public

The common good was displaced from its preeminent position in the public philosophy of the West by the emergence of serious religious disagreement about the meaning of the good life at the dawn of modernity. Because of this history, recovering the common good as a plausible social aim today requires careful consideration of the role of religious communities in public life. Today in both Europe and the United States religious pluralism is significantly greater than in the past, due to immigration, conversions to non-Western religions, the emergence of new religious movements, and the rise of agnosticism and unbelief.[1] Widespread popular awareness of these religious differences is also higher today than in most of past history. International communication and travel have made Westerners newly conscious of the importance of non-Western religions in the lives of many of the peoples of the world. Because of this heightened awareness of religious diversity, there is considerable apprehension today about the dangers of religious involvement in politics in both popular and more theoretical discussions. These anxieties are based in real events, such as the divisive role played by religion in the conflicts of the Middle East, northern India, the former Yugoslavia, Northern Ireland, and numerous other places. Worries about the conflict-prone tendencies of religion are not the result of secularist paranoia. Religious beliefs and loyalties have a marked proclivity to deepen social divisions.[2] They create communal

---

[1] On the growth of religious diversity in the United States, see Diana L. Eck, *A New Religious America*. See also Eck and the Pluralism Project at Harvard University, *On Common Ground: World Religions in America*, interactive multimedia computer optical disc (New York: Columbia University Press, 1997).

[2] See Mark Juergensmeyer, *Terror in the Mind of God: The Global Rise of Religious Violence* (Berkeley: University of California Press, 2000).

bonds that do not coincide with those linking the citizens of nation-states. Religious loyalty can therefore threaten the basis of the unity of states and set subdivisions of the human race at odds with each other.

Does growing religious pluralism mean that a shared under-standing of the common good has become even less possible today than when religious conflict drove it off the Western public agenda in the seventeenth century? Is it even possible that a proposal to bring back the common good as a social objective may invite new religious conflicts by encouraging believers to use coercive power to advance their religious understandings of the good life? If so, the only reasonable response is "no thanks."

Despite the cogency of these concerns about the danger of reli-gious involvement in public life, this chapter will argue that religious communities can make important contributions to bringing both the idea and the reality of the common good back to a central place in public life. Avoidance of new forms of religious conflict and oppression does not require that religion be kept a strictly pri-vate matter. We are not compelled to choose between religiously inspired conflict and the subordination of religious values to a pub-lic philosophy whose motto is "live and let live." There is a third alternative: religious communities can and do contribute to the public good of a community that is both peaceful and supportive of the freedom of its members.

This chapter will present some empirical evidence to argue that this third alternative deserves more serious consideration than it often receives. There are significant groups of religious believers who are in fact corporately involved in public life and who con-tribute to the common good in peaceful and freedom-supporting ways. Evidence will also be presented that indicates that active par-ticipation by citizens in public life is seriously threatened today and that religious communities possess distinctive capacities to enhance such citizen participation. Both of these claims are based on factual descriptions of the involvement of some religious communities in public life today. Second, it will be argued that religious communi-ties can make distinctive and perhaps unique contributions to the strength of civic life and the good of democratic self-government. They can make a significant contribution to realizing the idea of the common good developed in the preceding chapter. The argument in this chapter is that such religious contributions to the common good are possible and should be taken seriously. The next chapter will go further by presenting a normative argument for why religious communities *ought* to understand themselves in ways that enable them to make such contributions to the common good. In particular, the next chapter will propose reasons why Christian churches should see themselves as agents of the common good and why the larger society should consider this possibility also.

PUBLIC RELIGION, CONFLICT, AND PEACE

The activity of religious communities in the public sphere has been a high-profile matter over the past decade both in the United States and globally. It is clear that something important is happening in the zone where the religious and political interact. But just what is going on has been interpreted in several ways.[3] Before making normative recommendations about religious contributions to the common good, we need to consider these readings of the *de facto* impact of religion on public life today.

A common reaction to the new visibility of religion in the public forum has been apprehension that it threatens the freedom and peace of public life. In the United States, an interpretation frequently heard in the public media and the academy is one of fear that public activity by religious communities could shatter the fragile moral bonds holding American society together. The visibility of the so-called religious right has been a particular cause of alarm. It has generated apprehensions that public activism by religious communities leads to divisive and moralistic politics. This fear reflects a presupposition that social peace and religious freedom are secure only when religious communities live their faith quietly and privately. This also seems to be the prevailing view among many ordinary Americans.[4]

---

[3] Peter Berger sums up a review of the conflicting trends by concluding that only "one statement can be made with great confidence: Those who neglect religion in their analyses of contemporary affairs do so at great peril." "Secularism in Retreat," *The National Interest* 46 (Winter, 1996/1997), 12.
[4] See chapter 1 above.

Apprehensive readings of the effects of political involvement by religious communities are also common in discussions of the global picture. These interpretations cite the role of the Islamic resurgence in the politics of the Middle East and parts of Africa such as Sudan and Algeria, the resistance of Israeli ultra-orthodox religious parties to land-for-peace agreements between Israel and the Palestinians, the Hindu nationalism of the Bharatiya Janata Party (BJP) in India, and the religious dimensions of other tragic conflicts such as those in Bosnia and Northern Ireland. The title of a book by Gilles Kepel that was a best-seller in France has described this new salience of religion as *The Revenge of God*.[5] It examines movements such as the Ayatollah Khomeini's revolution in Iran, the militant Zionism of the Gush Emunim in Israel, the highly politicized Catholic lay movement Communione e Liberazione in Italy, and the Moral Majority inspired by Protestant fundamentalism in the United States.

Samuel Huntington has systematized such disparate cases of religious involvement in public life into a grand narrative that claims to tell the story of where global politics is headed. His much-noted thesis is that world politics in the post-Cold War era will be driven by a clash of civilizations and cultures rather than of ideology or economics. Civilizations are communities distinguished from each other by "history, language, culture, tradition, and, most important, religion."[6] This diagnosis raises the specter of religious conflict on a global scale. If it is true, religion in public is a very dangerous thing indeed.

According to this account, religious communities are unlikely to be agents of the common good of pluralistic societies or of an interdependent globe. Rather they can be expected to deepen divisions by drawing sharp boundaries between the faithful and the infidels. Wilfred Cantwell Smith, a noted scholar of comparative religion, has argued that religions have an essentially "fissiparous quality." In Smith's view, religious beliefs create boundaries between people, not only when distorted or misused but by their very nature. For

[5] Gilles Kepel, *The Revenge of God: The Resurgence of Islam, Christianity and Judaism in the Modern World*, trans. Alan Braley (University Park: Pennsylvania State University Press, 1994). French original: *La Revanche de Dieu: Chrétiens, Juifs et Musulmans à la reconquête du monde* (Paris: Editions du Seuil, 1991).

[6] Samuel P. Huntington, "The Clash of Civilizations," *Foreign Affairs* 72 (Summer, 1993), 22, 25.

religion binds persons together into "partial wholes"[7] – the communities of those who believe in Yahweh, Jesus, Allah, or Krishna,
and those who are outside the community of belief. This divisive
quality of religion seems to be exacerbated by the conditions of intellectual and social life today. The very complexity and pluralism
of our situation generates an uneasiness about personal identity.
Religious communities with clearly drawn borders respond to this
unease by providing clear answers to the questions "Who am I?
Where do I belong?"[8] In giving communal support for a sense of
meaning and purpose in life, religious communities strengthen personal identity and simultaneously reinforce inter-group boundaries.
So, it is argued, religion is emerging as a new source of conflict in
the post-Cold War world. According to this interpretation, if there
is a viable notion of common good in this context it will be the
common good of some sub-group. Thus pursuit of the common
good will be a threat to peace and to the freedom of those outside
the community of religious belief.

Indeed, Huntington maintains that a strong identity requires that
groups define themselves over against and in opposition to those
who are different. He states unabashedly that "It is human to hate.
For self-definition and motivation people need enemies."[9] Since
the end of the Cold War has removed the basis for defining identity
through ideological enmity, new space has been created for religion
to define in-group/out-group boundaries. For example, in the post-
Cold War world, Westerners can no longer define themselves in

7 Wilfred Cantwell Smith, "Divisiveness and Unity," in Joseph Gremillion, ed., *Food/Energy and the Major Faiths* (Maryknoll, NY: Orbis Books, 1978), pp. 73–74.

8 Huntington, *The Clash of Civilizations and the Remaking of World Order* (New York: Simon and Schuster, 1997), p. 97.

9 *Ibid.*, p. 130. Since Huntington holds this view, it should not be surprising that many commentators read him as calling for a renewal of the sense of national purpose in the United
States and the West more generally in terms of an opposition between the "West and the
rest," especially Islam. More recent writings suggest this is a misreading. Huntington now
seems to suggest that neither Islamic nor Confucian societies at present provide serious
enough threats to lead to a strong sense of national purpose in post-Cold War America.
Also neither multiculturalism nor commercial interests can provide an adequate sense
of national purpose for the United States. So until a new enemy with sufficient power
emerges, the United States should exercise restraint in international involvement. Oddly,
therefore, Huntington implies that it is peaceful pluralism, not conflict, that make the common good difficult to define. But for Huntington, a universally inclusive understanding
of the common good is an illusion. See Huntington, "The Erosion of American National
Interests," *Foreign Affairs* 76, no. 5 (September/October, 1997), 28–49, esp. 49.

terms of anti-Communism. As the free market achieves legitimacy in the former USSR, in the South Africa governed by quondam allies of the South African Communist Party, and even in the People's Republic of China, it is hard to define being Russian, African, or Asian in opposition to market capitalism. According to this scenario, the end of the Cold War has removed the cork that kept the divisive power of religious loyalty bottled up for several generations. So this narrative projects a future where conflicts are driven by rivalries between civilizations formed by religious traditions.

Is this hypothesis an adequate account of what is happening at the intersection between religion and politics today? I will argue that it is not. Making such an argument, however, does not mean denying the evidence that religion is indeed a factor in a number of the conflicts on the global stage today or that religious communities have been party to some of the more raucous political discords in the United States. The argument here has the more modest aim of showing that a narrative depicting religion as inherently divisive and generative of conflict is entirely too sweeping and grandiose. Some religious communities today do generate inclusive understandings of civic community. So it is clear that religious communities can do so. As the medieval scholastics used to say, *ab esse ad posse, valet illatio* (from reality to possibility is a valid inference). Furthermore, the greater the evidence that real-life communities of believers make such actual contributions to the good of an inclusive community, the more "realistic" will be the normative argument that they ought to do so. Such a normative argument will be made in the next chapter.

The thesis that religion is an inherently conflictual force is based on a selective sample of the movements that exemplify a public role of religion today. In the United States, citing the "religious right" of the Moral Majority or the Christian Coalition as illustrative of the role of religion in public life ignores much both of American history and of contemporary American reality. More hopeful observers hark back to religious involvement in the abolitionist, labor, and civil rights movements in the United States to propose a more positive scenario.[10] In line with these historical precedents,

---

[10] For a historical account of the role of religion in the origins and growth of the civil rights movement in the United States, see Charles Marsh, *God's Long Summer: Stories of Faith and*

politically significant activity by religious groups can help transform American public life for the better today. When religious communities advocate the cause of the disenfranchised, the poor, and those who are marginalized because of their race, class, or gender, the outcome will be a more just, free, peaceful, and ultimately more united society.

Such activity has been evident in some of the important contributions of the US Catholic bishops concerning economic justice and world peace. It is evident in the long-standing public role of the black churches as advocates of civil rights and economic justice for all. The fact that the black churches and their leaders continue to play a significant role in American politics was perhaps most evident in the presidential candidacy of Reverend Jesse Jackson and the leadership position of Reverend William H. Gray III in the US House of Representatives during the period when the Christian right was becoming most visible. A commitment to an inclusive understanding of the common good is also found in the activities of Evangelical Christian groups like the Sojourners community. This understanding has been programatically articulated by the Sojourners' leader Jim Wallis and has been given theoretical backing by the president of a major evangelical seminary, Richard Mouw. In other words, a kind of religious engagement that aims to contribute to an understanding of the common good that reaches beyond in-group/out-group boundaries is certainly not absent in the United States.[11]

Civil Rights (Princeton, NJ: Princeton University Press, 1997), and David J. Garrow, *Bearing the Cross: Martin Luther King, Jr., and the Southern Christian Leadership Conference* (New York: William Morrow, 1986). For a contemporary appeal to such history, see Harvey Cox, "The Transcendent Dimension: To Purge the Public Square of Religion is to Cut the Values that Nourish Us," *Nation* (January 1, 1996), pp. 20–23.

[11] On Catholic contributions of this sort, see Thomas M. Gannon, ed., *The Catholic Challenge to the American Economy: Reflections on the US Bishops' Pastoral Letter on Catholic Social Teaching and the US Economy* (New York: Macmillan, 1987); for the contributions of the black churches see Peter J. Paris, *The Social Teaching of the Black Churches* (Philadelphia, PA: Fortress Press, 1985), Andrew Billingsley, *Mighty Like a River: The Black Church and Social Reform* (New York: Oxford University Press, 1999), and Robert M. Franklin, *Another Day's Journey: Black Churches Confronting the American Crisis* (Minneapolis, MN: Fortress 1997); for Evangelical contributions see Jim Wallis, *The Soul of Politics: A Practical and Prophetic Vision for Change*, foreword by Garry Wills, preface by Cornel West (Maryknoll, NY: Orbis Books: 1994), Wallis, *Who Speaks for God? An Alternative to the Religious Right – A New Politics of Compassion, Community, and Civility* (New York: Delacorte, 1996), Richard J. Mouw and Sander Griffioen, *Pluralisms and Horizons: An Essay in Christian Public Philosophy* (Grand Rapids, MI: Eerdmans, 1993).

Similarly, it requires considerable selection of evidence to propose the grand hypothesis that future international conflict can be
mapped as "the West versus the rest," with the Christian West committed to the values of "democracy, free markets, limited government, human rights, individualism, [and] the rule of law" and "the
rest" resisting these values as contrary to their religious traditions,
particularly in Asian and Islamic civilizations.[12] This predilection
for a conflictual and exclusionary interpretation of religion is most
evident in Huntington's apothegm "Islam has bloody borders."[13]
While it is certainly true that Islamic societies have been involved in
a number of wars and civil conflicts of recent history, exclusion and
reaction against the outsider are not of the essence of either normative Islam or the behavior of most Muslims. The Islamic world
is itself internally quite pluralistic in its stance toward the West
and democracy. The vast majority of Muslims are peaceful and
certainly do not fit the stereotypical image of violent terrorists.[14]

So Pierre Hassner, the director of the Centre d'Études et de
Recherches Internationales in Paris, has rightly challenged the effort to explain all post-Cold War conflicts in light of a putative
"closed and conflictual character" of civilizations and religious
traditions.[15] This description fits some religious communities and
does not fit others. It fits those that are most spectacularly visible
precisely because they are conflict-prone. It is a mistake, however, to
generalize about the public role of religion from these cases. The
characteristics of the most conflict-prone and exclusive religious
groups are certainly not universal attributes of religion as such. It
is also the case that many of the conflicts in the world today that
have religious dimensions are not simply clashes between faiths;
rather religion is often a flag that serves as a rallying point for other
politicized aspects of group identity, such as ethnicity or nationality. Northern Ireland and the former Yugoslavia are examples of
religion playing this role.

[12] Huntington, *The Clash of Civilizations and the Remaking of World Order*, p. 184.
[13] *Ibid.*, pp. 254-258.
[14] See John L. Esposito, *The Islamic Threat: Myth or Reality* (New York: Oxford University Press, 1992), p. 5.
[15] Pierre Hassner, "Morally Objectionable, Politically Dangerous: Huntington's *Clash of Civilizations* 1," *The National Interest* 46 (Winter, 1996/97), 64.

When high walls are constructed on the basis of religion as such, the religious communities involved can often be properly called "fundamentalist." A major study of fundamentalism around the world, sponsored by the American Academy of Arts and Sciences, concluded that the "the essence of fundamentalism" is "militant, mobilized, defensive reactions to modernity."[16] This description of fundamentalism was drawn inductively from the empirical characteristics of a variety of religious groups in the United States and world-wide. The phenomenon of fundamentalism depends on a particular kind of assessment of modern pluralism – one that sees it as a threat to religious identity itself. Fidelity to religious belief, therefore, is seen as requiring that the identity of believers be defined over against non-believers. Fundamentalism reveals at least as much about how the social-cultural environment of a religious community is being interpreted as it does about essential characteristics of religious belief itself. The phenomenon of fundamentalism, therefore, is not "fundamental" to all strongly held religious conviction.

The Fundamentalism Project found that "reactivity" to modernity was a central mobilizing characteristic of groups such as the Moral Majority and the Christian Coalition in the United States, Communione e Liberazione in the Catholic world, Gush Emunim and Kach in Israel, Hamas and Hizbollah in Islamic countries, and some of the exclusivist Hindu groups in India. The stance of reaction to the presence of others with different ultimate convictions generates many of the other characteristics of fundamentalist movements, such as literalist readings of selected parts of their tradition's holy scriptures, authoritarian organization of the internal life of the religious community, and the drawing of sharp boundaries between the truly faithful and both unbelievers and lukewarm adherents of the faith. These characteristics make fundamentalist movements adversaries of all efforts to find common ground with those outside the community of the faithful. In the extreme they can lead to rejection of efforts to live in peace with others or to deny religious freedom to those who are religiously different.

---

[16] Gabriel A. Almond, Emmanuel Sivan, and R. Scott Appleby, "Fundamentalism: Genus and Species," in Martin E. Marty and R. Scott Appleby, eds., *Fundamentalisms Comprehended, The Fundamentalism Project*, vol. v (Chicago: University of Chicago Press, 1995), p. 409.

Interpreting the public role of religion in light of such examples, therefore, virtually guarantees that a new "war of religions" scenario will be written. In such a script, the idea of religious communities contributing to a common good that includes the good of those who are not in-group members becomes a mirage. When such interpretations are in the air, it is not surprising that keeping religious faith quietly private seems the only reasonable option. If all manifestations of religion in public were of this reactive and exclusivist type, the choice today would be a reprise of that faced by Europe during the seventeenth century: you can have freedom and peace or you can have pursuit of the public good by religious communities, but you cannot have both.

Fortunately, this is not the real choice we face. There are publicly influential religious communities who do not define themselves in reaction to those outside. There are large groups of religious believers who accept what has been learned through modern Western experience about the values of religious freedom and an inclusive understanding of civic affairs. These religious communities are dedicated to the values of peace, human rights, and greater justice for all persons and groups in society. They affirm these values as implications of the most basic or fundamental convictions of their faith and religious tradition. Such communities of believers can be found in most of the major religious traditions of the world. Both their existence and the way they understand themselves are important clues to discovering how the common good might become a viable social goal in a pluralistic society.

The most well-known recent examples of public religious engagement that takes religious freedom, non-violence, and the quest for an inclusive community with deep seriousness are the movements led by Gandhi and Martin Luther King. R. Scott Appleby has highlighted many contemporary movements with the same characteristics.[17] For example, in the early 1990s the Buddhist primate of Cambodia, Samdech Preah Maha Ghosananda, led a series of "pilgrimages of truth" through Cambodia to build popular support for UN-sponsored elections aimed at overcoming the fear

---

[17] The examples that follow are drawn from R. Scott Appleby, *The Ambivalence of the Sacred: Religion, Violence and Reconciliation* (Lanham, MD: Rowman and Littlefield, 1999), chaps. 4 and 7.

left in the wake of Khmer Rouge atrocities and continuing threats. Hundreds of thousands of Cambodians joined in support of the pilgrims, who themselves numbered in the tens of thousands. Other Buddhist religious leaders such as Sulak Sivaraksa of Thailand and Thich Nhat Hanh of Vietnam have been at the forefront of a developing "engaged Buddhism" that actively promotes universal human rights and inclusive social justice through non-violent means.[18] In the Muslim world, the largest Islamic party in the world's most populous Islamic country has supported democracy and civic participation for non-Muslims under the leadership of Abdurrahman Wahid, former president of Indonesia.[19] Influential Islamic thinkers have been developing Muslim understandings of universal human rights and leading political movements to secure these rights. In Iran, Abdolkarim Soroush, an Iranian intellectual who advocates human rights as central to an Islamic understanding of right government, has stimulated a serious debate about the nature of an Islamic republic. A Sudanese lawyer, Abdullahi Ahmed An-Na'im, works to overcome that country's long-standing ethnoreligious conflict as well as advocating a broad human rights agenda for African Muslims and Africans more generally.[20] In the struggle for India's independence from British colonial rule, Gandhi went well beyond seeking to defend his own Hindu traditions to a struggle for democracy, human rights, and the peaceful coexistence of Hindus and Muslims both in India and what are now Pakistan and Bangladesh. This struggle was certainly one of the most significant public manifestations of religion in the twentieth century. It was fully committed to the values of freedom, democracy, and peace that are so often invoked in arguments that religion should be a strictly private affair.

Other recent examples are more familiar to Westerners because they are rooted in Christianity and thus closer to home. In Northern

[18] See also Christopher S. Queen and Sallie B. King, eds., *Engaged Buddhism: Buddhist Liberation Movements in Asia* (Albany, NY: State University of New York Press, 1996).
[19] For a study of the developments in Indonesian Islam, see Robert W. Hefner, *Civil Islam: Muslims and Democratization in Indonesia* (Princeton, NJ: Princeton University Press, 2000). See also the forthcoming Boston College dissertation by Benyamin Intan on "'Public Religion' and the *Pancasila*-based State."
[20] Abdullahi Ahmed An-Na'im, *Toward an Islamic Reformation: Civil Liberties, Human Rights, and International Law* (Syracuse, NY: Syracuse University Press, 1990).

Ireland, ecumenical communities composed of Roman Catholics and Protestants have played notable roles in the efforts to heal deep sectarian divisions and bring peace. In post-apartheid South Africa, Anglican Archbishop Desmond Tutu's chairmanship of the Truth and Reconciliation Commission is the culmination of his long-term role in seeking a peaceful path to a truly common justice in that country. Tutu's struggles rose simultaneously from his religious faith and from a conviction that the good of each person is integrally connected with the good of all. His opposition to Apartheid – apartness – is the very antithesis of the notion that religion is essentially divisive. Tutu's Christianity, like that of many other religious leaders and lay believers in South Africa, is the root of commitment to a public good that is truly common.

The public role of Christianity, and of Roman Catholicism in particular, in promoting democracy was noted by Huntington in an essay written shortly before he advanced his "clash of civilizations" hypothesis. Huntington observed that since the Second Vatican Council the Roman Catholic church has been one of the most visible religious forces in the domain of world politics and that this involvement has been an effective force for the global advancement of democracy over the past several decades.[21] From 1974 to 1989, more than thirty countries in Europe, Asia, and Latin America moved from authoritarianism to democracy. In most of these countries the majority of the population is Catholic and Catholicism has shaped their cultures in important ways. From Portugal and Spain in the mid-1970s, to South America in the late 1970s and early 1980s, to the Philippines in the mid-1980s, to Poland and Hungary in the late 1980s, "Catholic societies were in the lead, and roughly three-quarters of the countries that transited to democracy between 1974 and 1989 were Catholic."[22]

In light of these conflicting trends, it is not surprising that there is considerable confusion today about what is to be expected when religion becomes a public force. For religious communities are not

---

[21] For evidence of the strong alliance of Catholicism and democracy that has developed since the Second Vatican Council, see Huntington, "Religion and the Third Wave," *The National Interest* 24 (Summer, 1991), 29–42. This article is based on Huntington, *The Third Wave: Democratization in the Late Twentieth Century* (Norman: University of Oklahoma Press, 1991).

[22] Huntington, "Religion and the Third Wave," 30.

following a single path in the public domain. Some reject modernity, pluralism, and the high value placed on human rights and democracy in the West. Among these anti-modern groups, some are drawn toward authoritarian and even violent responses to the extension of the terrain where democracy and inclusive civic community hold sway. On the other hand, significant bodies of religious believers not only accept inclusive democracy as compatible with their faith; they are being led to active promotion of a civic life based on these values by their religious faith itself. Thus simple conclusions that the appearance of religion in the public square is a threat to freedom, peace, and the unity of society are unjustified. The related thesis that pursuit of a vision of the common good by religious communities will automatically generate conflict and oppression is similarly unjustified.

There seems to be a propensity to regard all public religion with suspicion and to lump very different forms of religious activity together as "fundamentalist," "dogmatic," "authoritarian," or "the religious right." When this suspicion shapes the discussion, somehow Mahatma Gandhi, the Reverend Martin Luther King, Archbishop Oscar Romero of San Salvador, Archbishop Desmond Tutu of Cape Town, Rigoberta Menchú of Guatemala, Bishop Carlos Belo of East Timor, and the numerous followers of each of these leaders get left off the list of significant religious influences in public life. Perhaps this is because acknowledging their influence would imply that we are not faced with choosing between the alternatives of divisive religion on the one hand and the privatization of religion on the other. There is a third option: religious traditions, interpreted properly, have the capacity to contribute to the common good of public life in a way that is fully compatible with pluralism and freedom.

Thus the question that must be addressed before reaching a conclusion about the effect of public advocacy of the common good by religious communities is: "What kind of religion are we talking about?" Discussions of the public role of religion in both academic and popular venues rarely raise this question. They tend to proceed as if religion were a single, undifferentiated phenomenon. It is odd to find discussions that are sensitive to the reality of pluralism so silent on the evident plurality of the ways that religion can and does seek to influence the public sphere. In chapter 6 we will address the normative question of what religious and theological convictions would enable religious communities to make contributions to an inclusive common good. But before doing so it will be helpful to explore some evidence for why such contributions are desirable from the point of view of civic life itself.

RELIGION STRENGTHENING PUBLIC LIFE

Active citizen participation in public life is itself a constitutive part of the pursuit of the common good. Active participation by citizens brings a democratic public life into existence. Where such citizen participation is strong, a key element of the common good is on the way to being realized. Where it is weak, the common good is diminished and the people do not freely determine the conditions of the life they share together. They are reduced to pursuing what good they can in their private lives. This is not a formula for a free society, for without active citizen engagement public life will fall under the control of administrative bureaucracies or authoritarian elites. In the present historical circumstances, where the web of social interdependence is more and more tightly woven, it is a formula for the loss of freedom. In fact, the complexity of contemporary social life is making active participation by citizens in public life more difficult to sustain. This appears true even in societies with written democratic constitutions, including the United States.

This decline in civic participation is directly relevant to the issue of the role of religion in public life. There is significant evidence that religious communities support active engagement in public life by their members. Religious communities have the capacity to strengthen public life in a time when other social pressures encourage a retreat into privacy. Thus it will be argued here that religious communities can play an important role in promoting the good of active self-governance. This calls for moving from a stance of suspicion toward religion as a threat to public freedom to a stance that looks to religion as a potential contributor to greater public freedom.

The need for such a change in presuppositions about the likely impact of religious engagement in public life is implied by several recent empirical studies of political participation in the United States, one of which relies on research outside the United States as a point of reference for its analysis. Robert Putnam has argued that the United States has been undergoing a notable decline in overall civic participation in recent decades. The United States has been experiencing a depletion of the "social capital" that is requisite for effective democracy. Putnam describes social capital as "the connections among individuals – social networks, and the norms of reciprocity and trustworthiness that arise from them." These connections enable people "to act together more effectively to pursue shared objectives."[23] Social capital, therefore, is a prerequisite for pursuit of the common good. It includes a rich associational life in groups like the Elks club, the League of Woman Voters, labor unions, and churches. In more classical terms, a high level of social capital is another way of speaking about the strength of civil society. Civil society is a complex web of human communities including families, neighborhoods, churches, labor unions, corporations, professional associations, credit unions, cooperatives, universities, and a host of other associations. Calling this network of associations "civic" points to their importance in public life even though they are distinct from the state.

Putnam cites extensive data to argue that the associational life of civil society in the United States is weakening today. For example, participation by Americans in religious services and church-related groups has declined by about a sixth since the 1960s. Membership in labor unions in the non-agricultural sector has dropped by more than half. Participation in parent–teacher associations declined from 12 million in 1964 to 5 million in 1982 before recovering to 7 million in 1993. Volunteer activity declined by about one sixth between 1974 and 1989. Putnam illustrates the trend with a

---

[23] Robert Putnam, *Bowling Alone: The Collapse and Revival of American Community* (New York: Simon and Schuster, 2000), and Putnam, "Tuning In, Tuning Out: The Strange Disappearance of Social Capital in America," *PS: Political Science and Politics* 28, no. 4 (December, 1995), 664–665. See also Putnam, *Making Democracy Work: Civic Traditions in Modern Italy* (Princeton, NJ: Princeton University Press, 1993), "The Prosperous Community: Social Capital and Public Life," *The American Prospect* 13 (Spring, 1993), 35–42, "Bowling Alone: America's Declining Social Capital," *Journal of Democracy* 6, no. 1 (January, 1995), 65–78. Putnam traces the recent history of the term social capital in pages 19–20 of *Bowling Alone* and acknowledges his indebtedness to James Coleman's *Foundations of Social Theory* (Cambridge, MA: Harvard University Press, 1990).

provocative example: between 1980 and 1993 the number of Americans who went bowling increased by 10 percent while bowling organized in leagues declined by 40 percent. Bowling alone, Putnam suggests, is a whimsical symbol of a serious reality: the decline of the associational life needed to undergird and support democratic politics.[24]

The argument that strong associational life in civil society is essential to self-governance is in harmony with the republican tradition's conviction that some level of commitment to the common good among citizens is essential to a functioning democracy. It also coheres with the Roman Catholic tradition's stress on the principle of subsidiarity as one of the key normative bases of politics. According to this principle, civil society is the soil in which the seeds of human sociality grow. When communities are small or of intermediate size, they enable persons to come together in ways that can be vividly experienced. The bonds of communal solidarity formed in them enable persons to act together, empowering them to shape some of the contours of public life and its larger social institutions such as the state and the economy. In a democratic society, government does not rule but rather serves the social "body" animated by the activity of these intermediate communities. Pope Pius XI formulated the principle of subsidiarity this way: government "should, by its very nature, provide help [*subsidium*] to members of the body social, it should never destroy or absorb them."[25] Civil society, not the state, is the primary locus in which human solidarity is realized. The strength of civil society is essential to realizing the common good of participatory government. In Putnam's words, it is a prerequisite to "making democracy work."

Putnam's studies add a particularly helpful element to the ideas drawn from the civic-republican and Catholic traditions in setting the context for discussions of the public role of religion. Before undertaking his recent work on American civic participation, Putnam conducted long-term empirical research in Italy on the newly decentralized form of regional governance that was launched there in 1970. He concluded that the new institutions of regional

---

[24] Putnam, "Bowling Alone," 69–70.
[25] Pope Pius XI, *Quadragesimo Anno* (Washington, DC: National Catholic Welfare Conference, 1942) no. 79.

government were successful in encouraging strong democracy in those regions of Italy that possessed a richly developed life in civil society. They did not succeed where the communities of civil society were weak. Both the state and the market worked to serve the needs of the people better in the Italian north because of the presence of strong bonds of civic life resulting from extra-governmental social solidarities. These solidarities were embodied in associations like "tower societies, guilds, mutual aid societies, cooperatives, unions, and even soccer clubs and literary societies."[26] In the south of Italy, on the other hand, the new regional governmental institutions were considerably less effective and citizen satisfaction with them notably lower because the mutual bonds of civil society were less developed there. Thus the stronger the civic context, the better the government and the more successful the economy. Appealing to a congenial example of northern Italian civic life, he observed that

The harmonies of a choral society illustrate how voluntary collaboration can create value that no individual, no matter how wealthy, no matter how wily, could produce alone. In the civic community associations proliferate, memberships overlap, and participation spills into multiple arenas of community life. The social contract that sustains such collaboration in the civic community is not legal but moral. The sanction for violating it is not penal, but exclusion from the network of solidarity and cooperation.

Thus by induction from empirical study rather than deduction from moral or political theory, Putnam concluded that de Tocqueville was right: effective democratic government depends on civic virtue and the vigorous bonds of civil society that promote it.[27]

Another recent empirical study shows that religious communities play a particularly important role in counteracting the decline in civic life detailed by Putnam. Sidney Verba, Kay Lehman Schlozman, and Henry Brady's *Voice and Equality: Civic Voluntarism in American Politics* is the most comprehensive and detailed study of participation in political activity in the United States yet produced. One of the major findings of *Voice and Equality*, somewhat to the surprise of its authors,[28] is that religious institutions make a major contribution to political participation in the United States. Political

---

[26] Putnam, *Making Democracy Work*, p. 181.   [27] *Ibid.*, pp. 182–83.
[28] Personal conversation with Kay Lehman Schlozman.

activity is broadly defined as "activity that is intended to or has the
consequence of affecting, either directly or indirectly, government
action."[29] This activity takes a number of forms: voting, working
in election campaigns, contributing money to candidates and political causes, becoming active in local communities, contacting
public officials, joining political parties or other political organizations, attending rallies, protests or demonstrations, serving on
governing bodies like school or zoning boards. They state their
overall conclusion this way:

> We show that both the motivation and the capacity to take part in politics
> have their roots in the fundamental non-political institutions with which
> individuals are associated during the course of their lives. The founda-
> tions of political involvement are laid early in life – in the family and in
> school. Later on, the institutional affiliations of adults – on the job, in non-
> political organizations, and in religious institutions – provide additional
> opportunities for the acquisition of politically relevant resources and a
> sense of psychological engagement with politics.[30]

Voice and Equality thus provides further evidence of the importance
of strong civil society for the realization of self-governance.

It also shows that churches and other religious communities are
key sources for a strong public life. Three factors are at the basis of
political involvement: the *motivation* to become politically active, the
capacity to do so, and involvement with networks of recruitment
through which requests for political activity are mediated.[31] Each
of these factors is strengthened in the lives of individual citizens
who are actively involved in a church or other institutional religious community. That the factors of motivation and recruitment
for political activity are present in religious communities is perhaps intuitively evident. Pastors preach about matters that touch
the well-being of the polis; religious values orient those who hold
them to pursue the realization of these values in the public domain.
Churches can provide an institutional base for political mobilization, as has been evident across the ideological spectrum from the
civil rights movement to anti-abortion campaigns.

---

[29] Sidney Verba, Kay Lehman Schlozman, and Henry Brady, *Voice and Equality: Civic Voluntarism in American Politics* (Cambridge, MA: Harvard University Press, 1995), p. 9.
[30] *Ibid.*, pp. 3–4.   [31] *Ibid.*, p. 3.

Less obvious is the fact that active involvement in church life has a significant, measurable impact on the capacity of Americans to become politically involved. Having money and time – factors that are independent of church membership – contributes to the capacity for political involvement. But so do certain civic skills that are cultivated by church membership, such as writing letters, going to meetings, taking part in making decisions, planning or chairing meetings, giving presentations or speeches. These skills are of course heavily dependent on one's family background, level of education, and the sort of job one holds. In other words, possession of such skills is significantly correlated with social-economic status. The higher one's social-economic status, the more likely one is to become politically active. But the acquisition of these skills is directly and significantly correlated with active involvement in a church. The communal participation that takes place in churches helps people learn them. In addition, churches enable Americans to develop these skills in a way that is independent of their social-economic status. In the United States, religious affiliation is not stratified by socio-economic status, race, ethnicity, or gender.

In other words, opportunities for the development of skills relevant to political participation are accessible in a more equal way to those active in churches than in American society at large. Indeed, the inequalities in other factors that encourage political activism, such as a successful family of origin, a high level of education, and a high paying job, lead to unequal levels of political participation. Church membership, on the other hand, provides a counter-weight that encourages more equal political participation. Thus Verba *et al.* reach a provocative conclusion about the United States: "The domain of equal access to opportunities to learn civic skills is the church."[32]

It is important to note that religious influence on political participation is tied to involvement with institutionalized religious bodies, not simply to a personal "spirituality," individualistically understood. In United States popular culture today, a distinction is often drawn between spirituality and institutionalized religion. It is sometimes suggested that the renewal of personal spiritual

[32] *Ibid.*, p. 320.

experience can knit up the raveled sleeve of modern society without the divisiveness that sometimes accompanies institutional religious commitment. Once again, however, the empirical data suggest otherwise. Sociologist Robert Wuthnow's survey-based research has shown that, in the United States, people's concern with "spirituality" translates most readily into active civic engagement when this concern is lived out in the context of an organized religious community.[33] When religion or spirituality is understood as a purely private affair between an individual and his or her god without the mediation of an institutional religious community with a public presence in society, little impact on civic participation can be detected. Wuthnow interprets survey data to suggest that spiritual sensitivities have little or no influence on voluntary activity aimed at helping the needy unless one is involved in an organized religious community. When a religious person is involved in an organized church, however, higher levels of piety correlate with higher levels of sustained effort to respond to the needs of the poor and disadvantaged.

This suggests that the *kind* of religion one practices is linked with both the level of one's civic involvement and the form that involvement will take. In Wuthnow's view, the spread of individualistic religious styles that separate spirituality from institutional religious commitment are therefore likely to have a dampening effect on levels of civic voluntarism.[34] He also suggests that when individualistic religion does lead to political activism it is less likely to be the sort of activism concerned with the plight of the poor and the disadvantaged. This may in part explain why televangelism is linked with conservative politics in the United States today.[35] Praying alone, or in front of a television set, may be as apt an indicator of the decline of social capital in the United States as is bowling alone.[36] If one is seeking to strengthen civic life in a democracy, encouragement of the privatization of religion does not appear to be a fitting normative objective.

33 Robert Wuthnow, *Acts of Compassion: Caring for Others and Helping Ourselves* (Princeton, NJ: Princeton University Press, 1991), p. 156.
34 *Ibid.*
35 See Jeffrey K. Hadden, "Religious Broadcasting and the Mobilization of the New Christian Right," *Journal for the Scientific Study of Religion* 26 (1987), 1–24.
36 Putnam has hypothesized that television is one of the prime causes of declining civic participation in the US today. See his "Tuning In, Tuning Out," esp. 677–81.

The implications of all these empirical findings for discussion of the role of religion in American public life are considerable. Civic participation is declining and this decline is traceable to the loss of the social capital of strong civic associations. But political participation is sustained by active involvement in extra-political civic communities, and the churches are among the most important of these communities. The percentage of Americans who are actively involved with religious communities is considerably higher than in many other developed democracies. Religion has a correspondingly more important influence in American politics. So one can conclude that churches play a key role in sustaining the civic involvement that is essential to the health of the American republic. Strong and civicly active churches help "make democracy work." Indeed, it seems that churches play an especially key role in the political empowerment of those with lower social-economic status. Thus if more active, more egalitarian representation in democratic politics is judged desirable, more church activism, not less, seems called for.

Churches, of course, do not exist simply to encourage active participation in politics. As religious communities they have properly religious ends that transcend the goods that can be achieved politically: worship of God; response to the deepest questions of human beings about the meaning of life, love, work, and death; the nurturing of moral values and virtues that enable people to live in accord with that meaning. Thus it would be a serious mistake to assess the vitality of religious communities solely in terms of their contribution to civic activity. Nonetheless, religious belief has consequences for the whole of human life, not only that part which occurs on Sunday morning. The Catholic church, for example, stressed the impact of its properly religious mission on public life when the Second Vatican Council stated that "this religious mission can be a source of commitment, direction, and vigor" in building up the human community and in initiating action "for the benefit of everyone, especially those in need."[37] Though churches are very different kinds of communities from bowling leagues, they have considerable impact on social life. Indeed, the fact that their

---

[37] Vatican Council II, *Gaudium et Spes (Pastoral Constitution on the Church in the Modern World)*, no. 42, in *Vatican Council II: Constitutions, Decrees, Declarations*, ed. Austin Flannery (Northport, NY: Costello Publishing Co., 1996), pp. 209–210.

distinctive identity addresses the meaning of the whole of human existence suggests that they will have social influence that ranges much more widely than communities with more narrowly defined purposes. Churches and other religious communities are therefore uniquely positioned to make contributions to sustaining a vision of the common good and to empowering their members to participate in the pursuit of the common good.

Religious institutions, of course, are not ideologically neutral venues for the development of politically relevant skills. Churches have distinctive identities and missions of their own that are shaped by their theologies and moral beliefs. These theologies and ethical convictions influence the issues around which church members are motivated and recruited to become politically active. The range of these issues is large. In the United States today they extend from abortion, on both the pro-life and pro-choice sides of the debate, to the debates about death with dignity, to issues concerning economic justice, values, and prayer in schools, war, human rights, and a host of other concerns that are simultaneously political, moral, and religious. *Voice and Equality* suggests that the center of gravity of the religious agenda in American public life today is tipped toward more conservative social concerns. It would nevertheless be useful to remember that the involvement of churches in political life has ranged over a wide array of issues in the history of the United States, from abolition, prohibition, and the labor movement, to the civil rights movement, opposition to the Vietnam war and the nuclear arms race. It is also relevant that different churches and segments within churches have played quite different roles in leading their members to civic engagement at different points in American history. For example, Protestants were notably more active in the abolitionist movement than were Catholics in the nineteenth century, while immigrant members of the Catholic church were more heavily involved in the labor movement and urban politics in the first half of the twentieth century than their Protestant counterparts.

Whether the churches' capacity to encourage civic engagement will in the end serve or threaten the common good does not have a predetermined answer. The answer depends on *how* the religious communities understand their aims and how those aims are related to the goals of other social groups. Taking these caveats into account, we nonetheless need to pay attention to aspects of the involvement of religious communities in public life that are rarely attended to in contemporary debates on the subject. Does it really make sense to start from the suspicion that the presence of religious communities in the public square will be a threat to democratic freedom? The success of a democratic republic depends upon the active participation of its citizens and this participation is declining. Churches can play an important role in countering this decline and thus in strengthening the common good of democratic societies. The focus of the discussion should not be on *whether* religion should enter public affairs but on *how* to achieve wise forms of political engagement by religious communities and their members.

This suggestion that religious communities can make significant contributions to public life is based on analysis of the situation in the United States. It is reinforced by consideration of the role played by some religious communities in other parts of the world. For example, the Christian churches were a significant influence in this revival of civil society and the strengthening of social capital in formerly Communist states. The power of the dissident workers and intellectuals of the "velvet revolutions" of 1989 grew out of their success in creating the solidarity of a genuine civil society, not out of direct seizure of state power or out of the barrel of a gun.[38] What were initially extra-governmental bonds of community at Gdansk's shipyards and Prague's Magic Lantern Theater empowered men and women to effect a stunning transformation of supposedly untransformable totalitarian regimes. Religious belief and religious community provided essential support for the men and women who ended totalitarian rule in many formerly Communist countries.

The public role of religion in the revolutions of 1989, of course, varied considerably from one country to another. The churches were surely not the sole agents of this transformation.[39] Nor were all Christian churches equally involved. But there is no question that the commitment of the churches was often crucial in sustaining

[38] See Bronislaw Geremek, "Civil Society and the Present Age," in *The Idea of Civil Society* (Research Triangle Park, NC: The National Humanities Center, 1992), pp. 11–12.
[39] Neils Neilsen, *Revolutions in Eastern Europe: The Religious Roots* (Maryknoll, NY: Orbis Books, 1991).

the many overlapping communities of civil society that refused to submit to state domination. Several years before the revolution in Poland, Adam Michnik, a Jewish intellectual and Solidarity activist, predicted that the role of the Catholic church would be crucial in challenging the regime. He described the church's role this way:

> The problem faced by Polish society is that civil society doesn't exist. Society is not recognized as capable of organizing itself to defend its particular interests and points of view . . . [T]he present totalitarian system insists that every person is State property. The Church's view is that every person is a child of God, to whom God has granted natural liberty . . . It follows from this that in Poland and other communist countries religion is the natural antidote to the totalitarian claims of the State authorities.[40]

In East Germany, Czechoslovakia, Hungary, as well as in Poland, the recovery of freedom, the revival of civil society, and the public presence of the churches were closely connected phenomena. There is also evidence that the Christian churches played important roles in "opening up" political space for self-governance in a number of Latin American countries and that churches are seeking to do so in sub-Saharan African contexts as well.[41]

We can conclude, therefore, that religious communities can play an important role in sustaining and strengthening public life without either controlling or being controlled by the state. The *res publica* is much larger than the sphere of government. Public life includes the activities of all those communities and institutions that form the rich fabric of civil society. It also includes all the public discourse, conversation, and argument that constitute a culture and the interaction of subcultures within it. Religious beliefs and loyalties are among the factors that energize the communities and institutions

---

[40] "Towards a Civil Society: Hopes for Polish Democracy," interview with Adam Michnik by Erica Blair, *Times Literary Supplement*, (February 19–25, 1988), p. 199.

[41] On the role of the churches in Latin America during the 1970s, see, for example, Daniel H. Levine, ed., *Churches and Politics in Latin America* (Beverly Hills, CA: Sage Publications, 1979), especially the essays by Brian H. Smith, Thomas Bruneau, and Alexander W. Wilde. On more recent church efforts in sub-Saharan Africa outside South Africa, see John M. Walligo, "Christianity and Liberation in Africa: Some Obstacles," and Laurenti Magesa, "Has the Church a Role in Politics?" in L. Namwera, *et al.*, eds., *Towards African Christian Liberation* (Nairobi: St. Paul Publications-Africa, 1990), pp. 27–46 and pp. 69–85; Jean-Marc Éla, "Christianity and Liberation in Africa," in Rosino Gibellini, ed. *Paths of African Theology* (Maryknoll, NY: Orbis Books, 1994), pp. 136–153.

of civil society, for they give people communal resources, affective motivations, and cognitive reasons for active participation in public life. Where these people are citizens of a democracy, their religious beliefs and loyalties will in turn have an important influence on government, law, and policy-formation. In democracies, where state and church are separated and religious freedom respected, the influence of religious communities on law and state policy will be indirect. The public influence of churches will not be the result of their direct control of political institutions. Rather, the effect of religion on government will be mediated through its influence in the multiple communities and institutions of civil society and on cultural self-understandings of citizens. This indirect influence of religion on government occurs through the activity of self-governing citizens, such as informal discussion of political questions, voting, running for office, contributing to political campaigns, writing to elected representatives, lobbying, etc.[42] Where the state has authoritarian pretensions, religious communities have the capacity to energize opposition and, in the extreme case, even revolution. In both democratic and non-democratic contexts, therefore, churches can serve the common good of self-governing societies in ways the "war of religions" paradigm too often obscures.

Acknowledging the legitimacy of this kind of presence of religious belief in public life follows from a commitment to religious liberty. To attempt to forbid or restrict this presence because of the fear of the possible influence of religion on government policy would effectively tell citizens who are believers to leave their most important convictions at home when they enter the public domain. More drastically, it would tell those who are unwilling to keep their beliefs to themselves that they are not welcome in the public sphere at all. When the public role of religion in civil society and culture is

---

[42] John Courtney Murray argued that the relation between "religion and government" in a constitutional democracy will be misunderstood unless it is seen in the context of and as subordinate to "the larger problematic of 'religion and human society.'" "The Issue of Church and State at Vatican Council II," in J. Leon Hooper, ed., *Religious Liberty: Catholic Struggles with Pluralism* (Louisville, KY: Westminster/John Knox Press, 1993), p. 215. J. Bryan Hehir has used the term "indirect" to describe the influence of religion on government via its influence on citizens, civil society, and culture. See Hehir, "Church-State and Church-World: The Ecclesiological Implications," in The Catholic Theological Society of America, *Proceedings of the Forty-First Annual Convention* (1986), 58.

acknowledged as legitimate, eliminating all religious influence on government could only be accomplished by suppressing some citizens' participation in self-government. This could hardly be what is required by a commitment to democratic freedom. In fact, resistance to such restrictions on the public role of religion has been a major force for the democratization of authoritarian regimes in recent decades. In numerous places from eastern Europe to Latin America to parts of east Asia, religious communities have helped constitute and strengthen civil society as a domain free from the authoritarian control of the state's apparatus.

The engagement of the populace in public affairs is intrinsic to the good of a free society, not simply an external condition necessary for realizing this good. It brings people out of a narrow world of isolation into the shared world where goods can be attained that can never be enjoyed in private. Most important, participation in public life makes it possible for citizens to attain the good of free and equal persons engaged in self-government. When religious communities understand their role in public rightly, they possess considerable power to contribute to the shared freedom of a self-governing people. When religious communities encourage their members to undertake interactive and mutually respectful engagement in the life of civil society they can make very valuable contributions to common good. By playing a public role in civil society and culture, therefore, religious communities can strengthen the public life of a free society in democracies and help bring it into being where it has been suppressed by authoritarian or totalitarian regimes. We must now ask what demands such a role in support of the common good makes on the self-understanding of religious communities and on the Christian churches in particular. That is the subject of the next chapter.

CHAPTER FIVE

Christianity in a community of freedom

Religious communities have the capacity to contribute to the common good of a free republic. This chapter will explore how this potentiality can be actualized. Specifically, it will address the question of how pursuit of the common good in a pluralistic context should be an integral part of a Christian religious self-understanding. It will explore why Christians should be actively engaged in building up a community of freedom along with those who are not Christian. A Christian religious understanding of the full human good is not only compatible with commitment to the civic good of a free society but calls Christians to civic engagement that builds solidarity in freedom. One does not have to choose between promotion of a strong understanding of the civic good and full commitment to Christian faith. The two are essentially related.

The proposal that Christianity can make genuine contributions to the common good of a free society makes significant demands on both Christians and non-Christians. It cannot be otherwise, for placing conditions only on Christians or only on non-Christians will not lead to a community of mutual freedom and solidarity. The possibility of achieving such a community is a high-stakes affair in the public life of both nation-states and the world as a whole. Past and present religious conflicts provide ample evidence of just how high. Exploring the public role of Christianity from both secular and theological perspectives, therefore, is essential to revitalizing the pursuit of the common good.

Sustaining this kind of Christian contribution to a community of freedom requires that several conditions be met. The first concerns the way the place of religion in the public realm is normatively envisioned by the non-Christian and secular members of the larger society. If a secular understanding of the public role of religion makes demands that Christians cannot accept on their own terms, Christians will not be able to accept these demands. So the first section of the chapter addresses the question of whether a public role for Christianity is possible that could be affirmed by secular and non-Christian thinkers. This means raising questions about the interpretation of the direction of history that maintains that the growth of modern freedoms requires that religion play a diminishing or vanishing role in public life. In other words, that the claim that a free society is a thoroughly secularized society must be challenged.

The second part of the chapter will address the issue in properly religious and theological terms. It will propose a theologically normative approach to how Christians should understand the relation between their religious vision of the good life and the civic good that can be realized within earthly history. Unless Christians can fully affirm that support for the civic good of a pluralistic society is compatible with their faith, they will not support this civic good. An argument that support for the common good is a Christian duty, therefore, must address this question in explicitly theological terms. Urging Christians to support the common good on non-religious grounds would be to ask them to abandon or dilute their beliefs. This should be acceptable neither to Christians themselves nor to anyone who has a robust respect for religious freedom. So the theological compatibility of Christian faith with support for the civic good is an important issue both for Christians and for non-Christians alike. This theological issue will be the focus of the second part of the chapter.

RECONSIDERING SECULARIZATION

The contention that Christians can fully support the good of a civic community of freedom requires that they affirm the religious freedom of those who are not Christian. One way to reach this affirmation is by identifying the truth claims of Christianity with "truth for Christians." In this approach, Christianity becomes a personal belief that gives meaning to the lives of those who are Christians but that makes no claim about what others should believe about the

meaning of life. This stance toward religious belief, of course, provides strong backing for tolerance. In the United States today, such
a "quiet faith" or "personal religion" seems increasingly common
in the self-understanding of many believers.[1] But such a stance has
little to say to those who believe that Christianity is a privileged
understanding of both God and the human good. It cannot tell
them why one who believes that the Christian vision of the good
life is the true one, rather than "true for Christians," should respect the freedom of people who hold other religious beliefs or
none. Nor does it distinguish between appropriate and inappropriate ways that Christians might bring their understanding of the
good life into the larger world of politics and social life. This calls
for a more substantive discussion of the relation between Christian
faith and respect for religious freedom than advocacy of a simple
relativism provides. It requires showing how the Christian understanding of God and the human good can also lead to respect
for the freedom of non-Christians and to solidarity with them in
the pursuit of the civic good. This calls for theological argument
about the implications of Christian belief in a religiously diverse
world.

Such an argument must show that strong Christian convictions
do not lead to a kind of communitarianism that seeks to overcome
the fragmentation and individualism of public life by reorganizing
all of society around a single integrating value scheme. Such a
communitarianism either denies, ignores, or seeks to suppress the
reality of pluralism.[2] When a religious vision of the good is identified
with an agenda for the whole of public life, with no room left
for critique of that religious vision or for serious exchange with
other forms of belief, religious freedom is threatened. Indeed, where
the common good of historical, public life is defined entirely in
religious terms, one may be justified in suspecting that religious
authoritarianism will not be far behind. From what has been argued
above, this cannot be the path toward the common good of a
community of freedom.

[1] See chapter 1.
[2] Seyla Benhabib has called this approach "integrationist communitarianism." See her *Situating the Self: Gender, Community and Postmodernism in Contemporary Ethics* (New York: Routledge,
1992), p. 77.

In Roman Catholic discussions over the past century, this kind
of communitarianism was known as "integralism." This is a theological stance that stresses the integral unity of religion, daily life,
politics, the sciences, the economy, and the whole gamut of human
endeavor. Such a posture manifests the deep Catholic instinct to see
all things human as potential mediators of the divine presence and
grace. It can be found in other Western Christian traditions as well,
especially in the family of Protestant churches deriving from or influenced by John Calvin. This pursuit of unity is an impulse rooted
in the belief that there is one cosmos, one universe, founded on the
one God who is creator and Lord of all that is. Thus it takes religious
truth claims about the cosmos with the seriousness their substantive
content deserves. From a religious standpoint, therefore, the "integralist" impulse for unity can appear as an appropriate expression
of genuine religious conviction. It can become perverse, however,
if the unity of all things in relation to God is interpreted to mean
that all knowledge can be reduced to theology or that all social
institutions ought to be extensions of the church. In the words of
the theologian Karl Rahner, it can lead to a way of thinking that
simply assumes that "human life can be unambiguously mapped
out and manipulated in accord with certain universal principles
proclaimed by the church and watched over by her in the manner in which they are developed and applied."[3] This integralist
approach confuses the unity of the cosmos in God with the subordination of all life to the church; it mistakes the fact that all forms of
human knowledge can lead to knowledge of God with the claim
that theology is the only genuine form of knowledge. Such mistaken
claims were firmly rejected by the Catholic Church at the Second
Vatican Council when it affirmed both the civil right to religious
freedom for all persons as well as the legitimate autonomy of secular institutions and intellectual disciplines.[4] The Council affirmed
these conclusions while also maintaining the traditional Catholic
commitment to the importance of the common good. This was a

---

[3] Karl Rahner, "Theological Reflections on the Problem of Secularization," *Theological Investigations*, vol. x (New York: Herder and Herder, 1973), p. 322.

[4] See Vatican Council II, *Dignitatis Humanae (Declaration on Religious Freedom)*, no. 2, and *Gaudium et Spes (Pastoral Constitution on the Church in the Modern World)*, no. 36, in *Vatican Council II: Constitutions, Decrees, Declarations*, ed. A. Flannery, pp. 552–553, 201–202.

major development in official Catholic teaching. Indeed, it is fair to call it a revolution in the Catholic approach to the role of Christian faith in public life, with important consequences for Catholic understandings of both the Christian community and the common good. How did this happen?

Despite its revolutionary aspect, the framework for the Council's treatment of these questions has deep roots in the Christian theological tradition. The recent Catholic explication of this tradition, however, has a distinctively contemporary accent that it will be useful to highlight before turning to the deeper roots. The contemporary formulation has been shaped by some important distinctions that can be drawn concerning the meaning of the secular and the historical trend of secularization. On one common reading of modern history, the claim that societies are becoming more secular is a hypothesis that religious belief will exert declining influence in the public sphere. On this hypothesis, the withering away of religion or at least the exclusion of religious communities from the public square will more or less automatically solve the religion-and-politics issue. It has become apparent that things are not working out this way, as religion continues to play important public roles. To address this counter-evidence, sociologist of religion José Casanova has distinguished three possible meanings of secularization. Secularization can mean: (1) *decline of religion* in the modern world, which will continue until religion finally disappears; (2) *privatization of religion*, i. e., the displacement of the quest for salvation and personal meaning to the subjective sphere of the self, a displacement that renders religion irrelevant to the institutional functioning of modern society; (3) functional *differentiation of the role of religion* from other spheres of human activity, primarily the state, the economy, and science.[5] These distinctions are quite helpful in clarifying central insights of the Christian theological tradition that speak to the contemporary problematic.

The first two meanings of secularization are contrary to fact. Religion is not declining world-wide and in the United States the level of religious belief remains notably higher than in earlier periods of

---

[5] José Casanova, *Public Religions in the Modern World* (Chicago: University of Chicago Press, 1994), chap. 1. This account neglects the theoretical richness of Casanova's account for purposes of simplicity in this context.

American history. The decline-of-religion version of secularization is largely based on the experience of modern western Europe and cannot be generalized to the rest of the world. Claims that religion is becoming a more private affair can also be factually questioned, as chapter 5 has shown. But the differentiation of religious belief and activity from other dimensions of social and intellectual life need not mean that religion is declining or that it is becoming more and more private. Showing that such differentiation does not mean decline or privatization is a key to the theological task of clarifying the relation between Christian faith and the common good today. Such differentiation has been roundly endorsed by recent Catholic theology and shown to be fully compatible with essential doctrinal convictions of normative Christian tradition.[6]

"Differentiation" means distinction, not isolation into separate, airtight compartments. The differentiation of religion and various dimensions of public life has a different connotation than does "separation." In the United States, separation of church from state is very often equated with the restriction of religion to an entirely private sphere walled off from governmental power. In contrast to this, differentiation of religion from the domain of state power does not rule out all religious influence in public life or in politics broadly conceived. Separation of church from state is a matter of the relation of two institutions, with each having a different role and mode of activity. Religious influence in public and even political life can occur, however, even where state and church are institutionally distinct. There can be public influence by religion that is exercised without control of state by church. Thus there is a third alternative to "integralism" on the one hand and the privatization of religion on the other. In this third alternative, religious communities can have an impact on public life while, at the same time, free exercise and non-establishment of religion are fully protected. This alternative

---

[6] Not all recent Catholic thought has supported such differentiation of the religious and the secular, and those who have endorsed it have not all had the same reasons for doing so. It is nevertheless true that normative Catholic doctrine, as expressed by the Second Vatican Council, has affirmed the interpretation of Catholic thought advanced here. For a subtle treatment of recent Catholic theological currents on this issue, see Joseph A. Komonchak, "Vatican II and the Encounter between Catholicism and Liberalism," in R. Bruce Douglass and David Hollenbach, eds., *Catholicism and Liberalism: Contributions to American Public Philosophy* (Cambridge: Cambridge University Press, 1994), pp. 76–99.

to church – state unity on the one hand and strictly private religion on the other has been the historical achievement of the approach to the problem in the United States. It is an ironic fact that the strong role religion continues to play in American public life has been made possible by the equally strong distinction between church and state in the United States, while the privatization of religion in western Europe has been the historical result of reaction to a long history of church – state symbiosis on the European continent.[7]

Such differentiation without privatization was the route proposed for the Catholic community in the framework developed at the Second Vatican Council. Vatican II affirmed the civil right of all persons to religious freedom. It stated that "the right to religious freedom has its foundation in the very dignity of the human person, as this dignity is known through the revealed Word of God and by reason itself." Respect for the dignity of persons implies that "all persons are to be immune from coercion on the part of individuals or social groups and of any human power."[8] Immunity from religious coercion leads to a firm rejection of church efforts to co-opt the power of the state for its own purposes. Non-establishment of religion is an institutional consequence of this freedom of religion. But this does not mean religion is to be a strictly private affair. For Vatican II also affirmed that engagement by religious communities in public life is itself part of the meaning of religious freedom: "It comes within the meaning of religious freedom that religious bodies should not be prohibited from freely undertaking to show the special value of their doctrine in what concerns the organization of society and the inspiration of the whole of human activity."[9] Thus non-establishment of religion and a public role for religion are both affirmed; they are not conceived of as binary alternatives to each other.

A third alternative is possible because separation of church from state need not be violated when religious communities have public influence. Non-establishment of religion and a public role for

---

[7] For a discussion of the way the public presence of religion has been facilitated by separation of church and state in the United States, see Jeffery K. Hadden's presidential address to the Society for the Scientific Study of Religion, "Religious Broadcasting and the Mobilization of the New Christian Right," 1–24.

[8] Vatican Council II, *(Dignitatis Humanae) Declaration on Religious Freedom*, no. 2.

[9] *Ibid.*, no. 5.

religion are both social expressions of religious freedom. They can be distinguished from each other but need not be contradictory. Non-establishment is called for because religious freedom cannot be adequately protected where government power is placed behind one religion to the exclusion of others. This rules out the coercive enforcement of religious belief by the state. But religious freedom cannot mean that believers be required to express and act on their faith strictly in private. To demand this would be to tell religious believers what the scope and limits of their faith can be. Religious freedom can also be violated by the demand that religion remain strictly private. So casting the issue as a choice between non-establishment or public religion is a serious oversimplification. This either/or way of formulating the issue is based on a misunderstanding of the multileveled interaction of religion with social life. It is a false dichotomy that follows from misconceiving freedom as in opposition to life in common with others. When the possibility of a community of freedom is recognized, freedom and interaction in social solidarity can be seen as companions rather than adversaries. Thus religious freedom as non-establishment and religious freedom expressed in a public role for religion can be distinguished without being portrayed as opposed to each other.

A THEOLOGICAL ARGUMENT

This framework can help in the retrieval of important theological traditions that help clarify how the Christian community can contribute to the common good while fully supporting the freedoms so highly valued in the modern West. Several Christian theologians important in the Catholic tradition, especially Augustine, Thomas Aquinas, and their recent interpreters, are particularly important to such an undertaking, since the idea of the common good has been a distinctive emphasis in the Catholic tradition. A retrieval of their thought can also address fears about the possible impact of religious promotion of the common good that are based on some of the behavior of the Roman Catholic community in the past. The goal here is neither a historical study of past Catholic practice nor a comprehensive examination of the thought of Augustine and Aquinas. Rather, the aim is to draw on them in the interest of a

Christian theological approach to the common good in a free, pluralist society. The argument will be pursued further in subsequent chapters of this book.

Augustine's theology of the relation between Christian faith and public life is developed in *The City of God*. This great work sheds considerable theological light on how the Christian community is differentiated from the public sphere without being either isolated from it or dominant over it. *The City of God* was written in response to the charge that the growth of Christianity was the cause of the decline of the Roman empire. Some Roman patriots laid the responsibility for Rome's fall on the rise of Christianity as a significant presence on the Roman scene. There are echoes of this kind of complaint today in suggestions that influence by religion on public life or public philosophy can threaten the stability of the polity.[10] The analogy is ironic, however, for Roman objections were based on the claim that Christianity drew its adherents away from religiously based support for the common good of the republic. This is quite a different thing from the contemporary concern that the Christian community could threaten the peace and freedom of society by becoming too active in public. This irony suggests that the problem of religion in public will be characterized differently in different historical circumstances. In the eyes of Augustine's Roman contemporaries, the problem was that Christianity was too private a form of religion. In a society like ours, where the weakening of public life has again emerged as a significant problem, Augustine's reply to this charge again has considerable pertinence.

Augustine argued that Christianity was not guilty of the excessively apolitical spirit with which it was charged. At the same time he maintained that Christian faith could not be identified with a political program. The theological arguments by which Augustine reached both of these conclusions remain relevant to clarifying the

---

[10] For example, Richard Rorty has written that "Contemporary liberal philosophers think that we shall not be able to keep a democratic political community going unless the religious believers remain willing to trade privatization for a guarantee of religious liberty," in "Religion as Conversation-Stopper," *Common Knowledge* 3, no. 1 (1994), 3. Robert Audi argues a somewhat more nuanced version of this position in "The Separation of Church and State and the Obligations of Citizenship," *Philosophy and Public Affairs* 18 (1989), 259–296, and has further refined it in "The State, the Church, and the Citizen," in Paul Weithman, ed., *Religion and Contemporary Liberalism* (Notre Dame, IN: University of Notre Dame Press, 1997), pp. 38–75.

role of Christians in public life today. This role is to be neither one of domination over political existence nor retreat from it. In contemporary terms, Augustine said *yes* to the differentiation of religion from politics, but *no* to control of the polity by the church, *no* to control of the church by the polity, and *no* to the withdrawal of the church into the domain of private subjectivity.

The outline of Augustine's theological argument is particularly evident in his rethinking of Cicero's definition of a republic. According to this definition, the existence of a republic requires agreement among the people about what is right or just and about the good they share in common.[11] In Book II of *The City of God* Augustine relied on Cicero to suggest that Christianity strongly supports the virtues and values that are required in a republic. Only citizens who have thoroughly embraced such virtues and values will be capable of sustaining a genuinely common life. Decades before the birth of Christ, Cicero had already concluded that "it is through our own faults, not by any accident, that we retain only the form of the commonwealth, but have long since lost its substance."[12] Cicero's arguments for this sober conclusion were that common commitment to the ways of justice had decayed in Rome to the point where these ways were no longer practiced and in fact no longer even known among the citizens. Drawing on Cicero, Augustine turned the critics' argument that Christianity caused Rome's fall on its head. The decline of the republic was not due to the public acceptance of Christianity but to the absence of the virtues Christianity brings to public life in a unique way. The source of Roman instability was not too much Christianity but the fact that Christianity had not yet appeared on the scene.

The initial phase of Augustine's argument even suggests that *only* Christianity is capable of sustaining a genuine republic. This part of his argument might suggest he was advocating an "integralist" or even theocratic definition of a true commonwealth. On explicitly theological grounds, Augustine questioned whether Rome had ever been a true republic at all, even in the earlier heroic period before the decline lamented by Cicero. According to Cicero's definition,

---

[11] Cicero, *De Re Publica*, I, xxv, 39. This definition is cited by Augustine in *The City of God*, trans. Henry Bettenson (London/New York: Penguin Books, 1972), II, 21.
[12] Cicero, *De Re Publica*, v, i, 2.

there could be no republic in the absence of public "agreement with respect to justice and partnership for the common good." Augustine initially interpreted this to mean that *de facto* consensus on a concept of justice is a necessary but not sufficient condition for the existence of a commonweal. To create a genuine commonweal, there must be social and cultural agreement on what is *truly* just, *truly* the common good. Citing the classic formula that justice means rendering to all persons what is due to them, Augustine argued as a Christian theologian that this means rendering to God what is due to God, namely worship and love. Thus a true commonweal is an assembly of people united in the worship and love of the one true God rather than idols. In addition, in a commonwealth the people must be bound together by a love whereby each citizen loves his neighbor as he loves himself, for love of neighbor is the active work in the moral domain that gives expression to love of God.[13] A true commonweal, therefore, is a people bound together by faith in Christ, love of God, love of the neighbor in God, and obedience to the moral exigencies of the gospel. Thus the only republic that embodies Cicero's definition truly and fully is the one Augustine calls the City of God – the Jerusalem whose cornerstone is Christ and whose animating source is the Holy Spirit of God's love and grace.

Thomas Aquinas was in full agreement with this stringently theological understanding of the common good. For St. Thomas, the ultimate good of all creatures – the full common good – is God. Human beings achieve their ultimate fulfillment – their good – only by being united with God, a union that also unites them to each other and indeed with the whole created order. "God's own goodness . . . is the good of the whole universe."[14] There could hardly be a more "theocentric" and theologically based definition of the foundation of the moral life. Everything human beings are to do, in both personal and social life, should be directed to one end: union with the God who is their maker and redeemer.

Such a high theological definition of the full good of human society is precisely the sort of thing that critics of the idea of the common good dread might be imposed upon believer and unbeliever alike,

[13] Augustine, *The City of God*, XIX, 23.
[14] Aquinas, *Summa Theologiae*, Ia, IIae, q. 19, art. 10.

even by force of arms, should the social balance of power permit this. They fear that such religious beliefs about the full meaning of the good life will become the basis of a political program to which they have not freely consented. Paradoxically, such an exclusively theological definition of the good can easily lead believers to write off the possibility of finding common ground with those outside the community of faith. Endorsing such common ground, even if it could be identified, would be seen as compromise at best and a work of Satan at worst. So it can lead believers to withdraw from public life. In both the scenario that would forcefully impose a theological conception of the good and in the scenario that abandons pursuit of common ground entirely, the idea of the *common* good of a pluralistic society becomes a mirage. There is reason to be apprehensive, therefore, that a theological understanding of the common good may be either a prelude to the return of religious persecution, or a form of perfectionism that further undermines what little is left of the idea of citizenship.

This, however, is not where Augustine left the matter and his theology will be misunderstood unless this is recognized. Augustine was neither a theocrat nor a religious separatist. The reasons he was neither of these things are crucial to an adequate theological approach to the role of the Christian community in a community of freedom and solidarity today. For Augustine argued that an understanding of the human good in its full theological depth shows why Christians should also pursue the more limited goods that can be attained in secular, terrestrial history. There is a common good that humans can share together in history, even though it falls short of the full good of the Reign of God. The distinction of this terrestrial common good from the eschatological City of God grounds opposition to theocracy, while the relation of the City of God to historically achievable goods grounds an important public role for the Christian community.

Rejection of the idea that the Christian understanding of the full good should be politically imposed throughout society follows from Augustine's deep conviction that human fulfillment can only be attained in the communion of saints. This fullness of the City of God transcends history. It is an eschatological reality that surpasses all the human goods that can be achieved in historical politics, no matter how high a form politics might take. For this reason, placing all one's hopes for happiness and justice in a historical, earthly city risks becoming a kind of idolatry. Thus Augustine rejected the belief central to classical thought that the good of the *polis* or *civitas* is the highest human good.[15] Pursuit of the good through political means must therefore be carefully distinguished from the religious vocation of the believer and living out one's religious belief cannot be simply identified with a political agenda.

In other words, Augustine's insistence on the transcendence of the City of God desacralizes politics. It distinguishes what can be achieved politically from what Christians ultimately place their hope in. Every social good achievable in history is a limited good. This provides Christian warrant for a kind of politics that does not seek to achieve the final human good that can be attained only in the kingdom of God through the gift of God's grace. An exclusively religious politics is a form of false messianism. It makes the political sphere the bearer of counterfeit messianic hopes, often because of an inability to come to terms with the historical imperfection and imperfectability of public affairs.[16] It easily leads to fanaticism and tyranny on the one hand or to failure to seek the lesser goods that are in fact achievable in politics on the other. Genuine Christian faith counteracts false political expectations by placing hope where it belongs, namely in God. In counteracting such false hopes, it can free believers to pursue the goods, including the common good, that can be achieved within terrestrial cities.

Augustine's thought, therefore, bears some similarity to some modern liberal understandings of the limited role of government.[17]

---

[15] For a succinct discussion of these themes in Augustine's political theology see P. R. L. Brown, "Political Society," in R. A. Markus, ed., *Augustine: A Collection of Essays* (New York: Doubleday, 1972), pp. 311–329, esp. p. 323. Compare Augustine's transcendent vision of the *civitas Dei* with Aristotle's affirmation of the primacy of the political: "If all communities aim at some good, the state or political community, which is the highest of all, and which embraces all the rest, aims at good in a greater degree than any other, and at the highest good." *Politics*, 1252a, 3–6. trans. in *The Basic Works of Aristotle*, ed. Richard McKeon, p. 1127.

[16] For a recent example of the use of Augustine in making such an argument, see Cardinal Joseph Ratzinger, *Church, Ecumenism and Politics: New Essays in Ecclesiology* (New York: Crossroad, 1988), p. 216.

[17] On this point see Paul J. Weithman, "Toward an Augustinian Liberalism," *Faith and Philosophy* 8, no. 4 (1991), 461–480; Edmund N. Santurri, "Rawlsian Liberalism, Moral Truth, and Augustinian Politics," *Journal for Peace and Justice Studies* 8, no. 2 (1997), 1–36.

We can draw upon this theology to argue for limits to the use of state power in pursuit of the good and also to suggest that the Christian community should not seek a "theocratic" control of political and social life. The roles of both state and church in the attainment of the ultimate good are limited. Such a theology can provide warrants for many of the democratic values and institutions developed by modern Western democracies. In particular, it will stand opposed to any form of religious persecution and to governmental denial of religious freedom.[18] Restricting or enforcing religious belief (whether it be true, false, or some mixture of true and false) is simply beyond the scope of legitimate governmental power. Government is strictly incompetent to determine what religious beliefs are true and what are false.[19] Religious truth is beyond political understanding and therefore beyond what any government or politician can know when they are operating within their properly political roles.

Nevertheless, Augustine's theology supports a considerably richer understanding of the worldly common good than do many forms of liberalism. Despite his insistence that no earthly city can achieve the full communion of the City of God, he in fact maintained that the common life of a republic with a shared common good is possible within history. To be sure, if the consensus on justice and the good needed to make a republic is understood in a strictly theological way, only the City of God can be a commonweal in the full sense. But Augustine recognized that it would be somehow absurd to insist that all societies that lack the full faith

[18] I am aware, of course, that Augustine's attitude toward the use of governmental power for religious ends is not entirely consistent, as his justification of coercion of the Donatists shows. It can be argued, however, that his approach to the Donatists was in fact inconsistent with the main lines of his theology. In any case, it is entirely contrary to the appropriation of his thought being advocated here and in recent Roman Catholic theology such as that of the Second Vatican Council. On the Donatist case, see P. R. L. Brown, "St. Augustine's Attitude to Religious Coercion," *Journal of Roman Studies* 54 (1964), 107–116, and R. A. Markus's treatment of the question in *Saeculum: History and Society in the Theology of Saint Augustine* (Cambridge: Cambridge University Press, 1970).

[19] See the Second Vatican Council's *Declaration on Religious Freedom (Dignitatis Humanae)*, which states that "private and public acts of religion by which people direct themselves to God, according to their convictions, transcend of their very nature the earthly and temporal order of things . . . If [government] presumes to control or restrict religious activity it must be judged to have exceeded the limits of its power" (no. 3).

and love of the heavenly city were not cities at all. This led him to revise Cicero's definition and to propose a "more feasible" understanding of a commonweal. This redefinition enabled him to maintain that "a republic of a certain kind" could exist short of the City of God.[20] The revised definition of a *res publica* goes as follows: "a people is an assemblage of reasonable beings bound together by a common agreement as to the objects of their love."[21] Following this definition, the quality of a republic will be directly proportional to the qualities of the loves its people share in common. Societies united by noble loves or strong solidarities, and dedicated to high standards of justice, will be superior to those with lower goals and cultural values. According to this definition, Rome in its heroic early period could be counted a republic even though it lacked Christian faith and failed to worship the one God. When it ceased to share any common bonds of concord, however, it fragmented into disunity and ceased to be a commonwealth at all.

This redefinition of the meaning of a republic is one expression of Augustine's subtle understanding of the relation between the Christian vision of the ultimate good and the good attainable in worldly history.[22] These goods must certainly not be identified, but neither are they entirely unrelated. Civil society is not, or need not be, identical with the kingdom of Satan or the *civitas terrena*. Nor is the church identical with the heavenly Jerusalem or the *civitas Dei*. Elements of the City of God can be found in all dimensions of civil society and in the political community as well, while distorted loves and human sinfulness are present within the historical community of the church. The full good of the City of God can be really though imperfectly present in civic life to the extent that concern for the neighbor rather than introverted love of self or lust for domination are present there. By the same token, the evils of sin, pride, and domination can be found among those who make up the church. Within history the

---

[20] Augustine, *The City of God*, ii, 21.　　[21] *Ibid.*, 24.

[22] The question of the relationship between the City of God and the earthly city in Augustine's thought is admittedly complex. My interpretation is indebted to Eugene TeSelle's essays, "The Civic Vision in Augustine's *City of God*," *Thought* 62 (1987), 268–280; "Toward an Augustinian Politics," *Journal of Religious Ethics* 16, no.1 (1988), 87–108; and "Justice, Love, Peace," in Richard J. Neuhaus, ed., *Augustine Today* (Grand Rapids, MI: Eerdmans, 1993), pp. 88–110.

two cities are intermingled and interpenetrating, wheat and tares growing together.[23] This complex interweaving of good and evil manifests Augustine's deep sensitivity to the ambiguities and tensions of political, ecclesiastical, and indeed all terrestrial existence.

Christians live in the midst of both cities. They are resident aliens in the earthly city, who maintain a critical distance from its politics and values. At the same time, the love of neighbor that is an active expression of faith should lead them to work to make the civic community into the best city possible.[24] The fullness of this love of neighbor will ultimately be realized only as a gift of God in the communion of saints, the heavenly city. Though this ultimate end is beyond politics, it sets the direction for the historical project of constructing the earthly commonweal. In the civic life of terrestrial republics, therefore, different degrees of approximation to the full theological good are possible. Earthly republics can be more like the heavenly city or less so. Christians are called to contribute to transforming their society from lesser approximations of the heavenly city to ones that come nearer to the good that is their ultimate hope.[25] Their pursuit of such transformation calls for careful discernment of the possibilities opened up by historical circumstances.

This understanding of the relation of the Christian community to civic life takes history seriously. The relation between Christians and their co-citizens is a dynamic, historical interaction. It is not the imposition of a pre-given, Christian mold on the formless matter of society. Rather, the quality of relationships among the citizens of the earthly city, both Christians and not, should reflect something of

---

[23] As Augustine put it in a sermon on the fifty-first Psalm:

> Let us not therefore despair of the citizens of the kingdom of heaven when we see them engaged in . . . something terrestrial in a terrestrial republic; nor again let us forthwith congratulate all men whom we see engaged in celestial matters, for even the sons of pestilence sit sometimes on the seat of Moses . . . The former amid earthly things lift up their hearts to heaven; the latter amid heavenly words trail their hearts on the earth. But there will come a time of winnowing when they will be separated, the one from the other, with the greatest care. (*Enarrationes in Psalmos* 51, 6, Corpus Christianorum, Series Latina, vol. xxxix (Turnhout, Belgium: Brepols, 1956), 627. The translation is that contained in Erich Przywara, ed., *An Augustine Synthesis* (New York: Sheed and Ward, 1936), pp. 270–271.)

[24] TeSelle, "Civic Vision in Augustine," 279.

[25] This transformationist interpretation of Augustine has been influenced by H. Richard Niebuhr, *Christ and Culture* (New York: Harper and Row, 1951), pp. 206–218.

the love of the heavenly city. Christians should treat non-Christians as fellow citizens, not as adversaries or enemies. Christians can enter into the life of the *polis* with a spirit marked by a solidarity grounded in love of their neighbors. This means engaging in both mutual efforts to discern the civic good and joint action for this good together with fellow citizens. When Christians act this way in civil society, they will be building up the terrestrial common good as a real though imperfect image of the highest good of the heavenly city. In James Dougherty's words, such a theological vision "finds Jerusalem, old and new, within the secular, historical city, and proposes there to redeem the Time Being."[26] Redeeming the time means building the kind of commonweal that is possible in history, not withdrawing into an ecclesial ghetto or seeking to impose heavenly values by force.

The theological significance of common life in civil society can be further clarified with the help of the thinking of Thomas Aquinas. In a Thomistic perspective, the ultimate theological good and the good that can be achieved in the secular domain have an analogical relation to each other. They are both similar and different, mutually illuminating rather than opposed or contradictory to each other. When divine and human goodness are both called "good," this is because they have more in common than the fact that we use the same word to name them. They are good by analogy – both different in their goodness but also similar to the degree they are truly good.[27] Jacques Maritain's social-political development of Aquinas's understanding of the metaphysics of such analogy sheds light on the relation between the Christian understanding of God as the highest good and the common good of human society.

Maritain's position has been called personalist communitarianism, for its central affirmation about human beings is "that

---

[26] James Dougherty, *The Fivesquare City: The City in Religious Imagination* (South Bend, IN: University of Notre Dame Press, 1980), p. 144, cited in TeSelle, "Civic Vision in Augustine," 279.

[27] Aristotle hinted at such an understanding when he noted that the term "good" has many meanings when applied to different realities. For example, God is good, human intelligence is good, the moral virtues are good, having a place to live is good. God's goodness is of course different from any humanly achievable good. But there is something similar about divine and human goodness that invites the use of the same word "good" to refer to both kinds of goodness. See *Nicomachean Ethics* 1096 a, b.

personality tends by nature to communion."[28] This is the basis
of Maritain's (and St. Thomas's) understanding of the analogical
nature of the common good. The true good of persons is communion with other persons, not something that can be enjoyed
in solitude. This good is realized completely only in God. God is
supremely personal, for God is the supreme exemplar of love and
communion. Indeed as the first letter of John in the New Testament
expresses it, "God *is* love" (1 John 4, 8). Because personhood implies the capacity for communion, the highest realization of personality is God. The supreme exemplification of goodness is God's
love. Humans are persons of a lesser sort, for they are capable of
love and interpersonal communion to a lesser degree. So Maritain
maintains that "the idea of the person is an analogical idea which is
realized fully and absolutely only in its supreme analogue, God."[29]
Lesser, non-divine beings are personal to the extent that they are
in some measure "like God." This human likeness to God is their
capacity for relationships of love, mutual communion, and solidarity with each other. To the degree that humans actualize this
capacity in their relationships, their goodness becomes more like
the supreme goodness of God. The human good is thus analogous
to divine goodness. The fulfillment of human persons occurs in relationships of love, communion, and solidarity both with God and
with other human beings. Again, as the first letter of John puts it:
"if we love one another, God lives in us" (1 John 4, 12). In contrast
with this, the ultimate evil for human beings is isolation. Privacy,
radically understood, is hell in a more than metaphorical sense.

Maritain turns to the Christian doctrine of the Trinity to further illustrate the analogy between the divine and human good.
The doctrine of the Trinity, as elaborated in the Christian theological tradition, affirms that the One God is not an isolated
monad but rather is three persons in relationships of absolute self-
communication and communion. The self-communication in love
by the three divine persons is so total that God is radically one.
Relying on this doctrinal tradition, Maritain concludes that the essential relationality of personhood has its supreme exemplification
in the unity of the three persons of the divine Trinity. He follows

---

[28] Maritain, *The Person and the Common Good*, p. 47.   [29] *Ibid.*, p. 56.

Aquinas in affirming that the divine persons are "subsistent relations" – persons whose very identity as persons *is* their relationship one with the other.[30] This understanding of personality in God is analogous to the understanding of human personhood. In both the divine and the human, to be a person is to be-in-relation-to-other-persons. The mutual implication of personality and relationality has its highest exemplification in God's own being. It is reflected in the mutual implication of personhood and communal relationship in human beings.

Human society is thus a real though imperfect image of God. Human community is located on "an analogical scale" between the perfect society of persons that is the Trinity and simple aggregations of impersonal beings that do not form communities in the proper sense at all. In the unity of persons that is the Trinity, "each one is in the other through an infinite communion."[31] At the other end of the analogical scale are non-personal beings such as rocks, plants, and non-human animals. These can form collectivities whose members are in coordinated interaction with each other. The shared good of such an aggregation of non-personal beings is the harmonious interaction of a physical system, a hive, or a herd. This non-personal shared good is intrinsically valuable, as environmental concerns certainly reveal. But it is not the fuller good of self-conscious communication in language and love that human beings can achieve. It is not the good of a city or a *polis* that is realized in human communication and the joint action of self-government.

Human beings stand in an intermediate position between the divine and the impersonal on this scale of analogies. Humans are persons capable of communication, conscious relationships, mutual concern, and love. Humans are also physical, chemical, and biological beings that are linked with and dependent on each other, but always separated from each other in space and time. So

---

[30] For a discussion of this theme in St. Thomas see Catherine M. LaCugna, "The Relational God: Aquinas and Beyond," *Theological Studies* 46 (1985), 647–663.

[31] Maritain, *The Person and the Common Good*, p. 58. Here Maritain cites Thomas Aquinas, *Summa Theologiae* 1, 42, 5. The 1966 translation of *The Person and the Common Good*, published by University of Notre Dame Press, omits several lines from the French text on this page. For a more accurate and complete translation of this passage, consult the excerpts contained in Joseph W. Evans and Leo R. Ward, eds., *The Social and Political Philosophy of Jacques Maritain: Selected Readings* New York: Scribner's, 1955, p. 86.

Maritain concludes that the human good is both like the divine
good of full communion and love, but also different from the divine good because of the finitude and incompleteness of temporal
existence. The terrestrial common good of human society is thus
analogous to the full communion of the Trinity and to the full union
with God and neighbor that Christians hold will be a gift of divine
grace in heaven. But the life of the city can never be the complete
realization of this unlimited good as long as history lasts. "Human
society is located between these two; a society of persons who are
material individuals, hence isolated each within itself but nonetheless requiring communion with one another as far as possible here
below in anticipation of that perfect communion with one another
and God in life eternal."[32]

This Thomistic theological framework opens up important perspectives on the relation between the ultimate Christian vision of
the good and the meaning of the common good of human communities in history. Like Augustine's analysis, it implies that the full human good is the communion of all persons with God and with each
other in God that will be achieved in the heavenly city. This destiny
transcends *all* historically achievable goods. Christians, therefore,
are required by their faith to reject any attempt to achieve the full
common good, as it is understood theologically, by political means.
Reliance on the state to enforce the full Christian vision of the
good would in effect subordinate the transcendent City of God
to a limited earthly institution. The theological rejection of such
subordination has important political consequences. It leads to a
political theory that is thoroughly anti-totalitarian in its rejection of
all forms of state absolutism. No state can claim sovereignty, even
a democratic one; only God is authentically sovereign. The power
of government is limited in principle, and these limits are unambiguously supported only by constitutional forms of government.[33]

This limitation on governmental power is one of the sources
of the distinction between the state and civil society.[34] Society is

32 Maritain, *The Person and the Common Good*, p. 59.
33 Maritain, *Man and the State* (Chicago: University of Chicago Press, 1951), pp. 28–53, pp.
148–150. These ideas are also developed in a more American idiom by John Courtney
Murray, for example in a posthumous publication of some of Murray's writings: J. Leon
Hooper, ed., *Religious Liberty: Catholic Struggles with Pluralism*.
34 Maritain, *Man and the State*, chap. 1, "The People and the State."

a fuller and richer reality than the political sphere. Social life is not constituted by one kind of relationship among persons, for example the political relation, but by many kinds. Society is a braid or web made from many kinds of interactions, such as personal friendships, family ties, workplace interactions, religious communities, and numerous others. The political relationship is only one of the relationships that weave together to make a society. Civil society is constituted by a host of diverse social, economic, political, and cultural interactions. Each of these relationships is capable of realizing some aspect of the human good. But none of these aspects is the whole common good. The historical, earthly common good, therefore, is an ensemble of diverse goods. These include the goods achieved in family relationships, in voluntary associations, in political activity, in economic life, in the church, etc.

It is important to note that this ensemble of goods is not cleanly divisible into the political good on the one hand and a large set of "private goods" on the other. Many non-political goods are social and relational, so it is misleading to speak of all goods outside the sphere of the state as private. This use of "private" to describe all goods outside the purview of the state suggests that all non-political goods are the goods of individuals apart from their human relationships and community. The more appropriate distinction is between social goods and political goods, where the former are achieved in the multiple relationships that are constitutive of personhood and the latter in political action organized through government. The distinction between "social" and the "private" is the basis of Maritain's insistence that a "personalist" interpretation of the good is fundamentally different from individualism.[35] His opposition to an all-encompassing state is based on a defense of civil society

[35] For a defense of Maritain against the charge that his "personalism" is a form of individualism, see I. Th. Eschmann, "In Defense of Jacques Maritain," *The Modern Schoolman* 22 (1945), 183–208, esp. 207. Eschmann is responding to a not-too-veiled critique of Maritain in Charles DeKoninck, *De la primauté du bien commun contre les personnalistes. Le principe de l'ordre nouveau* (Québec/Montréal: Editions de l'Université Laval/ Editions Fides, 1943). It is true, however, that Maritain's understanding of the ultimate relationship of the human person to God in contemplation is not mediated by any creature. This aspect of the theology presented in Maritain's *Person and the Common Good* has rightly been questioned by Dean Brackley in his "Salvation and the Social Good in the Thought of Jacques Maritain and Gustavo Gutierrez," Ph.D. Dissertation, University of Chicago (1980), pp. 107–122.

that rejects individualistic presuppositions. Since the freedom and dignity of persons are achieved in interaction with other persons, respect for this freedom and dignity calls for respect for the many forms of relationship in which persons can participate. Each of these relationships is the locus of part of the common good that can be achieved in history.

Since the many forms of relationship are actualized in mutual communication and moral interdependence, each of them can be in some way analogous to the ultimate common good of the union of human beings with God and with each other in God. In the Thomistic theological approach based on analogy, as in the Augustinian understanding of the interpenetration of heavenly and earthly cities, the Christian vision of the full human good can be a model for what can be achieved in all human relations. The full communion of divine love is an exemplar for all lesser goods, whether in friendships, family life, the work place, politics, or the church. The distinction of the full Christian vision of the good from the political good does not render this vision irrelevant to public life. All aspects of public life can be real though imperfect reflections of the fullness of communion that is the ultimate Christian hope. Though Christians reject coercive use of the state to implement the kingdom of God, they see themselves called to work for the transformation of social life into a more fitting reflection of the good that is their ultimate hope.

The Christian religious vision of the city of God, therefore, affirms and seeks to realize the basic capacities of human beings for positive interaction and relationship. Its transcendent vision of the common good does not contradict the shared goods that can be attained in history. Further, these capacities for mutual relationship and communication can only occur in a human way when they occur in freedom. Relationships based on and expressive of personality are relationships built in freedom. If reciprocal freedom is absent, so is the mutuality that must be present if the communion and love of the City of God is to be reflected in this-worldly interaction among persons. For this reason, terrestrial approximations of the full good must themselves be attained in freedom. A worldly community of freedom is thus a prerequisite for worldly anticipations of the City of God, as well as being an approximation and analogy of the heavenly City. Christians, therefore, should be agents of both the common good and of the ways of a free society. Indeed they cannot be one without being the other.

This theological standpoint should allay some of the fears of critics of close links between the idea of the common good and religious aspiration.[36] It is certainly true that if religious hope becomes entirely politicized the dangers of totalitarianism are not far behind. In the face of this danger we must take seriously the theological warning that every form of human community is marked in some measure by sin and therefore falls short of the full communion of the kingdom of God. But this does not mean that opposition to false messianism must lead to self-protective individualism or atomism. Such individualism itself not only contradicts fundamental dimensions of the human good, but it can lead to forms of tyranny when the powerful arrogate social goods to their private benefit. Jeffrey Stout has expressed the subtlety of the Augustinian standpoint when he points out that it resists both political messianism and retreat into privatism. On the one hand, it points to the fact that "no sphere [of historical existence] can rightly occupy the position of be-all-and-end-all in our lives without throwing the rest out of proper proportion – neither vocation, nor family, nor voluntary association, nor private projects, nor politics." But on the other hand, each of these spheres is formed by relationships in which members of society find "some part of their identity," including that part that follows from being "citizens of a republic dedicated to the common good."[37] Thus the political good of the *polis* should be a central concern of those who recognize they have here no lasting city. For the communion of the kingdom of God can have an anticipatory, though incomplete, presence in the political sphere, just as it can in friendships, family life, and other terrestrial communities, including but not restricted to the church. An accurate reading of the tradition rooted in Augustine and Aquinas leads neither to totalitarianism nor to minimalist politics. A third

[36] I include among those with such fears not only secularists but also those Christians who fear too close an identification of Christian faith with politics. See, for example, Cardinal Joseph Ratzinger, *Church, Ecumenism and Politics*, p. 216, and Gilbert Meilander, *The Limits of Love: Some Theological Explorations* (University Park, PA: Pennsylvania State University Press, 1987), p. 140.

[37] Stout, *Ethics after Babel*, p. 235.

alternative exists, one that understands the common good as an ensemble of goods that embody the good of communion, love, and solidarity to a real though limited degree in the multiple forms of human interaction.

We can call this alternative a pluralistic-analogical understanding of the meaning of the common good. The theological argument just made shows why pursuit of the common good demands full respect for the many different forms of interrelationship and community in which human beings achieve their good in history. None of these forms of community may be absolutized or allowed to dominate all the others.[38] Each has a place within the framework of social existence, but none of them can be granted absolute status. The only absolute is God, with whom human beings enter into full relationship only in the heavenly Jerusalem, the City of God. But the political domain has the potential to become a partial embodiment of the full human good. This potential points to a form of politics that seeks greater human solidarity, not just toleration or the protection of individuals in their solitude. This will be a politics that seeks the common good in freedom – the common good of a community of freedom. Such a politics must be supported and sustained by a culture that values both freedom and solidarity, that sees solidarity as a prerequisite for shared freedom, and that sees freedom as self-rule as possible only in common action with others. As Augustine's revised definition implies, a commonweal will exist to the degree that the citizens share common loves. The quality of this republic will be proportional to the quality of the loves found among citizens and in the culture they share together. To the extent that the Christian community has a transformative influence on these loves it will have an immediate impact on culture. It will also have an impact on politics that is mediated by the culture citizens share. In both immediate and mediated ways, therefore, the Christian community can make important contributions to the common good of a community of freedom. Such a contribution is urgently needed in a world that is both more and more interdependent and less and less sure that a common life is possible.

[38] This is the central thesis of Michael Walzer's *Spheres of Justice: A Defense of Pluralism and Equality* (New York: Basic Books, 1983).

CHAPTER SIX

Intellectual solidarity

Any fruitful contribution by the Christian community to the common good will be one that is faithful to essential Christian religious convictions and also affirms that non-Christians are full members of a civic community of freedom. The discussion of the previous chapter shows that such a Christian contribution is entirely possible from a theological point of view. We now turn to an examination of what realizing this possibility will require more practically. This chapter will explore *how* Christians should bring their vision of the good life into the public sphere in a spirit of solidarity with their non-Christian fellow citizens. It will also address the question of *how* non-Christian citizens ought to respond to the presence of religion in the public sphere. The shared good of a community of freedom is incompatible with all forms of domination or exclusion of one group of persons by another, whether on religious or secular grounds. For this reason, an inclusively free community makes demands on both those inside and outside the church. This chapter will suggest what some of those demands are and why we should try to meet them.

A religiously pluralistic community, by definition, does not already share a common vision of the good life. Moving toward such a shared vision, even in outline, will take intellectual work. This common pursuit of a shared vision of the good life can be called intellectual solidarity. It is an intellectual endeavor, for it calls for serious thinking by citizens about what their distinctive understandings of the good imply for the life of a society made up of people with many different traditions. It is a form of solidarity, because it can only occur in an active dialogue of mutual listening and speaking across the boundaries of religion and culture. Indeed, dialogue that seeks to understand those with different visions of the good life is already a form of solidarity even when disagreement continues to exist. Intellectual solidarity thus requires certain orientations of mind on the part of both Christians and non-Christians alike. These intellectual dispositions are the principal concerns of this chapter. The third part of this book will address more concrete implications in areas like poverty in American cities and the challenges of globalization. Before turning to these more practical matters, however, we need to take some further theoretical bearings that will make it possible to address them creatively.

DELIBERATION, RECIPROCITY, CIVILITY

Intellectual solidarity is one of the key factors for the revitalization of the common good in our religiously and culturally diverse world. "Intellectual solidarity" will be used here to describe an orientation of mind that regards differences among traditions as stimuli to intellectual engagement across religious and cultural boundaries. It is an orientation that leads one to view differences positively rather than with a mindset marked by suspicion or fear. It starts from a posture that welcomes foreign or strange understandings of the good life into one's mental world in a spirit of hospitality, rather than standing on guard against them.[1] This receptive orientation expects to be able to learn something valuable by listening to people who hold understandings of the good life different from one's own. It also expects to be able to teach something valuable to those who are different by speaking to them respectfully about one's own understanding of the human good. Intellectual solidarity arises in this give-and-take of mutual learning among people who see the world differently. It is a disposition based on the hope that we can actually get somewhere if we decide to listen to what others think a good life looks like and in turn to tell them why we see the good life the way we do. Differences of vision are not so total that we are destined to remain eternally strangers to one another. Even the beginnings of dialogue create connections that make erstwhile strangers no longer alien to one another.

[1] See Thomas Ogletree, *Hospitality to the Stranger: Dimensions of Moral Understanding* (Philadelphia, PA: Fortress Press, 1985), p. 119.

The need for such mutual learning and teaching is evident in all domains of human life. Ideally such give-and-take occurs in all forms of human thought, from the acquisition of elementary skills to the highest levels of scientific understanding, literary imagination, and philosophical wisdom. Whether the task is tying one's shoes, playing soccer, writing a computer program, performing a piano concerto, or discovering whether human life is finally meaningful or absurd, human beings learn how to approach these matters in interaction with each other. One can become a better soccer-player, pianist, or philosopher only by observing others as they do these things, listening to them explain why they act or think the way they do, and speaking to them about what one has already learned about such matters oneself. Disengagement from this give-and-take will diminish one's capacity to do these things well. Total lack of interaction with others will destroy one's capacity to do anything at all. This is true not only in the acquisition of skills but also in intellectually demanding activities such as the arts and philosophy. In these endeavors, those who see some facet of the human good differently are potential sources for the enrichment of one's existing understanding. To withdraw from interaction with them or to adopt a thoroughgoing defensiveness toward them can be psychologically destructive. There can, of course, sometimes be good reasons for such withdrawal, and self-defense can regrettably be a necessity in some circumstances. But when these occasions arise something has already been lost. The fact of this loss shows that a predominantly on-guard posture toward those who are different will diminish one's overall intellectual and social possibilities.

Chapter 2 has pointed to some of the historical reasons why intellectual engagement with those holding different religious understandings of the good life has been replaced in the West by suspicion and wariness toward them. The experience of what people can do to each other in the name of their understandings of the good life, especially religious understandings, is deeply etched in Western historical memory. There are plenty of contemporary experiences in the world today to keep this memory alive. These experiences have formed a cultural presupposition that the way to protect freedom is through strategies and institutions that encourage people to leave each other alone. Such strategies aim at peaceful coexistence among people living in parallel worlds, safely insulated from each other by tolerance but with preexisting differences in place. Peace is attained by what John Rawls once called "the method of avoidance." This method recommends that in the political life of a pluralistic society "we try, so far as we can, neither to assert nor to deny any religious, philosophical or moral views, or their associated philosophical accounts of truth and the status of values."[2] By avoiding these issues in public life, this method provides space for people to go their own ways. It does this by asking everybody to keep many of their convictions about the good life to themselves.

Avoiding disputed values may keep the peace for a while, and it may protect a solitary form of freedom for a time. But when living in non-intersecting parallel worlds is not a realistic possibility, it is not enough. Today, for example, the thickening technological and economic interconnections among people mean that people's different ideas of the good life inevitably intersect with the ideas held by others. The outcomes of these intersections shape social policies and in many ways determine who gets what. Cultural and religious differences among whole civilizations are similarly being driven into new forms of interaction on the global stage. The earth today is no longer occupied by people living in largely self-contained, parallel civilizations whose occasional interactions can be lubricated by tolerance. Determining what this global world will look like and who will benefit from its new possibilities calls for a lot more than the "method of avoidance" can deliver.

In this new context, some moral and political philosophers have begun to propose that we need more than detached tolerance to live good lives. These thinkers are suggesting that a less defensive, more positive engagement with others can lead to a better life for all under present circumstances. They hint, in ways that are not fully developed, that pursuing intellectual engagement across the boundaries of religious, philosophical, and cultural traditions can open up possibilities that are especially important in the increasingly interdependent world of today. It can lead to a fuller freedom than individuals can attain when detached coexistence

---

[2] Rawls, "The Idea of an Overlapping Consensus," 12–13.

sets the overall agenda in public life. This view is presented, for example, by Amy Gutmann and Dennis Thompson. Gutmann and Thompson are deeply opposed to any imposition of a vision of the common good by coercive means. Yet they have written that "mere toleration . . . locks into place the moral divisions in society and makes collective moral progress far more difficult."[3] By making progress in understanding unlikely, disengaged tolerance is unlikely to produce the peaceful, harmonious coexistence it promises.

When society is becoming more densely and extensively interconnected, greater moral understanding of one another becomes essential if we are to avoid falling into deeper conflicts than we have experienced in the past. Without new forms of intellectual engagement on the meaning of the common good, the outcome of new forms of technological and economic interaction will likely be new conflict occasioned by rising frustration with the apparent inability to address actual social conditions. We need a form of cooperation that goes beyond coexistence in parallel worlds to conjoint action to which we all contribute. Such cooperation calls for intellectual communication among people from different traditions, civilizations, and religions holding different understandings of the good life. It calls for efforts at mutual understanding that move across the boundaries that tolerance leaves in place. This shows the special salience of the idea of intellectual solidarity today.

The hints in recent theoretical literature that point toward the need for this kind of solidarity appear most explicitly in discussions of democracy as a deliberative process. In the face of disagreements about the good life, the deliberative model of democracy proposes a third alternative to either coercion or disengaged coexistence. Gutmann and Thompson state the main idea of deliberative democracy simply: "when citizens or their representatives disagree morally, they should continue to reason together to reach mutually acceptable decisions."[4] Deliberative democracy thus begins from the *de facto* situation in which citizens hold different moral convictions about many public issues, stemming from their differing religious and philosophical visions of the good life. But deliberative

---

[3] Amy Gutmann and Dennis Thompson, *Democracy and Disagreement* (Cambridge, MA: Harvard University Press, 1996), pp. 62–63.

[4] *Ibid.*, p. 1.

democracy is premised on the hope that coexistence in parallel worlds is not the only alternative to efforts to abolish differences coercively. Engagement with others by listening, speaking, and thinking with them about the quality of the lives we must in fact live together can lead to enhanced prospects for both freedom and peace.

Such deliberating together can take several forms. It can occur in a conversational, exploratory mode, where the interlocutors seek deeper understanding of each other's vision of the good life or of some specific political dimension of this vision. Or it can be in the mode of argument, where the reasons are presented for why one position should be judged more adequate than alternative views.[5] Both conversation and argument are involved in genuine deliberation; both call for respectful engagement with persons holding conceptions of the good life different from one's own. Both suggest that disagreement, whether about specific public policies or about the larger meaning of how we live, does not mean we are so fated to mutual incomprehension that the best we can do is go our separate ways. Real deliberation is based on the hope that greater mutual understanding and perhaps some new areas of agreement can emerge when human beings listen to each other attentively and speak to each other respectfully.

Keeping such a hope alive is a necessity if the option of living in parallel worlds is less and less a real option. It has always been true that human beings cannot thrive or even survive without social cooperation. But this truth is especially relevant today as we face issues like the insufficiency of racial tolerance to overcome barriers dividing city and suburb in the United States and the challenges of new forms of financial, environmental, and technological interconnection on the global scene. The need to cooperate has not been annulled today simply because we are increasingly aware of our differing religious, philosophical, and moral convictions. Indeed, when such differences are especially evident, so is the need to find more intentional ways to cooperate.

Recent proposals that view democracy deliberatively are based on the hope that our disagreements are not so total that we cannot

---

[5] For a useful discussion of the relations and differences between conversation and argument, see David Tracy, *Plurality and Ambiguity: Hermeneutics, Religion, Hope* (San Francisco: Harper and Row, 1987), chap. 1.

learn from each other through conversation and argument about how to live well together. They presume that the public forum in a democratic society is not simply an arena where people come to assert their interests or to affirm conclusions they have reached before political debate begins. If the commitments one brings to political debate are taken as entirely settled, politics will not be a process of deliberation at all. It will be a process of negotiation or bargaining for the best deal that can be obtained under the prevailing configuration of power. When politics is a form of bargaining rather than deliberation, people bring their commitments to the public forum for implementation, not for transformation or evaluation. Understandings of the good life are taken as simply given, as having been definitively formed in a pre- or extra-political domain such as that of private religion or economic interest.[6]

When politics is a form of bargaining, a political statement characteristically takes the form "I want x." This statement might express an entirely self-oriented desire, such as wanting lower taxes for myself and my income bracket, independent of what such a tax law will do to the lives of the poor in American cities. Or it might express a desire that includes the good of others, such as wanting a health care system that provides insurance for all.[7] Many non-egotistic loyalties to the good of sub-groups are vigorously present in both national and international society already. Revitalizing pursuit of the common good in a diverse democracy is not simply a matter of overcoming crude egotism. Rather the issue is whether the commitments people bring to the public forum are simply demands, or whether they will be subject to deliberation through engagement with others in the political process. If they are the latter, they will not take the form "I want x," but will be addressed to fellow citizens in the form "x would be good for the community to which we belong."[8] They will be advanced as proposals about how we might see the good similarly.

[6] See Robin Lovin, "Perry, Naturalism, and Religion in Public," *Tulane Law Review* 63 (1989), 1521.
[7] As Rawls has observed, "Every interest is the interest of a self (agent), but not every interest is in benefits to the self that has it." *Political Liberalism*, p. 51.
[8] See Benjamin Barber, *Strong Democracy: Participatory Politics for a New Age* (Berkeley: University of California Press, 1984), p. 171.

To make a political proposal in this way is to call for discussion and argument. The need for deliberation is presupposed by the fact that such a proposal is made as an appeal to others to see the world the way I have come to see it. It is an invitation to discussion, not simply a declaration of what I want. To be sure, such a proposal can be made in an argumentative mode rather than in the more open-ended mode of conversation. The proposal may vigorously present reasons why we should jointly see the intertwining of our lives in a way that leads to changing the tax base or zoning laws to overcome the isolation of inner cities from the suburbs. They may propose changing national energy policies in ways that promise to protect the biophysical environment we share. Such arguments, however, have a very different form from bald assertions of what I want and seek to secure with the aid of power-alliances with those who think like I do. Arguments are different from simple announcements of what I already think. My thinking may in fact be right, but those who do not already think the same way are unlikely to be much affected by such an announcement. Nor are arguments simply strategies to recruit allies. Rather, argument presupposes that I have sufficient respect for the equality and reasonableness of other people that I am willing to give them evidence and warrants for my conclusions. It is based on the hope that, if I am right, my conclusions will also make sense to my fellow citizens.[9] A political argument, in other words, is a proposal about some aspect of how citizens should live together that is introduced in the public forum for consideration and deliberation. It is also a proposal about how citizens should act together through the social institutions and policies that form their common life. It advocates some aspect of a vision of the common good, along with the reasons why others should see that it will lead to a better life for all who must live together.

It is obvious, of course, that we have to be prepared for situations where deliberation leaves us far short of unanimity on all the public decisions that must be made in a democracy. Deliberative democracy is not governance by unanimous consensus. Democratic self-government, however, depends on citizens having certain personal virtues that make them willing to participate in a deliberative form

---

[9] See Tracy, *Plurality and Ambiguity*, pp. 25–26.

of politics rather than approaching the public sphere with an "I'll get what I want" attitude. Chief among these is the virtue of civility. Democratic self-government also depends on having in place an institutional framework that protects the possibility of genuine deliberation when public policy issues are being decided, and that leaves open the possibility of further deliberation on another day even when public decisions have been made. These institutions are those of a constitutional government that protects such basic human rights as freedom of speech, religion, and association. Without the protection of these freedoms citizens will be unable to participate in public deliberation when decisions are being made or to question policies that have already been determined. We will return to the question of this constitutional framework later in this chapter. But first we need to consider the personal virtue of civility among fellow citizens.

The term "civility" has a rather thin ring to the religiously attuned ear. It suggests a minimalist adherence to the niceties of social convention. Civility in the classic sense of the term, however, goes considerably deeper than *politesse* from a distance. Civility manifests citizens' commitment to cooperate with each other in a spirit marked by genuine reciprocity and mutual respect. It is a personal virtue that leads citizens to seek to live together cooperatively. This kind of virtue is grounded in the belief that all fellow citizens are free and equal. All are entitled to participate in determining what the cooperative arrangements of social life will be, especially the most important institutions of government and the rights and duties they respect. Reciprocity among citizens, therefore, means that when one makes a proposal about important matters of common social life, one respects the freedom and equality of all those the proposal will affect. Thus the person making the proposal should be able to argue that it would be at least reasonable for others to accept it. For if one advocates important political institutions or policies that one knows cannot be reasonably affirmed by one's fellow citizens, politics will become a form of manipulation or a pursuit of domination. Reciprocal respect for others' worth as persons rules this out. Similarly, reciprocity means that advocacy of important political institutions or policies includes a commitment to act in accord with them if they are accepted by others, even at the cost of one's own more immediate interests in particular circumstances.[10] The reciprocity and mutual respect of genuine political deliberation thus has important consequences for the way citizens enter the political process, for the kind of policy proposals they support or advocate, and for the overall institutional framework that governs the activities of political life.

The reciprocity that is a characteristic of civility is, therefore, quite different from coexistence in parallel worlds. Rawls has gone so far as to say that the political relationships that express it can be called forms of "civic friendship."[11] It is not the detached stance of people who have posted "do not disturb" signs on their doors and are prepared to respect such signs when they have been posted by others. Civility indeed respects the freedom and equality that advocates of tolerance are so concerned to protect. But it begins from the recognition that freedom and equality can only be achieved through mutual cooperation, interaction, and interdependence. Civility is a virtue that grows out of the bonds of connection among citizens and in turn strengthens these bonds. As a form of civic friendship, it recognizes both that citizens need each other to live good lives and that their contributions to the good of others are needed if a society that is good for all is to be created and sustained. The virtue of civility has consequences for the way a pluralistic society pursues the common good. Engaged political deliberation is a form of reciprocal, intellectual give-and-take with fellow citizens about the meaning of the common good in its many aspects. Such deliberation in the public sphere is the intellectual expression of mutual respect for the dignity of one's fellows in a community of freedom. It is the political face of intellectual solidarity – the virtue that creates a community of freedom in the midst of diversity and that leads to a deeper understanding of how to live well together.

CHRISTIAN DISTINCTIVENESS AND COMMON MORALITY

The question, then, is whether Christians can have a practical commitment to this kind of listening and speaking in the pursuit of

---

[10] This understanding of civility is significantly influenced by Rawls, "The Idea of Public Reason Revisited," *University of Chicago Law Review* 64 (1997), esp. 770. This essay has been reprinted in Rawls, *The Law of Peoples*.
[11] Rawls, "The Idea of Public Reason Revisited," 771.

a shared understanding of the common good. Is intellectual solidarity with non-Christians compatible with Christian beliefs about God, the human condition, and the vision of the human good grounded in these beliefs? This problem has confronted Christianity since the apostolic church first encountered the thought-worlds of Greece and Rome. It was a central challenge in the thirteenth century as medieval theology grappled with Aristotelian and Arab-Muslim thought. It arose, and was generally not well handled, when Christian thinkers first encountered the great intellectual traditions of India and China in the sixteenth and seventeenth centuries. Today it has been brought vigorously to the fore once again by new awareness of the multiplicity of cultures and ways of life in our shrinking world. The new global context demands that the public role of faith be considered in light of deepening awareness of religious and cultural diversity. Here this question will be considered in light of the ways it arises for the Roman Catholic church because of the importance of the idea of the common good in the Catholic tradition. But what is said here clearly has relevance for other branches of the Christian community as well.

A principal objection by some Christians to seeking intellectual solidarity with those outside the church is that this will inevitably lead to a subordination of the Christian ethic to the ethos of liberal democracy. By allowing its public discourse to be disciplined by what others regard as reasonable, the Christian community will end up abandoning any substantial reference to Christ and to the distinctive Christian form of life.[12] On the other hand, some "postmodern" thinkers regard intellectual solidarity as impossible. Diversity among traditions runs so deep that different ways of life and thought are simply incommensurable. Thus pursuit of reasonable discourse across traditions is like chasing a mirage. There is no standard of reasonableness that can bridge from one tradition

---

[12] For arguments along these lines, see Michael J. Baxter, "Review Essay: The Non-Catholic Character of the 'Public Church,'" *Modern Theology* 11, no. 2 (April, 1995), 255–258; Stanley Hauerwas, "The Church and Liberal Democracy: The Moral Limits of a Secular Polity," in *A Community of Character: Toward a Constructive Christian Social Ethic* (Notre Dame, IN: University of Notre Dame Press, 1981), pp. 72–86; George Lindbeck, *The Nature of Doctrine: Religion and Theology in a Postliberal Age* (Philadelphia, PA: Westminster Press, 1984); John Howard Yoder, *For the Nations: Essays Public and Evangelical* (Grand Rapids, MI: Eerdmanns, 1997). The prevalence of this perspective across Christian denominational lines is indicated by the fact that Baxter is a Roman Catholic, Hauerwas a Methodist, Lindbeck a Lutheran, and Yoder a Mennonite.

to another. What counts as rational is determined by the cultural practices of relatively local or ethnocentric groups.[13] Anything containing hints of universality must be rejected as an Enlightenment illusion at best or as an ideological screen for imperial aspiration at worst.

Problems such as these were very much on the minds of the Catholic bishops of the world when they assembled at the Second Vatican Council from 1961 to 1964, though the bishops formulated them somewhat differently. One of the defining objectives of the Council was to engage the diverse religious and cultural traditions of the world from a Christian perspective. The need to take global diversity with great seriousness was unavoidable given the backgrounds brought to the Council by the bishops themselves. The Council was an assembly of bishops drawn from almost all of the cultures around the world and from societies where all of the great world religions play significant roles. As theologian Karl Rahner has observed, Vatican II was a unique event in the history of the Catholic community in that it was "in a rudimentary form still groping for identity, the Church's first official self-actualization as a world Church" rather than as a European religion to be exported to the rest of the world along with European culture.[14] This historical and sociological context had considerable influence on the way the Council approached the effort to sustain and deepen the church's fidelity to the gospel while it also sought to renew and strengthen the church's contribution to the common good of the world community.

The Council clearly rejected the idea that Christian identity could be renewed by strategies that reaffirm Christian identity through church domination or control of extra-ecclesial communities. The Conciliar documents on intra-Christian ecumenism, on the relation of the church to non-Christian religions, and on religious liberty all indicate this clearly.[15] The Council also rejected

[13] See Richard Rorty, "Postmodernist Bourgeois Liberalism," in Robert Hollinger, ed., *Hermeneutics and Praxis* (Notre Dame, IN: University of Notre Dame Press, 1985), p. 218.
[14] Karl Rahner made the bold proposal that the global situation of Vatican II marks a new epoch in Christian history in "Toward a Fundamental Theological Interpretation of Vatican II," *Theological Studies* 40 (December, 1979), 716–27. The citation here is from p. 717.
[15] See Vatican Council II, *Unitatis Redintegratio* (Decree on Ecumenism), *Nostra Aetate* (Declaration on the Relationship of the Church to Non-Christian Religions), and *Dignitatis*

any strategy that would cause the church to turn in on itself as an enclave concerned solely with the good of its own members. The *Pastoral Constitution on the Church in the Modern World* presents a third alternative to both the strategy of control and the enclave approach. It sees the possibility of solidarity across religious boundaries as an implication of Christian faith itself and also of the co-humanity of Christians and non-Christians. This vision is stated programmatically in the Constitution's opening words:

> The joys and hopes, the grief and anguish of the people of our time, especially of those who are poor or afflicted, are the joys and hopes, the grief and anguish of the followers of Christ as well. Nothing that is genuinely human fails to find an echo in their hearts. For theirs is a community of people united in Christ and guided by the holy Spirit in their pilgrimage towards the Father's kingdom, bearers of a message of salvation for all of humanity. That is why they cherish a feeling of deep solidarity with the human race and its history.[16]

This theme of solidarity is a leitmotif throughout the entire *Pastoral Constitution*.

The possibility of such solidarity despite significant differences in religious and cultural traditions is a deep presupposition of the Catholic understanding of the Christian tradition itself. St. Paul in the letter to the Romans, Thomas Aquinas, and the major social encyclicals of the modern popes, for example, all maintain that Christian believers and unbelievers alike can know the most basic requirements of the human good. Christian morality is not a morality for Christians only. The desire to find common moral ground between Christians and non-Christians is theologically warranted by the belief that one God has created the whole of humanity and that all human beings share a common origin and destiny. Since reason is one of the Creator's greatest gifts to human beings, the use of reason to discover the human good and the consequent norms of social morality is fully compatible with Christian biblical faith. Indeed, this theological framework implies that the demands of social morality must be reasonable; as expectations about how human

---

Humanae (Declaration on Religious Freedom), all in *Vatican Council II: Constitutions, Decrees, Declarations*, ed. A. Flannery.

[16] Vatican Council II, *Gaudium et Spes* (Pastoral Constitution on the Church in the Modern World), no. 1, in *Vatican Council II: Constitutions, Decrees, Declarations*, ed. A. Flannery, p. 163.

beings should live together they must "make sense" in light of critically appropriated experience.[17]

There are analogues to this traditionally Catholic approach in Lutheran and Calvinist understandings of the "orders of creation" and the "common grace" discernible in the structures of the created world, even though the followers of Luther and Calvin are less confident in our ability to discern these without the aid of revelation than are Catholics. But even for Luther and Calvin, a theologically warranted affirmation that critical reflection on human experience is the basis of social morality gives Christians a solid basis to hope that they can find common ground with non-Christians in determining how they should live together in society and the polity. Christians can enter into reasonable deliberation with non-Christians about the common moral issues all humans must face. Thus according to these classic theologies, Christians can enter into intellectual solidarity with non-Christians in pursuit of the social and political good, even though they have divergent beliefs about ultimate questions of human destiny and salvation.

Nevertheless, it would be naive to think that these classic theological arguments can be simply repeated in the face of contemporary challenges. In fact, the Second Vatican Council was aware that differences in social location and cultural tradition have important influence on what people see as reasonable interpretations of the good, and thus as the reasonable demands of social morality. On such normative matters, though "there is growing exchange of ideas, there is still disagreement in competing ideologies about the meaning of the words which express our key concepts."[18] Thus one

---

[17] On the inclination of and need for human beings to live together in society as a distinctive manifestation of their rational nature, see Thomas Aquinas, *Summa Theologiae* I, II, q. 94, art. 2. Natural law is of course a highly controverted matter in both moral philosophy and moral theology, and it is not my intent to deal with these controversies here. Let me simply state that I presuppose that "natural" means "reasonable" in light of careful reflection on the full range of human experience. Thus what is affirmed as natural must "make sense" in light of critically appropriated experience. Margaret A. Farley has argued that a natural law approach to the human good means that things should generally "make sense." See Farley, "Moral Discourse in the Public Arena," in William W. May, ed., *Vatican Authority and American Catholic Dissent* (New York: Crossroad, 1987), pp. 168–186, at 174–175; "Response to James Hanigan and Charles Curran," in Saul M. Olyan and Martha C. Nussbaum, eds., *Sexual Orientation and Human Rights in American Religious Discourse* (New York: Oxford University Press, 1998), pp. 101–109, at 105–106.

[18] Vatican Council II, *Gaudium et Spes*, no. 4.

can discern in some of the texts of Vatican II an incipient emergence of what has since come to be called the postmodern suspicion of universalism. This postmodern critique has been aimed at the eighteenth-century Enlightenment's belief that reason is independent of social context and of the inherited presuppositions of cultural traditions.[19] In line with such suspicions of Enlightenment rationalism, the Council called for the renewal of the Christian vision of the human good in light of biblical faith and Christian theological conviction.[20] Reason alone was treated as an insufficient basis for an ethic that is faithful to the gospel.

Thus it is clear that the Council wanted to have it both ways on the issue of universal solidarity versus the particularism of traditions. The Council affirmed the deep roots of its vision of the good life in the gospel of Christ; it also upheld the possibility of bringing Christian convictions about the common good into fruitful engagement with alternative conceptions. This double agenda is evident in the entire first part of the Council's *Pastoral Constitution on the Church in the Modern World*. This document's treatment of three fundamental topics – the dignity of the human person, the importance of the vocation to community in solidarity, and the religious significance of this-worldly activity – is supported by distinctively Christian theological warrants as well as by claims regarded as intelligible to non-Christians on the basis of critical reflection on their experience.

For example, the Council affirmed that the dignity of the human person is discernible in the transcendent power of the human mind, in the dignity of conscience, and in the excellence of liberty. This dignity can be recognized by all human beings and makes claims upon all, both Christian and non-Christian. Nevertheless, human dignity is known in its full depth from Christian revelation.

[19] It is clear that Catholicism has not accepted the presuppositions of Enlightenment rationalism. But some eighteenth- and nineteenth-century Catholic thinkers, including moral theologians and social ethicists, were subtly affected by this rationalism in their apologetic efforts to defend Catholic thought in the face of the challenges raised to it by Western European modernity. They adopted the methods of their rationalist adversaries to counteract the substance of rationalist arguments. For discussion of the effect of such apologetic efforts on theological responses to modern atheism, see Michael J. Buckley, *At the Origins of Modern Atheism* (New Haven, CT: Yale University Press, 1987).

[20] See especially Vatican Council II, *Optatam Totius* (Decree on the Training of Priests), no. 16, in *Vatican Council II: Constitutions, Decrees, Declarations*, ed. A. Flannery.

From the biblical account of the creation of human beings in the image and likeness of God, Christians affirm that human beings are marked with a sacredness that is properly religious. Further, human beings have a sacredness that rests on the redemption and re-creation brought about by Christ: "The truth is that only in the mystery of the incarnate Word does the mystery of the human person take on light . . . the revelation of the mystery of the Father and His love, fully reveals human beings to themselves and makes their supreme calling clear."[21] Such a theological claim challenges the rationalist idea that Christian ethical reflection can rely exclusively on philosophical reason. It shows that the church's vision of the common good is a religious one that flows from the heart of Christian faith. This common good, however, can only be adequately identified and understood through a "living exchange" between the Christian community and the diverse cultures of the world.[22] Thus the Council is seeking to bring a distinctively Christian understanding of the human good into active engagement with the many cultures of a world increasingly conscious of itself as divided and pluralistic.

DIALOGIC UNIVERSALISM

Thus the Second Vatican Council reaffirmed the pursuit of the common good in a divided world while it simultaneously urged renewal of a distinctively Christian vision of the human good. This approach can be called dialogic universalism.[23] It is universalist, for it presumes that human beings are sufficiently alike in that they all share certain very general characteristics in common and that the same general outlines of well-being are shared in common as well. For example, the good of all human beings requires that basic bodily needs be met, that intelligence be developed and educated, that freedom of conscience be respected, and that participation in social and political life be a real possibility.[24] At the same time

---

[21] *Gaudium et Spes*, no. 22.   [22] *Ibid.*, no. 44.

[23] I originally used this phrase in my *Claims in Conflict: Retrieving and Renewing the Catholic Human Rights Tradition* (New York: Paulist Press, 1979), chap. 3, p. 131. What is said here is a development of that earlier discussion.

[24] See *Gaudium et Spes*, nos. 14–17, 25. There is a significant resemblance between what the Council says unsystematically about common human characteristics and what Martha

the pursuit of the common good is dialogic. Cultural differences are so significant that a shared vision of the common good can only be attained in a historically incremental way through deep encounter and intellectual exchange across traditions. It is also dialogic because it sees engagement with others across the boundaries of traditions as itself part of the human good.

In other words, it is possible to read Vatican II as affirming that Christian intellectual solidarity with non-Christians is both a demand of human reasonableness and an implication of the distinctively Christian understanding of the human good. For when the Council stressed the particularity of its theological understanding of the human good, it continued to affirm the possibility of identifying universal human goods across cultural and religious boundaries. These universal goods, however, were not presumed to be identical with the values already held dear in Western European civilization or in the moral tradition of the church itself. Knowledge of what these universal goods are will be the outcome of inquiry and dialogue. The church's contribution to this dialogue must draw deeply from two thousand years of Christian tradition to be sure. Christianity has much to teach our diverse world about the terrestrial good of society and the polity. But dialogue calls for listening as well as speaking. This expectation that one can learn from listening means that one cannot presuppose that a vision of the common good adequate to new historical circumstances is already fully present in the church's tradition. Still less can the traditional Christian or Western understandings of the common good simply be proposed to or imposed upon others. An authentically human and authentically Christian conception of the common good calls for openness to new insight within the church as well as outside it.

Openness to such development is a consequence of taking other persons from other traditions seriously enough to lead one to think one can learn from them. In other words, it calls for intellectual

Nussbaum develops more systematically in a number of her writings, including "Human Capabilities, Female Human Beings," in Martha C. Nussbaum and Jonathan Glover, eds., *Women, Culture, and Development: A Study of Human Capabilities* (Oxford/New York: Clarendon/Oxford University Press, 1995), pp. 61–104. The resemblance stems from the influence of Aristotle on Nussbaum and of Aristotle through the mediation of Thomas Aquinas on the Council.

solidarity with them. The Council saw this as a requirement of both reasonableness and of Christian faith itself. As *Gaudium et Spes* put it, "All we have said up to now about the dignity of the person . . . provides a basis for discussing the relationship between the church and the world and the dialogue between them."[25] Such dialogue with other traditions and modes of thought has marked much of the Christian tradition throughout its historical development in the past. The most creative moments of dialogue in the past have made the Christian intellectual tradition what it is today; carrying on this tradition creatively calls for similar intellectual solidarity with others today. As the Council put it, the church

> has profited from the history and development of humankind. It profits from the experience of past ages, from the progress of the sciences, and from the riches hidden in various cultures, through which greater light is thrown on human nature and new avenues to truth are opened up. The church learned early in its history to express the Christian message in the concepts and languages of different peoples and tried to clarify it in the light of the wisdom of their philosophers.[26]

This stance of dialogue with cultures and the sciences was broadened by other documents of the Council to include inter-Christian ecumenical dialogue and dialogue with the other great world religions.

This commitment to dialogue is simultaneously an expression of fidelity to the gospel and of respect for the other. Christian faith entails care and respect for all persons, and respect for their dignity means listening to their interpretations of the human good. They are God's creatures for whom Christ died and rose, not aliens. Further, Christian love calls for the building up of the bonds of solidarity among all persons, and such solidarity requires efforts to understand those who are different, to learn from them, and to contribute to their understanding of the good life as well. Intellectual solidarity with them forges a bond that goes beyond tolerance understood as leaving others alone to the positive engagement with others that true dialogue demands. For Christians, such dialogue, therefore, embodies a dynamic interaction between the biblical faith handed on to them through the centuries of Christian tradition and the intelligence that is a preeminent manifestation of the *imago Dei* in all human beings.

There are illuminating analogies between the practice of intellectual solidarity in the religious sphere and in other areas of intellectual life. Following postmodern critiques of the Western Enlightenment, it has become apparent that all reasoning is embedded in history. All rational inquiry is shaped by the traditions that have formed the inquirer's presuppositions and within which the inquirer has been educated. Neither the questions addressed nor the modes of thought available to address these questions are the products of a timeless pure reason. New questions arise from the anomalies that have become apparent within an ongoing tradition of inquiry. Responses to these questions are in part dependent on the resources provided by received traditions. This dependence of rational inquiry upon tradition is evident not only in ethics and theology but in other domains of knowledge as well.

For example, in physics the questions addressed by Newton in the late seventeenth and early eighteenth centuries were not the same as those that confronted the Greeks in classical times. Newton's efforts would have been impossible had he not learned from the Greeks. What he learned from the Greeks, however, led to questions that neither Aristotle nor Ptolemy ever raised. Newton's breakthrough responses to these new questions generated both new methods of physical analysis and new conclusions about physical reality. He drew on the past traditions of physics in the very act of revolutionizing physics. Similarly in the twentieth century, the inadequacies that had subsequently emerged within a Newtonian account of the world gave rise to further new questions. These questions led Einstein to recast the framework of the Newtonian world. Thus the demands of reasonableness in physics led to different methods of analysis and conclusions about the structure of the universe in the differing historical periods of Ptolemy, Newton, and Einstein. This process of beginning from the received insights of a tradition and addressing unsolved problems in light of new data can lead to the gradual and continuous development of knowledge. But at certain key moments, like those faced by Newton and Einstein, it can also bring about revolutionary change in taken-for-granted modes of thought.[27] This is true in religion and ethics just as it is in the sciences.

But this historical change in the questions and methods of thought in differing periods in the history of physics does not mean that Ptolemy's, Newton's, and Einstein's theories are equally true and therefore equally false. Consciousness of the historical contextualization of these questions and methods does not imply historical relativism. Einstein was compelled to raise new questions because of perceived inadequacies in the physics he had learned. Once these questions have been seen as necessary ones, Einstein's conclusions can be judged more adequate than Newton's and to lead to a truer picture of the physical world. A thoroughgoing relativism in physics is not a consequence of our awareness that physics has a history. Indeed, such a relativism would bring physical inquiry itself to a halt, for if all conclusions are judged of equal truth-value there is no purpose in pursuing any inquiry at all.

This insight borrowed from the sciences can illuminate the deeper structure of the Second Vatican Council's stress on respect for the other and on dialogue across the boundaries of diverse communities as essential expressions of Christian fidelity to the gospel. It provides insight into how the Christian community can combine fidelity to the particularistic vision of the human good rooted in the gospel with a commitment to discerning the common morality needed in a pluralistic but interdependent world. The starting point of the Council's effort to contribute to the pursuit of a common morality is the gospel and the received Christian interpretation of the social and political implications of the gospel. But the new situation faced by the Council led it to propose that tradition-based convictions must be brought into active encounter with new social and cultural data. These new data include the visions of the human good held by non-Christian religious communities with non-Western histories, as well as those understandings of the good life held by secular thinkers within the West itself. The Christian

---

[27] This is a thumbnail sketch of Thomas Kuhn's well-known and much debated account of scientific revolutions. This sketch is an oversimplification, but I hope it is adequate to show that the point being made here about the development of Christian thinking about the common good through its encounter with new problems is not unique to religious and moral thought. See Kuhn, *The Structure of Scientific Revolutions.*

community has faced such new data in the past, in the encounter with Aristotelian thought in the thirteenth century and Indian and Chinese cultures in the early modern period, for example. In the former case, the serious dialogue of intellectual solidarity led to a revolution in the Christian intellectual tradition that enabled the church to remain faithful to the gospel in a very new context. In the case of the encounter with the culture of China, the early Jesuit efforts to achieve intellectual solidarity across cultural and religious borders was resisted by church leaders who saw it as a betrayal of the gospel itself. The result was an institutional failure both to bring Christianity to China and to enrich the Christian tradition with ideas that Chinese thought could have provided. If the interpretation presented here is correct, the engagement with Aristotle rather than the resistance to Confucius is the model the Council recommended as the way Christians should pursue the common good in the interdependent, pluralistic world of today.[28]

Intellectual solidarity and the method of dialogue, therefore, do not imply relativism. In fact, the commitment to dialogue and mutual inquiry suggests just the opposite – that there is a truth about the human good that must be pursued and that makes a claim on the minds and hearts of all persons.[29] Christians will contribute to the common good of society and the *polis* by starting from what they know about this terrestrial good from the gospel and from their tradition. They will speak about this good openly in social deliberation about how people should live together in the interconnected polities of today on an increasingly interdependent planet earth. Intellectual solidarity demands such forthright speech. But it demands open-minded listening as well. Such dialogue can generate incremental developments in the Christian tradition's understanding

---

[28] For a most perceptive discussion of the depth of the Council's innovations and how they centered on a new "dialogic" approach to events and communities outside the church itself, see John W. O'Malley, "Reform, Historical Consciousness, and Vatican II's Aggiornamento," *Theological Studies* 32 (1971), 573–601, and O'Malley, "Developments, Reforms, and Two Great Reformations: Towards a Historical Assessment of Vatican II," *Theological Studies* 44 (1983), 373–406.

[29] See Alasdair MacIntyre, *Whose Justice? Which Rationality* (Notre Dame, IN: University of Notre Dame Press, 1988), chap. 18. See also MacIntyre, *Three Rival Versions of Moral Enquiry: Encyclopaedia, Genealogy and Tradition* (Notre Dame, IN: University of Notre Dame Press, 1990), chap. 10, which relates this treatment of how traditions develop to the task of the university.

of the good life and incremental changes in other traditions as well. It may on occasion lead to revolutionary changes in the vision of the common good for one or all of these traditions. Such a revolutionary shift is almost certainly called for by the new reality of global interdependence today. When reasonable deliberation and discourse lead to such developments in the Christian vision of the good, this will be a manifestation of fidelity to deep Christian theological convictions, not a betrayal of such convictions.

In other words, the challenge of today's pluralistic and interdependent world leads to a developmental way of conceiving of the relationship between faith and reason. Faith and reason are related to each other in a historically unfolding process, in which Christian belief shapes the way the human good is interpreted while the pursuit of an inclusive community influences the interpretation of Christian belief. This interaction calls Christians both to remain faithful to the distinctiveness of the gospel and simultaneously to recognize that their faith in God calls for the use of human intelligence to discover the common bonds that make an inclusive human community possible. To declare that such intellectual solidarity is unattainable would be to maintain that the idea of the common good is a utopian fantasy as well. Such an outcome would be both a betrayal of the Christian tradition and treason to the possibilities human intelligence can discover. Both Christian faith and the reasonable hopes of humanity lead us to expect more.

Intellectual solidarity – the active engagement of listening and speaking with others whose beliefs and traditions are different – is the key to such dynamism. Dialogue, therefore, is both a means and an end, both an instrumental procedure and a substantive good. Where such dialogue is absent, the chances of obtaining a vision of the common good of the world we have entered at the beginning of the twenty-first century will be small to the point of vanishing. The Second Vatican Council launched the Roman Catholic community on this path of dialogue and many other Christian subtraditions have also embarked on it. The challenges of life together on a shrinking planet suggest it is not too much to ask it of non-Christian religious communities and of non-believers as well. This intellectual solidarity is itself an important dimension of the common good in a diverse world. It is a procedural way of conducting public affairs that will lead to better understandings of how we should live together. It also embodies the mutual respect that makes shared freedom a substantive reality. Commitment to this agenda of dialogic universalism thus makes demands of all religions, all cultures. To the extent such a commitment is present, the common good will be on the way to being realized.

HUMAN RIGHTS: INSTITUTIONALIZING SOLIDARITY

Intellectual solidarity as a dimension of the common good also has important implications for the institutions that shape public life. In particular, it suggests that institutions that secure and protect human rights for all are essential to the common good of a community of freedom. In light of the argument we have been developing, human rights should be understood as guarantees of the most basic requirements of solidarity. Human rights are the moral claims of all persons to be treated, by virtue of their humanity, as participants in the shared life of the human community. These moral claims will be practically guaranteed when respect for them is built into the basic structure of society, i.e., into the main political, social, and economic institutions that set the overall terms of social cooperation.[30] When understood this way, the protection of human rights is part of the common good, not an individualistic alternative to the common good. It also suggests that a universalist human rights ethic is required by a Christian commitment to solidarity, not a secularist adversary of the Christian ethos.

Consider freedom of religion, speech, association, and assembly. Securing these freedoms for all is morally required by any ethic committed to the genuine dialogue in which intellectual solidarity becomes a reality. Where these freedoms are denied, dialogue is impossible. When these freedoms are curtailed without just cause, those who suffer the restrictions are treated as if they had lesser dignity or worth than others. They are treated as outsiders. In the extreme, they are treated as if they were not human beings at all.

[30] See Rawls, *Political Liberalism*, p. 11.

This is the basis of the US Catholic bishops' definition of human rights as "the minimum conditions for life in community."[31]

Respect for these freedoms is a requirement of the respect due to the equal dignity of all persons as members of the human community. Where the rights to these freedoms are not respected, persons are not being treated in accord with the Christian vision of human dignity as achieved in communion with others. Nor are they treated in a way that is reasonable, for reasoned reflection on human experience shows that human beings cannot achieve the basic requirements of their dignity alone. Thus the Second Vatican Council stated that the right to religious freedom "has its foundation in the very dignity of the human person, as this dignity is known through the revealed word of God and by reason itself."[32] This claim is also made of the full range of human rights that appear in the United Nations Universal Declaration. All these rights were linked by the Council to the core of Christian faith: "by virtue of the gospel committed to it, the Church proclaims the rights of the human person."[33] Its continuing affirmation of a morality based on reasonableness led to the same conclusion. The Council affirmed that the common good includes all those social conditions that allow persons and groups "to reach their fulfillment more fully and more easily," and the Council specified these social conditions in a list of human rights.[34]

The location of this commitment to human rights within the framework of solidarity has important implications for the way rights are understood. Seen in this context, the classic rights to freedom of religion, speech, association, and assembly are not primarily rights to be left alone. Rather they are persons' moral claims to be treated as participating members of society. These moral claims must be institutionally protected if deliberation about the

[31] National Conference of Catholic Bishops, *Economic Justice for All: Pastoral Letter on Catholic Social Teaching and the US Economy* (Washington, D.C.: United States Catholic Conference, 1986), nos. 77–84, esp. section heading at no. 77. I have sought to give a more theoretical explication of this perspective in "A Communitarian Reconstruction of Human Rights: Contributions from Catholic Tradition," in R. Bruce Douglass and David Hollenbach, eds., *Catholicism and Liberalism: Contributions to American Public Philosophy*, pp. 127–150.
[32] *Dignitatis Humanae*, no. 2.   [33] *Gaudium et Spes*, no. 25.
[34] *Ibid.*, no. 26, see nos. 73–75. For the classic reason-based argument for human rights in recent official Catholic teaching, see Pope John XXIII, *Pacem in Terris*, esp. nos. 8–38, in O'Brien and Shannon, eds., *Catholic Social Thought*, pp. 132–137.

common good is to be possible. Institutional protection of religious expression is a prerequisite of any genuine dialogue across religious traditions. The same is true for freedom of speech, association, and assembly. Where these freedoms are stifled, dialogue and deliberation become impossible. The result will be a politics of authoritarian tyranny or of the cynical manipulation of public opinion. Tyranny and manipulation by their very nature serve the private good of some narrowly defined group of people, not the common good of all. Put positively, when these freedoms are exercised in active dialogue with others, a common life comes into existence among citizens in the midst of their religious and cultural differences. Securing these basic rights, therefore, is both a prerequisite for solidarity and an expression of solidarity.

The rights to religious freedom, free speech, and association are thus primarily positive social empowerments rather than simply negative civil immunities from coercion.[35] Religious freedom enables religious believers and non-believers alike to enter into a community of discourse that seeks to discover the truth about how they should live together. A commitment to intellectual solidarity leads to a quite different view of religious freedom from one that tolerates religion as long as it remains a private matter within the individual's conscience or inside the sacristy. Seen from a perspective that regards solidarity as essential to human dignity, religious freedom is the freedom to speak religiously in public. It is freedom to suggest ways that religious understandings of the good have a bearing on the realities of public life. Adopting this view, the Second Vatican Council stated that "It comes within the meaning of religious freedom that religious bodies should not be prohibited from freely undertaking to show the special value of their doctrine in what concerns the organization of society and the inspiration of the whole of human activity."[36] The free exercise of religion is a social freedom and the right to freedom of religion includes the right to seek to influence other people's understandings of the good life through public persuasion and argument. The dialogic ethic underlying this claim means that protection of active engagement

[35] See J. Leon Hooper, *The Ethics of Discourse: The Social Philosophy of John Courtney Murray* (Washington, D.C.: Georgetown University Press, 1986), pp. 154–56 and all of chap. 6.
[36] *Dignitatis Humanae*, no. 4.

of religious believers in public life, not privatization of religion, is part of the substantive meaning of the right to religious freedom.

All understandings of the good life are dynamic and developing, and we come to such understandings only through a social process of active engagement with others. For such a process to occur people must be willing to both listen and speak. At the Second Vatican Council, the Catholic church came to affirm the importance of religious freedom by listening to voices from beyond the church that had been affirming this right for several centuries. John Courtney Murray, principal drafter of Vatican II's *Declaration on Religious Freedom*, observed that the Council's affirmation of religious freedom brought the Church "at long last, abreast of the consciousness of civilized mankind, which had already accepted religious freedom as a principle and as a legal institution."[37] The development of doctrine that occurred at the Council, in other words, was a result of the church's willingness to learn from secular society as well as its readiness to recognize how this learning could enrich its own tradition. The Council's achievement thus shows how active participation in intellectual and cultural dialogue is essential to the discovery of how we should live together in a diverse world. This learning will occur through active conversation with the full array of intellectual currents present in culture. Religious freedom empowers Christians for such participation while simultaneously demanding that they exercise the intellectual humility that enables them to listen as well as speak.

The continuing need for a dialogical or deliberative approach to the interpretation of human rights is evident in the context of the increased awareness of the religious diversity of both the world and of Western societies. Human rights, of course, are proposed as protections for the sacredness of persons independent of their religious or cultural traditions. They are held universally by all persons. Western Enlightenment thought interpreted this claim to universality to mean that human rights are moral standards that stand independent of all traditions, cultures, and religions. The contemporary awareness of the historical embeddedness of rationality, however, raises serious doubts about this claim that rights transcend history

[37] John Courtney Murray, "The Declaration on Religious Freedom: Its Deeper Significance," *America* 114 (April 23, 1966), 592.

and communal traditions. This has led some recent theorists to reject the very notion of human rights as an Enlightenment illusion.[38] Such a rejection of the existence of human rights, however, would be a serious setback for the growing sense of solidarity across cultures in a world where violations of human dignity continue today on a massive scale. Since the moral vocabulary of human rights has become the single strongest way to address this human degradation, to declare on theoretical grounds that it is an illegitimate way of speaking will have serious negative consequences for the lives of many people. But a defense of the idea of universal human rights must take account of the ways the justification of human rights norms and the interpretation of their concrete implications vary in notable ways from one philosophical, ideological, or religious tradition to another. Dialogue and deliberation across traditions once again come to the fore in this context.

For example, Judaism, Christianity, and Islam have a powerful influence on the way human rights are understood by the adherents of these faiths. In Judaism, the central place of communal identity and of the land of Israel leads to a reading of human rights that emphasizes the right of the Jewish people to national self-determination and to their possession of the land of Israel as an essential aspect of their national and religious identity. For many Israelis and Jews of the diaspora, rights have a distinctly communal reference.[39] Western Christians, on the other hand, understand rights in a way that gives greater emphasis to the rights of individual persons, for the universal mission of Christianity relativizes the importance of national or ethnic identity. The radical monotheism of Islam leads many Muslims to argue that universal human rights will only be secured in a society submissive to Allah – that is, in an Islamic republic. The religious beliefs of each of these communities, therefore, shape the intellectual and affective horizon against which they interpret human rights. This background of religious beliefs colors the concrete meaning of specific human rights and influences priorities for action in the pursuit of human rights.

[38] See, for example, Alasdair MacIntyre, *After Virtue: A Study in Moral Theory*, p. 67, and Richard Rorty, "Postmodernist Bourgeois Liberalism," pp. 219–20.
[39] See Ben Halpern, "Jewish Nationalism: Self-Determination as a Human Right," in David Sidorsky, ed., *Essays on Human Rights: Contemporary Issues and Jewish Perspectives* (Philadelphia, PA: Jewish Publication Society of America, 1979), pp. 309–335.

Thus both theoretical and practical defense of human rights must take into account the influence of these religious traditions on the ways rights are understood. Pursuit of respect for human rights requires an ongoing dialogue about how the universal standards sought by the discourse of human rights relates to the distinctive, particularist self-understandings of the religious communities of the world. This means that commitment to ecumenical and interreligious dialogue is a prerequisite for a global human rights ethic today.[40] Religious communities must be active participants in public deliberation about public institutions if we are to achieve a more humane common life within religiously diverse nation-states and across the boundaries of these states in today's interdependent world. The suggestion that only strictly secular discourse is legitimate in public and that religion must be kept private is more likely to produce fundamentalist reactions than a more humane life together. Participation of religious communities in deliberation about the common good is a much more promising path. This calls for the nurturance of a spirit of dialogue and intellectual solidarity among all concerned, believer and non-believer alike. Only along that path will we discover ways both to respect diverse identities and to promote the common good at the same time.

It should be noted, however, that this argument for religious presence in public life does not mean that religious liberty is a positive empowerment *but not* a civil immunity from coercion. Freedom from coercion remains an essential precondition for freedom as empowerment for participation. A community of discourse and deliberation can only be such when it is immune from coercion.[41] Pursuit of the common good through public deliberation and the protection of fundamental freedoms are therefore mutually and reciprocally connected to each other. This means, on the one hand, that religious understandings of the good life should not be excluded

---

[40] For one effort along these lines see the *Declaration Toward a Global Ethic* issued by the 1993 Parliament of the World's Religions held in Chicago, in Hans Küng and Karl-Josef Kuschel, eds., *A Global Ethic: The Declaration of the Parliament of the World's Religions*, trans. John Bowden (New York: Continuum, 1993), and commentaries on this Declaration from representatives of many traditions in Hans Küng, ed., *Yes to a Global Ethic*, trans. John Bowden (New York: Continuum, 1996).

[41] In the words of Vatican Council II, believers should "avoid any action which seems to suggest coercion or unworthy persuasion." *Dignitatis Humanae*, no. 4.

from public discourse. Believers have as much right to make their case regarding public affairs as those who do so on non-religious grounds. On the other hand, religiously based claims about the good life must be tested in the same free exchange of ideas as are all other proposals in a democratic society. Persuasion is the proper mode of public participation by religious believers, especially when they seek to influence law or public policy. Seeing religious communities as playing a deliberative role in pursuit of the common good in no way undercuts the right to religious freedom as an immunity from coercion. The institutional protection of the rights to freedom of religion, speech, and association are essential preconditions for the pursuit of the common good. Indeed, an institutional guarantee of these rights is part of the common good itself. The institutions of constitutional democracy, and the rights built into these institutions, are among the constitutive elements of a community where all citizens participate in the freedom of public life.

POLITICS, CULTURE, AND RELIGION

When human rights are linked with the common good in this way, the division of human life into quite distinct public and private domains is implicitly being challenged. A binary distinction between public and private life is difficult to sustain analytically. Government is surely a public affair. Calling everything that does not involve the exercise of governmental power "private" suggests that only the actions of government are relevant to the quality of public life. This overlooks the enormous influence of so-called "private sector" economic activities on the lives we share together in public. It also overlooks the public impact of commercial communications media and the entire domain broadly called culture, both of which shape and express publicly held values. The difficulty of drawing a sharp line between the private and public domains means it is equally difficult to conceive human rights simply as protecting private freedoms against unwanted encroachments by the public or by government. The linkage of human rights with the idea of the common good challenges the idea that rights are to the private sphere as the common good is to the sphere of government. This challenge is probably most evident in the claim that the right to religious freedom means the right of religious communities to be seen and heard in public and to propose their visions of the common good for deliberation in public.

Nevertheless, a further clarification is required to show that such a public role for religious visions of the common good will not simply lead back to a reprise of seventeenth-century Europe, with its limitations on civil freedom in the name of religious doctrine and its religious conflict. This clarification depends on replacing the binary public–private division of domains with the more complex distinction between government and civil society. Here civil society is understood to include the multileveled domain of culture and many of the activities regarded as strictly private today, such as family life and religious association. When social life is mapped this way, religious communities are seen as important participants in civic and public life while also being institutionally separated from state power.

This mapping of religious communities as public but not established, however, still leaves open the question of what sort of influence religious communities should have on institutions, policies, and laws in the governmental sphere. John Rawls, especially in his recent writings, can again help clarify the issue. Rawls rejects a dualistic contrast between the public or political sphere and the domain of the private. He proposes instead a tripartite distinction among the public or political sphere, the non-public sphere, and the private sphere. The "political" is the arena where the coercive power of government holds sway. The "non-public" is the sphere of civil society and of "the culture of daily life, of its many associations: churches and universities, learned and scientific societies, and clubs and teams, to mention a few." It is "social, and certainly not private."[42] Thus as an important influence in civil society, religion is not a private affair. Religious communities and traditions are part of what Rawls calls "the background culture" of political life.

Rawls's normative prescriptions on the social role of religion depend on his insistence that this background culture is "non-public."[43] Religious understandings of the good life can play important roles in shaping this background culture. Rawls,

[42] Rawls, *Political Liberalism*, pp. 14 and 220.
[43] Rawls, "The Idea of Public Reason Revisited," 768.

however, resists granting religious arguments about the common good the status of full "publicness." This is so because Rawls believes arguments based on religious conceptions of the human good fail to meet the standard of reciprocity, an essential quality of what he calls "public reason." A religious believer cannot reasonably expect that those of another faith or no faith will have reason to accept such arguments. So religious arguments cannot be proposed with the expectation that they will be mutually agreed to. Religious arguments may indeed be presented in public debate to clarify why the presenter holds a particular political view, including a religious idea of the good that supports constitutional democracy. This will reassure one's fellow citizens that one really does support a democratic regime and thus strengthen democracy. But if religious arguments about fundamental political institutions and laws are introduced in political debate, those who introduce them must accept the "proviso" that "in due course" they will also present reasons that others can be expected to accept.[44] Only in this way can reciprocal respect for the equal rights of citizens become politically institutionalized.

Rawls's recent approach to the social role of religion is generally compatible with the position being taken here. It is important to note, however, that the relation between the demands of reciprocal reasonableness and the political implications of religious visions of the common good is not a one-way relationship. Reciprocal reasonableness is not simply a given. It is not a predetermined yardstick by which religious understandings of the good life must be measured. To be sure, reciprocal reasonableness constrains what can be done in the name of religion. But it is also the case that serious religious discourse in civil society and the background culture can have significant impact on what citizens at large judge they can reasonably affirm. Religious discourse can influence what counts as reasonable even in political discourse, as the lives of Gandhi and Martin Luther King surely show. In the language of the Catholic tradition, the relation between faith and reason is not all in one direction: faith should be reasonable and "make sense," but reason can also be informed by faith. Further, it cannot be simply taken for

---

[44] *Ibid.*, 776, 783–787. In this essay Rawls has granted considerably greater scope for religion in the public sphere than did the normative prescriptions of *Political Liberalism*. He now calls his view the "wide view of public political culture," chiefly because he now grants religion a wider role in public life than he did in *Political Liberalism*.

granted that the political institutions that all citizens have reason
to accept at any given historical moment are in fact fundamentally
just institutions. Nor can it be presumed that citizens who affirm
institutions that aim to protect human rights will have identical
understandings of what human rights are. The cultural debates
about such questions will influence how citizens think about these
eminently public and political questions. Thus what Rawls calls the
"background culture" plays a formative role in shaping what is politically reasonable. Because religious communities are important
forces in civil society and culture, they can have significant influence
on what comes to be regarded as publicly reasonable. This fact is
overlooked if their role is restricted to the "non-public" domain.

Rawls is ready to accept this influence of religion and culture on
the political sphere, but only under the proviso that it be influence
under the constraint of reciprocity.[45] If this means that such influence must be exercised with due respect for the religious freedom
of all citizens, it is fully compatible with the idea of a community
of freedom for which we have been arguing. But if it means that
we should presume that existing constitutional democracies and
Rawls's own theory of democracy already know the best way for
us to live our common life together, it must be judged shortsighted.

Culture is a preeminently public domain. When religion plays
a role in culture, it is playing a public role that has political consequences. What citizens take to be reasonable is forged in the
interaction that forms the rich give-and-take among the diverse
communities that form culture and civil society, including religious
communities. There is a constant symbiosis and mutual influence
between the political and the cultural. For example, Martin Luther
King's appeal to the Bible as well as later classical sources that
have shaped the Christian tradition can thus be seen as an effort to
form (and reform) the public reason that prevailed in his time. At
the same time, he appealed to classic documents of the American
democratic tradition such as the Declaration of Independence
and the United States Constitution, showing that he did not aim
to speak to Christians only but to all citizens of his country. In
King's words one hears faith and reason interacting in a dynamic,

45 *Ibid.*, 799.

mutually illuminating way. Indeed it is sometimes difficult to tell when reading King's words about civil rights whether they were originally delivered as a sermon in a church or in an explicitly political, even legislative, context. Thus did King's faith become public and political in a way that was fully compatible with the aspirations of constitutional self-government.

The task of forming and sustaining a society in which people from diverse religious and cultural traditions can live well together is a never-ending historical project. We do not already possess reasonable criteria for how to do this that would settle matters once and for all if only everyone would see the wisdom of these criteria. There is no ideal earthly society that can be achieved once and for all. The terrestrial common good, even when it is recognized that human rights are an essential component of this good, will always remain imperfect and fragile. Only a political theory that grants quasi-divine status to democratic political institutions can deny this. Thus there will always be need for the most serious discussion and argument about what makes for a good society. This discussion must be public, and it will have major political impact. Without such public discourse, even the minimal good of a just order will be subject to forces of decadence. Religious communities that are committed to the civility of debate and argument have both the right and the duty to be fully present in this public exchange. When they are present there in intellectual solidarity with their fellow citizens, they will make an important contribution to the common good, even an indispensable one.

What practical pursuit of this sort of solidarity could mean for the life of the United States today remains an open question. The implications are even more problematic on the global level. The challenges raised by urban poverty and global interdependence nevertheless call for a significantly stronger orientation to solidarity than the "liberalism of fear" and its ethic of tolerance can provide. This chapter has not spelled out detailed responses to these challenges or policy proposals for meeting them. But it has shown, one hopes, that the Christian communities possess resources in their traditions that can guide their efforts to respond to these challenges without posing oppressive threats to modern freedoms. It is at least possible for religious communities to be agents of greater solidarity in cultural and political life. In the face of deep splits between the worlds of the urban poor and the suburbs, this requires an understanding of justice that takes the common good more seriously than we have in the West for the past several centuries. It raises the question of the scope of the community whose good should concern us. Is it the neighborhood, the city, the nation-state, the ethnic or religious community, or the entire globe? Finally, if all of these spheres of relationship are venues where we attain a common good or a common bad, how are the obligations of solidarity they generate related to each other?

Exploring these questions is the task of the chapters that follow.

PART III

Directions

CHAPTER SEVEN

Poverty, justice, and the good of the city

Human beings are dependent on one another not only for the higher achievements of cultural life we have been discussing but also for the necessities of material and economic well-being. For this reason, recovery of an active social commitment to the common good is a critical element in serious efforts to reduce poverty and advance economic justice. Poverty continues to be an entrenched fact of life for many people in Western societies today and it is vastly more widespread globally. Chapter 2 of this book has argued that the poverty of American core cities is a problem that an ethic of tolerance alone cannot handle. This chapter will argue that a revival of commitment to the common good and a deeper sense of solidarity are preconditions for significant improvement of the lives of the poor in large cities of the United States. The focus here will be on how effective efforts to alleviate the plight of the American urban poor call for public commitment to solidarity and the common good. Social allegiance to the common good can tackle poverty in a way that that the prevailing American ethos of individualism and tolerance cannot. The next chapter will extend this analysis to the larger international setting.

Commitment to the common good will not, of course, settle all the policy debates concerning poverty in the United States or elsewhere. But the lodestar of the common good can guide movement along a path toward better lives for the poor. It can orient public decisions toward a form of social interdependence in which the poor can begin to participate in the commonweal in a way that enables them to escape their plight. More specifically, the idea of the common good can generate an understanding of justice that is particularly relevant to overcoming deprivation. Such a normative understanding of justice will be outlined here, along with some of its practical implications for poverty-alleviation in American cities. This will further strengthen the case for the retrieval of a common good-based ethic as well as providing a practically relevant orientation for policy.

THE SOCIAL ISOLATION OF THE POOR

The need for a renewal of an ethic of the common good is suggested by the fact that deep economic and social divisions between suburb and inner city in the United States today are among the principal causes of urban poverty. To address these economic divisions Americans need a cultural orientation that places considerably higher value on interdependence, solidarity, and the common good than the predominant American culture grants these values today.

As noted in chapter 2, racial prejudice is no longer the principal cause of urban poverty in the United States today. Thus greater racial tolerance will not provide the principal solution. The decline in racial prejudice in American society over the past several decades has not solved the serious problems affecting the urban poor. It is true, of course, that racial discrimination continues today and that the legacy of the past enslavement of blacks has powerful continuing effects on their economic well-being.[1] Indeed, the poverty and low quality of life in US inner cities is a tragic legacy of the history of American racism. Owen Fiss has called it "perhaps the most pernicious vestige of racial injustice in the United States – the successor to slavery and Jim Crow."[2] The distressing fact is that African Americans in the United States have a shorter life expectancy than do the citizens of very much poorer regions of the world like China, the Indian state of Kerala, Jamaica, and Costa Rica. But there is more involved here than racial discrimination by itself can explain. There has been substantial growth in the black middle class of

---

[1] For an impassioned discussion of the continuing impact of the history of slavery and racial discrimination on the cultural and economic situation of African Americans, see Randall Robinson, *The Debt: What America Owes to Blacks* (New York: Dutton, 2000), esp. chaps. 1–4.

[2] Owen Fiss, "What Should Be Done for Those Who Have Been Left Behind?" *Boston Review*. (Summer, 2000), 7.

the United States in recent decades, and middle-class African Americans are much better off than their black brothers and sisters living in the heart of US cities. Those who suffer the most severe deprivations today are not blacks in general but African Americans in the inner city. For example, African American men living in Harlem have lower life expectancies than do males in Bangladesh, one of the poorest countries in the world.[3] The short life expectancy of inner-city blacks is not due to low incomes alone, for inner-city blacks in fact have much higher incomes relative to the cost of living than do those who outlive them in developing countries. Rather, it is the result of the weak community relationships evident in low levels of neighborhood cohesion, physical security against violence, quality of education, and access to medical care that are commonly found in American core cities. More than increased racial tolerance is needed to address these matters.[4]

The plight of inner-city African Americans is the result of social patterns that cut them off from the goods available in the larger society. These patterns have significant economic and class dimensions. It has been argued persuasively by the African American sociologist William Julius Wilson that poor, inner-city neighborhoods are increasingly "socially isolated" from the mainstream of American society. He defines social isolation as "lack of contact or of sustained interaction with individuals and institutions that represent mainstream society."[5] Its principal manifestation is a lack of jobs for which the inner-city poor have the required skills and to which geography and informal networks of interaction give them access. This social isolation is in part a matter of economics; the movement of capital and money determines the location of jobs. It is also the result of political decisions concerning land use, zoning, housing, and the funding of educational opportunities. These political decisions themselves affect the movement of capital and thus

[3] See Amartya Sen, *Development as Freedom* (New York: Alfred A. Knopf, 1999), pp. 21–24.
[4] The title of an early book by William Julius Wilson is *The Declining Significance of Race: Blacks and Changing American Institutions*, 2nd edn. (Chicago: University of Chicago Press, 1980). Wilson proposes policies aimed at overcoming the deprivation of the inner cities that are not race-based in "Race-Neutral Programs and the Democratic Coalition," *The American Prospect* 1 (Spring, 1990), 82–89, and in *The Bridge over the Racial Divide: Rising Inequality and Coalition Politics* (Berkeley: University of California Press, 1999).
[5] William Julius Wilson, *The Truly Disadvantaged: The Inner City, the Underclass, and Public Policy* (Chicago: University of Chicago Press, 1987), p. 60.

of jobs. The upshot of these economic and political choices is a high wall separating poor inner cities from middle-class suburbs. This wall marks a kind of caste or class boundary that is the principal obstacle to overcoming inner-city poverty in the United States today.

The existence of this boundary is evident in the way urban poverty increased during the 1970s and 1980s despite the improvement of economic well-being in the United States as a whole. Even though the overall economy grew during this period, poverty also increased. Reflecting rising inequality, the number of census tracts classified as ghetto poverty areas grew sharply, the concentration of the poor in these areas rose, and these changes hit minorities much harder than whites.[6] A sharp division between core cities and suburbs prevented the overall growth from benefiting those in the urban centers. This was manifest most directly in the disappearance of jobs for many in the inner city who were seeking them. This in turn led many of the poor in the inner city simply to give up trying to find work.

Wilson acknowledges that there continue to be serious problems with the behavior, motivation, and qualifications for work among the urban poor that partly explain their low participation in the work force. He calls this the problem of "ghetto related behavior," i.e., behavior that is more prevalent in the inner city than in the larger society, especially among young males. This behavior includes dropping out of school, single parenthood, drug use, and crime – all of which are closely correlated with not holding a job and with poverty.[7] But Wilson challenges the prevalent view that this behavior is the principal cause of joblessness and argues that the causality largely works the other way. When jobs have become unavailable, "ghetto-related behaviors often represent particular cultural adaptations to the systematic blockage of opportunities in the inner city and the society as a whole."[8] When persistent joblessness becomes general and routine, it has cultural as well as

---

[6] Wilson, *When Work Disappears: The World of the New Urban Poor* (New York: Knopf, 1996), p. 15. On how and why economic inequality increased in the United States in recent decades as aggregate economic conditions have improved see Sheldon Danziger and Peter Gottschalk, *America Unequal* (Cambridge, MA: Harvard University Press, 1995).

[7] Wilson, *When Work Disappears*, p. 52.   [8] *Ibid.*, pp. 72–73.

individual effects. "Giving up" becomes part of the social environment and culture of urban ghettos.

Social isolation of inner-city communities and the boundaries separating them from the larger society thus have multiplier effects on the way poverty and unemployment affect individuals. What is realistically imaginable to a family living in a poor neighborhood where many are jobless is significantly different from what seems possible to a poor family living in a neighborhood where most others have jobs. The former family's behavior is influenced not only by its own situation of unemployment but by the behavior and outlook of the many other jobless families around it. In a ghetto neighborhood of this kind, when residents live by productive values they receive fewer rewards and, in turn, find it much more difficult to transmit these values from one generation to the next. Thus social and economic isolation of poor urban neighborhoods magnifies the negative effects of poverty on family stability, crime, and drug-use. The social isolation of urban ghettos reinforces dysfunctional behavior and leads to a downward spiral in the quality of life.

The cultural impact of social isolation is particularly evident in the sensed "lack of self-efficacy" prevalent among poor, urban, black males. Cornel West does not flinch at calling it "nihilism" – the "collapse of meaning in life," the "eclipse of hope," "the profound sense of psychological depression, personal worthlessness, and social despair."[9] The structural and institutional disconnection of many urban neighborhoods from the social and economic life of the larger society thus has a profoundly negative impact on the aspirations and the behavior of many who live in the inner cities. It is the institutionalization of hopelessness.

This institutional diagnosis of the causes of ghetto problems shows the fallacy of arguing that reduction of urban poverty is primarily a matter of stimulating a stronger desire for work among individual urban poor people. A structural perspective certainly does not deny that there are genuinely harmful patterns of behavior in inner-city culture or that determined individuals can sometimes fight their way free of the negative pressures of their milieu. But it rejects the idea that that these behavior patterns are independent

[9] West, *Race Matters*, pp. 5, 12–13.

variables that adequately account for the extent of joblessness and poverty. Thus it challenges the belief of the sizable majority of middle-class Americans that "the problems of America's inner cities are largely due to people's lack of responsibility for their own problems."[10] As was noted earlier, most Americans believe that they are responsible for their own fates and that people can be pretty much what they want to be.[11] To those who hold this belief, the poor are no exception to what is true of almost everybody. If this were so, it would follow that the urban poor must want to live the style of life they lead even though it leads to poverty. The inner-city poor must in fact prefer drugs, single parenthood, and dropping out of school to behavior that will enable them to escape deprivation. This account of the causes of inner-city poverty, however, entirely neglects the cultural and structural obstacles to changes in behavior that are strongly operative in urban centers. The class patterns of social and economic isolation that cut the inner cities off from the suburbs play little or no role in such an account. Such individualistic convictions about the causes of the plight of the inner cities in turn lead to passivity in the face of urban poverty and even to hostility toward efforts to address its institutional, economic causes directly. So the problem remains and even deepens.

These individualistic presuppositions about the dynamics of urban poverty help explain how it has been possible for racial tolerance to have increased in the United States while the lives of the urban poor have not improved. Racial tolerance is an individualistic virtue; it rejects prejudice and discrimination against individuals on the basis of their skin color. This tolerance, however, does not generate positive action to address the institutional causes of urban poverty. Racial tolerance is fully compatible with the belief that poverty is the result of the dysfunctional behavior of the poor themselves and that alleviating it does not call for changed activity by the middle class or for alteration of the institutional relationships between cities and suburbs. White suburbanites are in

---

[10] See Wolfe, *One Nation After All*, p. 205, Table 5.4, also pp. 184 and 204–209, on the prevalence of this belief.
[11] See the data already cited in chapters 1 and 2: *General Social Survey*, question 673 G, codebook variable: OWNFATE; *New York Times* "The Way We Live Now Poll," *New York Times Magazine* (May 7, 2000), 66.

fact less racially prejudiced than they were a generation ago, but they also draw a very strong distinction between their responsibilities to the deserving poor and the undeserving poor. Alan Wolfe's interviews of middle-class Americans leads him to conclude that "there is no belief more strongly held in America than that welfare should only go to those who deserve it." [12] Because of the visibility of behavior like high unemployment, family instability, drug-use, and crime, the inner-city poor are seen as largely undeserving. Thus racial tolerance can increase without leading to improvement in the lives of inner-city African Americans because tolerance alone does not remove the economic and class walls that create social isolation.

For this reason, a stance that goes beyond tolerance is needed. If overcoming the pathologies of core cities is to become a significant item on the American agenda, it will require direct efforts to bridge the urban – suburban divide. Such bridging calls for a sense of mutual interdependence and an awareness that the good life of those in the suburbs is linked with a better life for those in the inner city. It requires a greater recognition that all citizens of a metropolitan area share each other's fate both in fact and from a moral point of view. In other words, a deeper awareness that the well-being of cities and suburbs are interdependent is needed if the poverty of core cities is to be addressed effectively. A revitalized vision that cities and suburbs share a common good, or a common bad, is a motivational precondition for dismantling the walls that isolate those in the inner city from the economic and cultural achievements of the middle class. Put positively, such a revitalized sense of the common good could energize social and political actions to enable the urban poor to become more active participants in the economic life of the larger society.

The need for such a renewed commitment to the common good is also evident from what has happened to the poor since the welfare reform legislation passed by the US Congress and signed by President Clinton in 1996. This legislation withdrew the entitlement of poor people to receive government assistance simply by virtue of their being poor. It was motivated by the belief that government support made it rational for poor people to avoid work,

[12] Wolfe, *One Nation After All*, p. 204.

encouraged single-parenthood, and otherwise reinforced destructive patterns of behavior. According to this account, withdrawal of the entitlement to welfare would remove perverse incentives that supposedly reinforced harmful behavior among poor people. Without guaranteed welfare benefits, they would have new motivation to work their way out of poverty.[13]

In fact, however, many ghetto residents have all along believed that work is the way to personal advancement and have sought to find jobs.[14] Thus it should not be surprising that in the booming economy of the post-welfare reform period, where jobs have become more available, many of the poor have sought and found work. Nevertheless many remain trapped in poverty despite holding jobs. The poor are still very much among us, but now many of them are working rather than on welfare. What the US Catholic bishops said in their 1986 Pastoral Letter *Economic Justice for All* is even more true today: "Many people are working but at wages insufficient to lift them out of poverty . . . Of the long-term poor, most are working at wages too low to bring them above the poverty line or are retired, disabled, or parents of preschool children."[15] Shortly after the 1996 welfare reform bill was signed by the president, Nobel prize-winning economist Robert Solow predicted that it would be the working poor who would bear the heaviest burdens of welfare reform. His prediction has been borne out: the problem today is poverty as such, poverty among those who work.[16] This contradicts the deeply held American belief that initiative and hard work will make a good life possible for all who are willing to

---

[13] The key books that made this argument and largely shaped the arguments of the welfare reform debate of the 1980s and 1990s were: George Gilder, *Wealth and Poverty* (New York: Basic Books, 1981); Charles Murray, *Losing Ground: American Social Policy 1950–1980* (New York: Basic Books, 1984); and Lawrence Mead, *Beyond Entitlement: The Social Obligations of Citizenship* (New York: Free Press, 1986).

[14] 66 percent of black respondents from a ghetto census tract in one survey saw "plain hard work" as very important for getting ahead, while only 3 percent denied its importance. Wilson, *When Work Disappears*, p. 67.

[15] National Conference of Catholic Bishops, *Economic Justice for All*, nos. 174–175.

[16] See Robert Solow, "Guess Who Pays for Workfare," in Amy Gutmann, ed., *Work and Welfare* (Princeton, NJ: Princeton University Press, 1998), pp. 23–44. Mary Jo Bane, Assistant Secretary of Health and Human Services in the Clinton administration until 1996, comments that, as a result of the welfare reform bill, "By and large, the welfare poor have become the working poor." "Poverty, Welfare, and the Role of the Churches," *America* (December 4, 1999), 10.

undertake them, for many people today work full time and are still poor.

The poverty of today's working poor continues to place severe strains on family life and on parents' ability to care for their children. Single mothers often have to choose between personally caring for their young children and earning enough to feed them. Much of this continuing poverty remains concentrated in inner cities, where despair, drug-use, dropping out of school, out-of-wedlock teen pregnancy, and other destructive forms of behavior persist. Now, however, it has become evident that oftentimes these phenomena are linked with poverty itself, not with dependency on welfare. Despite the claims that welfare reform would remove incentives that perpetuate both destructive behavior and poverty itself, it has not done so. Rather, harmful behavior persists, but now among the families of those who work for wages too low to raise them from poverty. Economic and class boundaries continue to isolate the poor in inner cities from the middle class who live largely in the suburbs. This isolation, not the racism of the middle class or the destructive behavior of inner-city residents, continues to be the key to the problem of urban poverty in the United States today.

Addressing this poverty will call for a recognition that we are deeply dependent on one another and on the institutional shape of society as we seek good lives. Hard work ought to raise people out of poverty and the human despair it often leads to. For this to be so, new avenues of interaction between city and suburb must replace the high barriers that separate the urban poor from the suburban middle class. In other words, addressing the reality of urban poverty in the United States today calls for a social strategy that embodies serious commitment to the common good that crosses the urban – suburban divide.

INTERDEPENDENCE AND SOLIDARITY

The interdependence of persons on each other is a fact of human life. The prevailing ethos of Western culture, however, often leads us to forget how human well-being thoroughly depends on reciprocal cooperation with other people. The initiatives that engender both economic and cultural flourishing are social activities; they are embedded in networks of human interaction and interdependence. Men and women depend on each other and the surrounding natural world in pursuing these goods. The autonomy and independence so highly regarded today are, to be sure, genuine marks of good human lives. They are aspects of the freedom and creative capacity that distinguish human beings from other animals and that raise men and women from the condition of slaves exploited for the benefit of others. But without careful attention to the ways humans are dependent on each other, the good life will be misunderstood and the path toward it misconstrued. This is especially relevant to the pursuit of economic justice and to efforts to overcome poverty.

The social boundaries between core cities and suburbs do not abolish the way that the well-being of their residents is in fact interconnected. The quality of lives of those in the suburbs and of those in the core cities are not independent variables. The fact of gated communities is a vivid reminder that such interaction has to be dealt with, though the gates of these communities are symbols of the negative way of doing so that is increasingly being chosen. Suburb and inner city are not separated from each other by vast empty spaces like those between stars in our galaxy or planets in our solar system. There is interaction between city and suburb, but it is interaction of a negative kind. Suburbs relate to inner cities in the mode of institutional self-defense and self-protection. Whether intentional or not, this stance leaves in place and even strengthens the structural barriers that prevent the poor from participating in the successes of the contemporary American economy in a way that befits their dignity as human beings. The isolation of the core cities described by Wilson, therefore, is in fact a form of interdependence with the larger society. But it is a pernicious kind of interdependence, like that between people inside and outside of a walled enclave.

This negative kind of interdependence, of course, is a complex reality. The pursuit of well-being by suburbanites and their families does not cause the poverty of those in the inner city in an immediate way, as if the middle class were directly taking resources from the urban poor. It is not like the relation between a thief and the victim

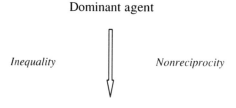

Figure 7.1. Unequal interdependence

of the theft. Rather this interaction is mediated by political, economic, and cultural institutions that affect both groups.[17] Seeking to overcome this negative interdependence, therefore, is not simply a matter of taking money from the middle class and giving it to the poor. Rather it requires changes in the social, political, and cultural frameworks within which both groups are living. Policies that tax the middle class and transfer funds to the urban poor may be part of an adequate response to urban poverty. But explaining why many in the inner cities are poor must be considerably more subtle than pointing out that they do not have enough money. In the same way, alleviating urban poverty calls for a more complex response than the transfer of funds.

As an aid to envisioning the kind of interconnection operative in the relation between cities and suburbs, consider two models of human interdependence that are polar opposites of each other. Call the first unequal interdependence and the second interdependence in solidarity. They are diagramed schematically in figures 7.1 and 7.2. The paradigm of unequal interdependence can shed some light on the relationships that now exist among suburbs and core cities. The model of interdependence in solidarity suggests the direction in which these links must move if the plight of the poor is to be addressed more effectively.

[17] See Glenn C. Loury, "Social Exclusion and Ethnic Groups: The Challenge to Economics," paper prepared for the Annual World Bank Conference on Development Economics," Washington, D.C. (April 28–30, 1999), 2, 15–16. Available on the website of the World Bank at http://www.worldbank.org/research/abcde/washington_11/pdfs/loury.pdf (downloaded June 2, 2000).

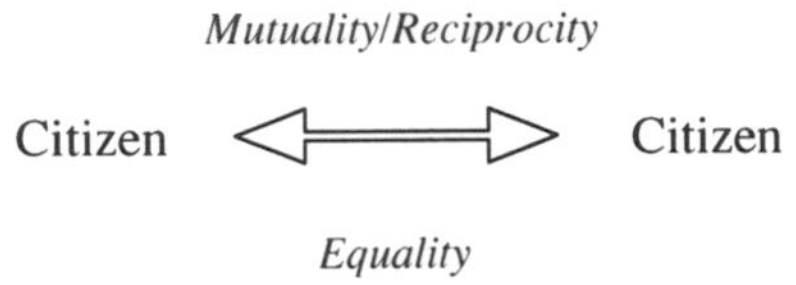

Mutuality/Reciprocity

Citizen   ⟵═══⟹   Citizen

Equality

Figure 7.2. Interdependence in solidarity

Unequal interdependence is the kind of relationship that exists between persons who hold very different amounts of power, both power that enables them to influence the shape of the larger society they live in and power to influence each other, whether directly and intentionally or indirectly and unintentionally. In a relation of unequal interdependence, one of the partners has the power to make things happen while the other partner lacks such power. It is a relation between an agent (in the sense of one who acts or initiates action) and a patient (in the sense of one who undergoes the effects of the action and must deal with its consequences). Thus in unequal interdependence, one side is primarily dominant and the other largely vulnerable. It is a relation of superordination and subordination. A nearly pure form of unequal interdependence is the relation of master and slave. The master is in control of what happens; the slave must simply cope with the decisions made by another. Slavery institutionalizes inequality and non-reciprocity in a radical way. A less radical but nonetheless still harmful form of unequal interdependence exists between rulers who are not accountable to those whom they rule. The people who live in a society with this kind of ruler are subjects, not citizens.[18] They do not share actively in governing themselves but must simply cope with decisions made by another.

Unequal interdependence is a social relationship, but it is a relationship that fails to give appropriate respect to the equal human dignity of the persons who are partners to it. In extreme forms such as slavery, tyranny, and colonialism, it does violence to the dignity of

[18] For a study of this pattern in the colonial rule of Africa by European powers, especially by Great Britain, and its continuing impact in African politics today, see Mamdani, *Citizen and Subject*. Both the pattern of slavery and that of African colonization continue to be relevant to the plight of the poor in American inner cities, even though I take it for granted that neither slavery nor colonialism provides an adequate model for explaining the plight of the urban poor in the United States today.

those who are reduced to a state of non-agency and simply coping. Such inequality might suggest that it should be called a relationship of dependence rather than interdependence. Indeed, slaves are thoroughly dependent on their masters. Nevertheless, in slave societies the institution of slavery shapes the lives and expectations of both parties, and the masters are dependent on their chattel in a perverse way. The slaves are foils for the masters' definition of their own identity. The masters' sense of self-worth depends significantly on having slaves at their disposal. In addition, the masters' economic well-being depends on the productive labor of the slaves. This dependence is the source of the masters' fear that the slaves will revolt or escape. Such fear is not unrealistic, for the masters stand to lose much that is important if the slaves should rebel or flee. The institution of slavery, therefore, is a two-way relationship, even though the relationship is non-reciprocal and unequal. Calling it unequal interdependence rather than simple dependence highlights this fact.

The relation of the poor in core cities to the middle class in the suburbs is certainly not slavery. Nevertheless, the paradigm of unequal interdependence illustrates one important aspect of the relation between ghetto neighborhoods and suburbs in the United States. Their interaction is real, but it is marked by non-reciprocity and inequality. The institutions of class and the differences in economic power that shape the relations between well-off American residents of the suburbs and the poor in inner cities affect the well-being of both groups. Both groups live in the context of a larger technological and cultural web that heavily influences their chances for economic success or failure. The urban poor, therefore, are not strictly speaking isolated from the larger society. They do not live in a parallel universe that never intersects with the world of the middle class. They are in fact interacting with the "main stream" society of the middle class all the time. But in this interaction, the urban poor are not full-fledged agents. Whatever agency they have is limited to figuring out how to cope with social conditions that are the results of decisions made elsewhere.

Zoning and land-use regulations, for example, establish significant topographical boundaries between poor and middle-class sections of metropolitan areas. These regulations in turn have powerful effects on the quality and availability of housing in inner-city neighborhoods. These boundaries also mark unequal zones of educational and other cultural opportunities. The resources required for genuine participation in the life of a technologically advanced society are available on the two sides of these boundaries in a very unequal way. These inequalities are in part a consequence of political decisions to fund education through local property taxes rather than on a metropolitan or statewide basis. The walls that prevent the inner-city poor from fully sharing in the social life of the larger society, therefore, have important political dimensions. They are not merely physical or geographical boundaries but are the cumulative effect of a long history of human choices. It is true, of course, that few contemporary suburbanites want the inner-city poor to face the lack of jobs, poor housing, inadequate education, and other sources of deprivation they face. In this sense, they do not intentionally erect the walls that are in place. Often the boundaries are the cumulative result of many choices made unreflectively and without attention to their consequences. Nonetheless, at other times choices to exclude the poor have been made quite reflectively and with full intent. Historical study of community boundaries, zoning, taxation, and education reveals a mixture of inadvertence and deliberate choice.[19] The most obvious, long-standing example of deliberate exclusion has been that based on race, and the legacy of racial exclusion continues despite the decline in conscious racism and the increased presence of middle-class blacks in the suburbs.[20]

The aggregate effect of the history of this mixed bag of many choices has been devastating for today's urban poor. It has led to an interdependence deeply marked by inequality and lack of reciprocity between suburbs and core cities. It has generated economic and political institutions that exclude the poor from sharing in the successes of the larger society, while it protects privileged opportunity and advantage for the middle class. The social isolation of the

[19] See Kenneth T. Jackson, "Gentleman's Agreement: Discrimination in Metropolitan America," in Bruce Katz, ed., *Reflections on Regionalism* (Washington, D.C.: Brookings Institution, 2000), pp. 185–217; Bruce Katz and Jennifer Bradley, "Divided We Sprawl," *Atlantic Monthly* 284, No. 6 (December, 1999), 26–42.

[20] See the *Multi-City Study of Urban Inequality* funded by the Russell Sage Foundation. Summaries of the results of this study as well as the data on which it is based are available at http://www.russellsage.org/special_interest/index.htm (downloaded May 26, 2000).

inner-city poor, therefore, is not primarily physical but moral. It stems from a lack of social, political, cultural, and, above all, moral commitment to the common good of larger metropolitan areas – the joint pursuit of a shared good by cities and suburbs built on the mutual and equal dignity of their residents.

What the urban poor need if they are to escape their isolation, therefore, is a transformed institutional framework that supports a more equal and reciprocal relationship with the larger society. Such interdependence among equal partners to a reciprocal relationship can be called interdependence in solidarity. It will have a very different shape from a relationship characterized by superordination and subordination. It is the kind of relationship that exists among citizens of a republic. The partners in such a relationship regard each other as equals. They make things happen in their social environment by acting together rather than some of them being agents and others having to cope with the consequences of actions they did not initiate.

This interdependence in solidarity has been a regular theme in the writings of Pope John Paul II and he has tied it directly to the idea of the common good. John Paul II has distinguished the *de facto* interdependence that is inevitable in human life from a moral interdependence that respects the dignity of persons in a reciprocal or mutual way. *De facto* interdependence can have negative or positive value. Its negative face is evident in the interaction of groups that are in conflict or at war, in relationships marred by domination or oppression, and where the institutions of the polity or economy unjustly exclude some people from relationships that are prerequisites for decent lives. In interdependence with a positive moral value the partners show mutual respect for each other's dignity as agents and their social institutions support the agency of all of them. Thus John Paul II has argued that the conflicts and patterns of exclusion present in contemporary social life point to "the need for a solidarity which will take up interdependence and transfer it to the moral plane."[21] In other words, he is urging movement from an unequal, non-reciprocal *de facto* interdependence to

[21] Pope John Paul II, *Sollicitudo Rei Socialis*, no. 26, in O'Brien and Shannon, eds., *Catholic Social Thought.*

a moral interdependence that promotes a common good founded on equality and reciprocity.

This positive form of interdependence will enhance the agency and well-being of all who are part of it. The possibility of such an achievement implies that agency and even human dignity, despite shorter-term conflicts and tradeoffs, are shared achievements. The goods of agency and dignity, especially in the longer term, are common goods. They must be mutually shared to at least a basic degree if they are to exist at all. No one can finally act solo, and no one can attain a good life alone. This implies that efforts to enhance one's agency or attain a better life by erecting barriers can, at best, be effective only as a short-term strategy. In conditions of crisis or imminent threat, such protections may of course be necessary. But when the result of the cumulative historical pattern of urban – suburban interaction is higher walls and deeper moats, those on both sides of the boundaries lose out. The barriers between city and suburb harm the well-being both of the urban poor and of the suburban middle class as well. These barriers impede the achievement of a quality of life that neither the poor nor the middle class can attain on their own. This is true from a moral point of view above all. But it is also empirically confirmed by both the negative effects on the poor and by the cumulative impact of urban sprawl on the suburban middle class as well.

When interdependence is understood in this way, it shows why the moral quality of people's relationships and the *de facto* quality of their lives overlap. The common good is both a moral and a descriptive concept. Over time, the moral quality of the patterns of people's interaction in a community inevitably influences whether their lives can be described as good from a pragmatic standpoint that is sufficiently capacious. When people interact in a way that expresses reciprocal respect for their dignity as persons their well-being becomes a shared good. The well-being of each party to the relationship is linked with the well-being of the others. The good of each is not in a zero-sum relationship with the goods of the others. Rather the good of each member increases or decreases as the common good grows or declines, for the well-being of each is linked with that of the others through their reciprocal relationship. The common good of such a community includes and supports the good of each member. The common good of the community and the good of the members are mutually implicating. This is the reason John Paul II calls commitment to the common good "the virtue of solidarity." Solidarity will not be found on the lists of cardinal virtues of prudence, justice, temperance, and fortitude that were central for the Greeks and Romans, nor among the theological virtues of faith, hope, and love enumerated by Christian thinkers in the past. John Paul, however, has proposed to add solidarity to these classic lists and to define this virtue as "a firm and persevering determination to commit oneself to the common good."[22] This virtue is not simply an affective sensitivity to the needs of others. It also calls for an intellectual recognition that interdependence is a necessary quality of human existence and that this interdependence must be reciprocal if the equal human dignity of the participants is to be respected in action. In addition, solidarity is not only a virtue to be enacted by individual persons one at a time. It must also be expressed in the economic, cultural, political, and religious institutions that shape society. Solidarity is a virtue of communities as well as of individuals.

One of the most important meanings of the concept of the common good, therefore, is that it is the good that comes into existence in a community of solidarity among active, equal agents. The common good, understood this way, is not extrinsic to the relationships that prevail among the members and sub-communities of a society. When these relationships form reciprocal ties among equals, the solidarity achieved is itself a good that cannot otherwise exist. Where such solidarity is absent, society falls short of the good it could attain and the lives of its members are correspondingly diminished. When a society not only falls short of the level of solidarity that it could reasonably aspire to but is shaped by institutions that exclude some members from agency altogether, the resulting interdependence becomes a genuine evil. It becomes a "common bad" that affects the quality of life of all members, especially of those who are excluded. The kind of interdependence that exists between US suburbs and core cities today provides a regrettable example of such shared harm. In the cities it leads to unemployment,

---

[22] *Ibid.*, no. 38.

inadequate housing, inferior education, drugs, crime, and despair for many of the poor. In the suburbs it leads to fear, the building of fences and gates, urban sprawl with its accompanying environmental degradation, and to what has been called a "frantic privacy" that makes the very notion of citizenship problematic.[23]

JUSTICE: PREREQUISITE FOR A GOOD THAT IS COMMON

The solidarity of a positively interdependent community can, of course, be attained to greater or lesser degrees. It is highest in close personal relationships among friends, who regard each other's well-being as their own. Thus Aristotle observed that in true friendship the good of each friend is shared in common with the others. But Aristotle also pointed out that close friendship is possible only with a limited number of people.[24] For this reason it may seem quite unrealistic to invoke solidarity as a guiding norm for the public life of large metropolitan areas in complex societies. A further reason for skepticism is John Paul II's statement that "there are many points of contact between solidarity and *charity*, which is the distinguishing mark of Christ's disciples."[25] To invoke solidarity as normative would thus seem to require that the demanding requirements of Christian charity become the operative values in the public life of large cities. This expects too much. A public philosophy that is relevant to the actual conditions of social life should not presuppose that all citizens will consistently love God with all their hearts and love their neighbors as themselves. Rawls, for example, makes a persuasive secular case that a public philosophy cannot be built on the expectation that such high levels of virtue will be found

---

[23] See Katz and Bradley, "Divided We Sprawl," 26. Again Pope John Paul II's words seem apposite to the condition of American cities:

> Today perhaps more than in the past, people are realizing that they are linked together by a common destiny, which is to be constructed together, if catastrophe for all is to be avoided. From the depth of anguish, fear and escapist phenomena like drugs, typical of the contemporary world, the idea is slowly emerging that the good to which we are all called and the happiness to which we aspire cannot be obtained without an effort and commitment on the part of all, nobody excluded. (*Sollicitudo Rei Socialis*, no. 26.)

[24] See Aristotle, *Nicomachean Ethics*, 1158a–1159b.
[25] Pope John Paul II, *Sollicitudo Rei Socialis*, no. 40.

among citizens.[26] This also follows from the Christian theological conviction that the fullness of charity will be realized only in the Kingdom of God. The fulfillment of love in God's reign is the Christian eschatological hope. But because men and women are limited both by their finitude as creatures and by their self-regarding disposition to sin, expectations about the achievement of solidarity in historical societies should not be too high.

These caveats, however, do not mean that solidarity should be written off as an inappropriate standard for the public life of American cities today. Despite Aristotle's cautions about the limited reach of friendship, he also observed that "friendship seems to hold states together." A basic level of concord is required if political communities are to avoid disintegrating into factions. In Aristotle's view, this concord among citizens is a form of friendship even though it is different in kind and intensity from that which exists among intimates.[27] In the same way, a kind of solidarity is required in the metropolitan areas of the United States today to prevent the social fragmentation and destructive isolation of the inner-city poor we have been describing. Just as Aristotle maintained that the quality of friendship appropriate to a relationship is determined by the kind of association in which it is present, the sort of solidarity we can expect in a metropolitan area must be appropriate to the relations that can exist within it. There are varieties of solidarity appropriate to differing sorts of relationship. Solidarity is not a univocal reality that is either present or absent. It can be present in a community in different ways and to different degrees. The fact that the shared good that can be sought in urban – suburban relationships is different from that attained by intimate friends does not mean solidarity should be written off the agenda for metropolitan areas.

In a similar vein, Thomas Aquinas recognized that seeking the common good is not an all-or-nothing affair. He suggested that a basic level of solidarity is essential to social life even though society falls short of being an ideal community due to the moral limits and weakness of its members. This is clearest in Aquinas's discussion of the scope and limits of what can be achieved morally through

[26] See Rawls, *A Theory of Justice* (Cambridge, MA: Harvard University Press, 1972), Section 22, "The Circumstances of Justice," pp. 126–130.

[27] Aristotle, *Nicomachean Ethics*, 1155a and 1160a.

the instrument of civil legislation. Aquinas held that all law should be directed to the promotion of the common good. At the same time, he recognized the limits of affection and the imperfection of the virtues that could be expected among the citizens of a city. Therefore civil law should not seek to forbid all vices or to enforce all virtues. Attempting to do so could in fact lead to greater social evils than those the legislation seeks to prevent. This does not mean, however, that civil law can have no moral objectives. It can and indeed must seek to assure certain minimal levels of the common good or solidarity. Civil law can proscribe behavior "without the prohibition of which human society could not be maintained." Similarly it can appropriately require the exercise of those virtues necessary for "the upholding of the common good of justice and peace."[28] Thus Aquinas distinguishes between the fullness of the common good and aspects of the common good that are necessary for social life to exist at all. These fundamental requisites of social life are dimensions of solidarity that are required by justice.[29]

From a common good perspective, therefore, justice calls for the minimal level of solidarity required to enable all of society's members to live with basic dignity. Levels of solidarity and love greater than this minimum, of course, can be hoped for and encouraged in personal friendships and in supererogatory acts of citizens. But as the plight of the urban poor reveals today, no one can be left out or excluded from the larger society without being unjustly harmed. All persons, including the urban poor, must be able to share in social life at least to the minimal level required to secure their dignity as human beings. Human dignity cannot be even minimally realized when persons are simply on their own. The norm of

[28] Thomas Aquinas, *Summa Theologiae* I-II, q. 90, art. 2; q. 96, arts. 2 and 3.
[29] Thomas Aquinas does not develop the distinction between minimal and maximal requirements of the common good in a fully adequate way. His distinctions have been clarified and developed in John Courtney Murray's treatment of the difference between the common good and public order (which includes justice and peace as key constituent parts). See Murray, *We Hold These Truths: Catholic Reflections on the American Proposition* (New York: Sheed and Ward, 1960), ch. 7, "Should There Be a Law?" pp. 155–174, and J. Leon Hooper, ed., *Bridging the Sacred and the Secular: Selected Writings of John Courtney Murray, S.J.* (Washington, D.C.: Georgetown University Press, 1994), "Memo to Cardinal Cushing concerning Contraception Legislation," pp. 81–86. Murray also treats this distinction in his notes to the Second Vatican Council's *Declaration on Religious Freedom*, in *The Documents of Vatican II*, ed. Walter M. Abbott and Joseph Gallagher (New York: America Press, 1966), esp. p. 686, note 20.

justice spells out the minimal requirements of the solidarity that is a prerequisite for lives lived in dignity. The requirements of justice establish a floor below which social solidarity cannot fall without doing serious harm to some of society's members.

The understanding of justice held by Thomas Aquinas and the later Catholic tradition can clarify this point. For Aquinas, the premier moral virtue is justice, which directs a person's actions toward the good of fellow human beings. Because human beings are simultaneously individual persons and participants in the common life of the civil community, virtuous citizens will seek not only their own individual good but also the larger good of the community.

Aquinas calls the obligations of justice that particular individuals or groups (such as firms) owe to other specifiable individuals "particular justice." Particular justice spells out obligations such as those of parents to their children, those that arise from promises, and those between the parties to a contract. An important form of particular justice is commutative justice, which requires reciprocity in exchanges among individuals. It calls for equivalence in what is gained and lost on both sides of an exchange. For example, commutative justice requires that employers pay their employees a wage that is equivalent to the value of the work the employees have done. If the employer fails to pay a wage with such value, the worker is not being treated in accord with the requirements of commutative justice and the employer is doing injustice.[30] Without such equivalence, the exchange will not be reciprocal and it can be questioned whether it is a free exchange at all.

The *quid pro quo* standard of commutative justice, however, does not give a complete picture of what justice requires. Determination of what constitutes an equivalent exchange of wages for work is dependent on an assessment of the social context within which the exchange takes place. Persons do not live as isolated individuals outside the institutionalized framework of the larger society. Their well-being is affected not only by the one-on-one exchanges they

[30] The issue of the meaning of a just wage is complex, since the determination of the dollar equivalent worth of a certain kind and amount of work is related to the complex issue of "just price." Also, since labor is not simply a commodity, the justice of wages has dimensions that go beyond those concerning the price of other goods. For an influential discussion of the issues that must be considered, see John A. Ryan, *A Living Wage*, revised and abridged edn. (New York: Macmillan, 1920), esp. chap. 3, "A Personal Living Wage."

enter into but also by the way the surrounding framework is organized and structured. This social framework in fact influences their
ability to engage in certain kinds of exchanges and can enhance or
diminish their freedom when they do. For justice to be done, therefore, the impact of these larger conditions of social interaction must
be assessed.

The issue of justice in wages was the historical issue that brought
these larger institutional and social dimensions of justice to the
fore in Catholic thought in the late nineteenth and early twentieth
centuries. Wage justice is still a very live issue today, especially in
current debates about minimum wages in the United States and
about sweatshop working conditions in some factories in developing
countries. But the way the larger social framework enters into an
understanding of justice goes beyond the question of wages and
sheds light on how solidarity is crucial to addressing the urban –
suburban divide.

Consider an inner-city resident who has been unemployed for a
long time and is no longer eligible for welfare support. This person's
dire straits could well lead to accepting wages well below the level
that commutative justice would require, since the alternative is no
income at all. On one level, an agreement to accept such wages
might appear to be entered into freely. But the worker's condition of
extreme vulnerability means that such a wage agreement would be
under immense pressure from the force of circumstances. It would
certainly not be an agreement between two persons with equal
freedom and agency. For this reason the reciprocity that is an essential dimension of commutative justice would not be present. The
reciprocity presumed by commutative justice cannot be present
among agents whose points of entry into an exchange is marked
by radical differences in power or vulnerability. In fact, it is impossible to determine whether the wages and the work exchanged
in such a context are in fact equal, since very low wages will be
subjectively worth much more to a person in extreme need than
to someone who is reasonably well off. A person who is well fed
would not likely be willing to work for more than a short time for
another loaf of bread. On the other hand, someone on the edge
of starvation would almost certainly be willing to work around the
clock for the same loaf. Michael Walzer calls the wage agreement

by someone in the latter situation an "exchange born of desperation."[31]

It is impossible, therefore, to determine whether a wage is just simply by virtue of the fact that it has been agreed to. Pope Leo XIII's 1891 encyclical *Rerum Novarum* argued that there is a demand of justice "more imperious and more ancient than any bargain." Justice requires that the worker's fundamental needs be taken into account when determining the fairness of wages. Injustice is being done if "through necessity or fear of a worse evil, the workman accepts harder conditions because an employer or contractor will give him no better."[32] The power relations operative in the social context of an exchange must be considered before determining that the agreement is just. Commutative justice alone cannot determine such matters.

The larger social conditions that must be considered are the concern of what Thomas Aquinas has called general justice and distributive justice. The US Catholic bishops use the terms contributive justice and distributive justice to describe the same realities. Figure 7.3 diagrams the three kinds of justice – commutative, contributive (or general), and distributive.[33] General justice for Aquinas is the virtue governing the duties of citizens to the common good of the larger community. In Thomas's words, "the virtue of a good citizen is general justice, whereby a person is directed to the common good."[34] The US Catholic bishops have named it "contributive justice," for it spells out the contribution to the common good that justice requires from individual people. The bishops state that this contribution includes working to produce the goods and services on which the well-being of society depends. Contributive

---

[31] Michael Walzer, *Spheres of Justice*, pp. 100 ff. Walzer draws the notion of "desperate exchanges" from Arthur Okun, *Equality and Efficiency: The Big Tradeoff* (Washington, D.C.: Brookings Institution, 1975), p. 20.

[32] Pope Leo XIII, *Rerum Novarum*, no. 34, in O'Brien and Shannon, eds., *Catholic Social Thought*, p. 31.

[33] See Thomas Aquinas, *Summa Theologiae* II-II, q. 58, arts. 5–7 and q. 61, arts. 1 and 2, and National Conference of Catholic Bishops, *Economic Justice for All*, nos. 69–71. I have recently learned that a similar though somewhat simpler diagram of the relation of these types of justice as understood by Aquinas was developed by Josef Pieper in his *The Four Cardinal Virtues: Prudence, Justice, Fortitude, Temperance*, trans. Richard Winston, *et al.* (New York: Harcourt, Brace, and World, 1965), p. 113.

[34] Thomas Aquinas, *Summa Theologiae* II-II, q. 58, art. 6.

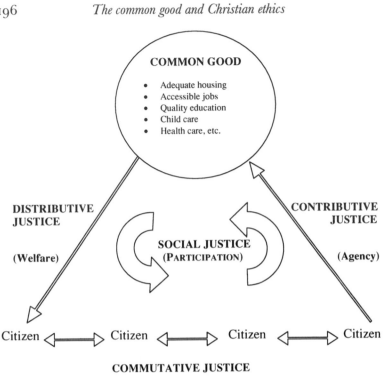

Figure 7.3.

justice requires that citizens be active members of the community, using their agency not only for their own good but for the good of the community as well. But they also suggest that contributive justice calls citizens to act in ways that lead to meeting the basic material needs of their fellow citizens, to the generation of jobs for the unemployed, to overcoming patterns of discrimination and exclusion, to the support of environmental quality, and to building up the general sense of community in society as a whole. Thus Figure 7.3 lists several social needs that are particularly relevant to the plight of the urban poor as elements of the common good. These include adequate housing, accessible jobs, quality education, child care, adequate health care, as well as other fundamental goods that are essential if citizens are to live in dignity. Contributive justice means that all citizens have a duty to help build up these aspects of social life in a way that is appropriate to their capacity to do so. These goods are all heavily dependent on how social institutions are structured. So contributive justice requires citizens to aid in the development of institutions that make employment, health care, and other social goods available to the members of society.

Distributive justice is, in turn, concerned with the way the members of society share in the goods that their life together makes possible. It deals with the allocation of the common good in a way that leads to the welfare or well-being of members. Aristotle and Aquinas both hold that this distribution need not lead to arithmetically equal shares for everyone. For example, distributive justice does not require that all incomes be of the same amount in dollars. Rather each person ought to share in the common good in a way that is proportionate to some relevant standard of desert.[35] The key question, of course, is what these standards of desert are. Michael Walzer has persuasively argued that the criterion of proportionality will be different for different kinds of goods.[36] For example, Nobel prizes should be given to individuals who have actually made important contributions to great literature or to world peace, and Olympic gold medals should be awarded to the fastest runners and most skillful divers. To distribute Nobel prizes or Olympic medals according to some other standard would vitiate their meaning. In a market economy, it is appropriate that income distributions be related to productivity and that rewards provide incentives for work needed to produce social well-being. In the distribution of goods such as health care, on the other hand, need is the suitable basis for proportionate shares. Those who are sick should get more than those who are well. Thus arithmetically equal distributions should not be expected for some goods. For other goods, however, strict arithmetical equality is called for. For example, the standard of "one person, one vote" is a condition for the recognition of the equal dignity of all citizens in a democratic society.

---

[35] Aristotle, *Nicomachean Ethics*, 1131 a and b; Thomas Aquinas, *Summa Theologiae* II-II, q. 61, arts. 1 and 2.

[36] In his *Spheres of Justice*, Walzer argues that "different social goods ought to be distributed for different reasons" (p. 6). My argument here fully agrees with this central thesis of Walzer's theory of justice, though it departs from him when he maintains that these reasons are always (or nearly always) culture-specific.

Some measure of equality is central to justice in all its forms. Disputes about whether this equality means arithmetical equality or proportional equality, and about the appropriate standard of proportionality, are the sources of most of the disputes about what justice requires in concrete cases. An adequate discussion of these disputes is impossible here. The task can be simplified, however, by noting the United States Catholic bishops' 1986 description of the bottom-line demands of justice: "*Basic justice demands the establishment of minimum levels of participation in the life of the human community for all persons.*" Persons can only live in dignity when they are capable of interacting with others in society, whether in the economic, political, or cultural spheres. This participation must be that of active citizens, for contributive justice requires that the members of society both possess and use their freedom and agency to build up the common good. Those citizens who fail to make active contributions in ways proportionate to their capacities fail to meet the minimal obligations of solidarity. Conversely, if the institutional arrangements prevailing in society prevent some persons from sharing in social goods to the level required by their dignity as members of the human community, the requirements of distributive justice are violated. Thus the negative requirements of a minimal level of solidarity are put this way by the US bishops: "The ultimate injustice is for a person or group to be treated actively or abandoned passively as if they were nonmembers of the human race."[37] These minimal requirements of solidarity establish a floor below which no one ought to fall in a just society.

This basic requirement of justice points to a minimal level of social solidarity that is required if persons are to be treated as members of society at all. The condition that results when this minimum is not being met can be called "marginalization" – exclusion from social life and from participation in the common good of the human community. It can be envisioned as in Figure 7.4.

There are many forms of unjust exclusion, as there are multiple dimensions of justice. Political marginalization occurs when people cannot vote, have their speech or association restricted, or face the straightforward repression of a tyrannical government.

37 National Conference of Catholic Bishops, *Economic Justice for all*, no. 77.

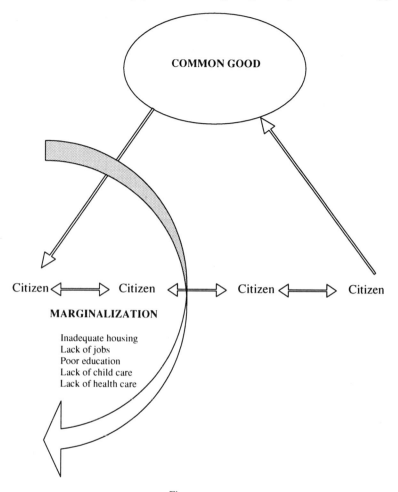

Figure 7.4.

Marginalization can also take economic forms. The poor of inner cities in the United States are *de facto* interdependent with the larger society in ways that make it impossible for them to find work even after searching for lengthy periods, perhaps even for a lifetime if they do not become so discouraged they give up trying. Poor educational resources deny them the opportunities needed to change their qualifications and to advance their children's abilities to enter into an economy that is bringing numerous benefits to the middle class. Basing access to quality education on incomes that have been made possible by education itself creates a vicious circle that excludes many in the inner city. The same kind of vicious circle arises when public education is funded by taxes tied to existing property values, for this means that poor neighborhoods will lack public funding for the educational efforts needed to change the environment they live in. Urban sprawl and restrictive zoning regulations reinforce this cycle. They strengthen the political boundaries between city and suburb that make it nearly impossible for the urban poor to challenge these realities. In other words, the urban poor are effectively marginalized. They are implicitly told by the community: we don't need your talent, we don't need your initiative, we don't need *you*.[38] This marginalization is less tied to race today than in past American history. This is one of the more encouraging developments of recent American history. But a sizable group of citizens continues to be excluded from the common good to the degree required by their dignity as members of society. This is an injustice that must be righted.

THE COMMON GOOD OF A METROPOLITAN COMMUNITY

Meeting the minimal demands of justice for all citizens, therefore, requires lowering the structural and economic barriers that prevent the inner-city poor from sharing in the common good of their larger metropolitan areas. As urban economist Alice Rivlin has put it, the centers of many US metropolitan areas have become the holes in the donuts of suburban prosperity.[39] Reducing the barriers between suburban affluence and urban poverty will require concerted work by citizens, acting precisely as citizens. It calls for efforts to reshape the social and political frameworks of metropolitan areas.

---

[38] See the documentation provided in *ibid*, chap. 3. The bishops' numbers are for 1986, but the situation is very similar today.

[39] Alice Rivlin, "The Challenge of Affluence," Adam Smith Award Lecture, National Association of Business Economists (September 11, 2000), 10. Available on the website of the Brookings Institution at http://www.brook.edu/es/urban/speeches/challengesofaffluence.pdf (downloaded July 10, 2001).

It is therefore a matter of social justice rather than fairness in the one-on-one exchanges governed by commutative justice. Social justice is a much used but rarely defined term. John Rawls describes it in a helpful way when he says that social justice governs "the basic structure of society," that is, the major political, economic, and social institutions that determine the division of advantages from social cooperation.[40] In the terminology used here, social justice requires an overall institutional framework that will enable people both to participate actively in building up the common good and to share in the benefits of the common good (see Figure 7.3). Social justice for cities, therefore, concerns the contours of the institutions shaping metropolitan economic, political, and cultural life. It requires a coordinated pursuit of both contributive and distributive justice through the major institutions of the metropolitan area as a whole. It will make demands on individuals, for individual people must contribute to the creation and maintenance of metropolitan institutions that are just. It will also benefit individual people, for socially just institutions enable individuals to have a just share in the larger metropolitan achievements. For social justice to become a reality, however, the social frameworks that enable individuals to contribute to and benefit from these community attainments must themselves be just.

The "subject" of social justice, therefore, is the major institutions that enhance or impede people's participation in creating and benefiting from the common good. To bring justice to the urban poor, metropolitan-wide institutions must be reformed so that the barriers to their participation are reduced. The large metropolitan areas of the United States have been the principal economic engines of the American economic success of recent years. Indeed, many metro-regions in the United States have economies that are larger than most of the countries in the world. For example, the economy of the New York metropolitan area is larger than Australia's, the Los Angeles metro-economy is larger than that of the Netherlands, Chicago's larger than Taiwan's, Argentina's, or Russia's.[41] The way

[40] John Rawls, *A Theory of Justice*, p. 7.
[41] United States Conference of Mayors, *US Metro Economies: The Engines of America's Growth, A Decade of Prosperity* (Lexington, MA: DRI-WEFA, Inc., 2001). Available at http://www.usmayors.org/citiesdrivetheeconomy/index3.html (downloaded July 11, 2001).

these regional resources are shared by residents should be determined, in part, by a standard of proportional equality. Those who contribute more to the common good can justly expect to benefit from it to a greater degree. But social justice requires more than quid pro quo. It also calls for all members of the community to be treated in accord with their dignity as members of a human community. This means recognizing that the ability to contribute is significantly shaped by the structures of community interdependence. For example, during the recent boom years in the United States the number of homeless people requiring emergency shelter has grown. The same is true of the number of hungry people needing food assistance, both in short term emergencies and over long periods of time. Many of these homeless and hungry people are children, and the chief causes of their need include the low-paying jobs, high housing costs, and unemployment faced by their parents.[42] The parents themselves face major institutional obstacles in their efforts to overcome their plight.

No one who is a citizen of a functioning community should be relegated to the sidelines of social interaction in this way. Poor people who are unemployed, inadequately housed, and undereducated in American inner cities are not part of a society that can be called a commonwealth. This marginalization of the inner-city poor is one measure of how far short the metropolitan areas of the United States are falling from being communities whose citizens are treated with the respect they deserve. The willingness of the well-off to tolerate such conditions and even take actions that perpetuate them shows how far the larger citizenry of the United States is from an effective commitment to the common good. When important economic and social institutions create barriers to basic levels of participation for some people, these institutions must be altered.

Making such changes will itself be a social project, especially when those who are excluded are powerless to change them by themselves. Such institutional transformation is precisely what is called for in the large metropolitan areas of the United States today.

---

[42] United States Conference of Mayors, "A Status Report on Hunger and Homelessness in America's Cities" (December, 2000). Available at
http://www.usmayors.org/uscm/hungersurvey/hunger2001.pdf
(downloaded December 16, 2001).

These institutions set the context for the creation and distribution of the goods of education, housing, and public safety. They raise class barriers that prevent the poor of the inner city from sharing to a minimally adequate level in goods that are readily available in the larger metropolitan region. These institutional barriers need to be challenged in the name of the basic requirements of social solidarity, the requirements of justice. Social justice, therefore, calls for action to lower the walls dividing the urban poor from the suburban middle class.

Efforts to overcome these barriers will have to take multiple forms. Bruce Katz, the director of the Brookings Institution's Center on Urban and Metropolitan Policy, has suggested a number of steps that could form a new urban agenda in the United States. Among the steps he proposes are the following. Government policies should seek to level the playing field between old city centers and new suburbs, for example, by directing funds toward affordable housing in cities and toward transportation systems that discourage sprawl and encourage the rebuilding of urban infrastructure. Poor working people and their families should have greater access to health care and child care, should be enabled to reconnect to the economic mainstream through means such as an increased earned income tax credit, and where necessary receive support through community health centers, Head Start programs for children, and community development agencies. To further overcome the urban – suburban divide, support for housing programs should be provided on a metropolitan-wide basis and should rely on regionally connected non-profit groups (religious and secular) that can link needy people to the jobs they lack. Urban schools need to be substantially improved or "fixed," but within the context of other proposed initiatives that look beyond schools alone to the neighborhoods and regions the schools serve.[43]

The policy initiatives that are needed are certainly a legitimate matter for debate among citizens. From the viewpoint of a public philosophy that takes the common good seriously, however, the need to address these issues is poignantly evident. When the

[43] Bruce Katz, "Enough of the Small Stuff: Toward a New Urban Agenda," *Brookings Review* 18, no. 3 (Summer, 2000), 4–9.

cumulative effect of the education, housing, transportation, land use, tax, and welfare policies puts minimally decent housing beyond the reach of many among the urban poor, a downward spiral of degradation is set in motion in inner-city neighborhoods that wounds the entire metropolitan region. It should also not be surprising that many who face such barriers simply give up. So all lose, especially the poor, when divisions between middle-class and core urban neighborhoods are as deep as they are in many of the metropolitan areas of the United States today. A public philosophy of the common good can set the direction for reversing this cycle.

Two parts of such a new urban agenda deserve special attention because of their current political visibility – education and the role of "faith-based" organizations in responding to the plight of the urban poor. The funding of education on a town-by-town basis from taxes on the assessed value of residential property also contributes to deepening the divisions between the city and suburb, between poor and middle-class neighborhoods. The glaring disparities in funding for education among towns and cities have recently stimulated a number of initiatives to attain greater equality on a state-wide basis. Such initiatives have begun to redress the inequality of funding for public education among cities and suburbs. They are therefore valuable steps toward overcoming the marginalization of the urban poor in the sphere of education.

Nevertheless, it is also clear that these initiatives have not significantly improved the quality of education available to the inner-city poor. In the face of the continuing inadequacy of the education available to the poor, new initiatives have been proposed, such as charter schools and public funding of basic education through vouchers for private and parochial schools. These hold considerable promise of improving the education available to the urban poor.[44] In fact there is something close to a consensus today that urban Catholic parochial schools succeed in bringing real educational advancement to inner-city children where urban public schools fail. This success in enabling the poor to participate in the common good of the larger community arises at least in part

[44] See Joseph P. Viteritti, *Choosing Equality: School Choice, the Constitution, and Civil Society* (Washington, D.C.: Brookings Institution Press, 1999).

from parochial school commitment to creating a strong sense of community among students, teachers, and staff. The educational philosophy of these parochial schools starts from a conviction that all children can flourish in an educational community that treats them as their equal dignity deserves. This commitment to equality leads parochial schools to make intellectually challenging demands on all their students, both poor and non-poor. An educational philosophy that links the worth of the person and the common good in community seems to be a kind of self-fulfilling prophecy. It can bring students a sense of hope that marginalization is not their fate. It thus enables them to become active participants in the larger community in a way those who face despair never will.[45]

This kind of educational philosophy raises strong questions not only for other educational philosophies but also for the live-and-let-live ethos that sustains the urban – suburban divide. If translated to the metropolitan level, such a philosophy would challenge the political and moral barriers that put urban and suburban education in effectively different worlds. This suggests that policy initiatives to overcome these boundaries – whether through voucher plans or metropolitan-wide reform of public education or both – should be guided by a philosophy that acknowledges that respect for equality and pursuit of the common good are allies, not alternatives. This will require a widely held view that justice requires a solidarity that reaches across existing class and caste divisions to include all those in the wider metropolitan region. Only such a conviction about the importance of the wider good can generate the sustained concern needed to transform educational institutions so that fewer of the children in metropolitan areas are simply left out.

In the United States, of course, the much disputed matter of the appropriate relation between church and state raises significant constitutional questions about such public support for religious schools. This constitutional matter will not be addressed here. But at least this much can be said from the viewpoint of a common good-based stance. The United States is virtually unique among

---

[45] See Anthony S. Bryk, Valerie E. Lee, Peter B. Holland, *Catholic Schools and the Common Good* (Cambridge, MA: Harvard University Press, 1993), and Terence H. McLaughlin, Joseph O'Keefe and Bernadette O'Keefe, eds., *The Contemporary Catholic School: Context, Identity, and Diversity* (London/Washington, D.C.: Falmer Press, 1996), esp. essays by Anthony Bryk, Bruce S. Cooper, and Richard Pring.

Western democracies in its insistence that religious freedom implies refusal to provide government funding for religiously connected elementary and secondary schools.[46] If one thinks that the sharp division between the private and public spheres is one of the major pathologies threatening American culture and political life today, envisioning private and public schools in similarly distinct spheres can be questioned. Abandoning such sharp distinctions could be the beginning of new wisdom on the reform of urban education today. But the abandonment of such sharp distinctions would also make clear that support for voucher programs is not a simple form of "privatization" of basic education. Means-tested voucher programs, for example, could only result from decisions by citizens that improvement of the quality of education available to the poor is a public responsibility and that vouchers are an effective way to provide it. This is far from a *laissez-faire* approach to meeting educational needs. It calls for a vision of the common good that includes the poor who are presently left out.

The social ministry of churches can also play a direct role in addressing the problems faced by those in poor urban centers. Religious communities bring spiritual resources to the poor that can help them overcome the despair that easily leads to giving up the fight to find a job or to overcome addiction.[47] These resources can also help preserve family stability and discourage teen pregnancy. They can aid those tempted to enter the world of drugs, gangs, and crime to find paths that lead to better lives for themselves and to better communities as well. In these ways, so-called "faith-based" approaches to the crisis in urban neighborhoods hold promise of making significant contributions to building up the common good of metropolitan areas by enabling the poor to help themselves in these ways. The churches can make important contributions to the common good of metropolitan areas by being agents of change in the thinking and action of their suburban middle-class members.

[46] See Charles L. Glenn, *Choice of Schools in Six Nations: France, Netherlands, Belgium, Britain, Canada, West Germany* (Washington, D.C.: US Department of Education, Office of Educational Research and Improvement, Programs for the Improvement of Practice, 1989).

[47] Mary Jo Bane, Brent Coffin, Ronald Thiemann, eds., *Who Will Provide? The Changing Role of Religion in American Social Welfare* (Boulder, CO: Westview Press, 2000); John DiIulio, "The Lord's Work: The Church and the 'Civil Society Sector,'" *Brookings Review* (Fall, 1997), 27–35; Joe Klein, "In God They Trust," *New Yorker* (June 16, 1997), 40–48.

Contact with the urban poor through volunteer service activities and through "twinning" of suburban and urban congregations can broaden the conviction among the middle class that enclaves and gated communities diminish their own lives as well as leading to deepening desperation in the city. Such initiatives are already well organized on a metropolitan-wide basis in a few cities in the United States and could have much greater impact if they were more broadly pursued.[48]

From the perspective required by social justice, however, such direct responses by the churches themselves are only a start. As Catholic Archbishop Roger Mahoney put it: "religious and community groups can touch hearts and change lives, but our efforts cannot replace needed government action to address the more than 40 million Americans without health care, the many children who go to bed hungry, and the millions of families who work every day, but cannot provide a decent future for their children. Our nation still needs significant public investments in health care, nutrition, child care and housing."[49] "Faith-based" responses to the problems facing core urban areas will be sorely inadequate if not accompanied by changes in the larger institutional context that is the occasion of so much despair and so much harmful behavior in central cities. The "principle of subsidiarity" indeed sees social vitality coming from less bureaucratic agents who are close to the grass roots and from the local level. But in his classic articulation of this principle, Pope Pius XI observed that "on account of changed conditions many things which were done by small associations in former times cannot be done now save by large associations."[50] Overcoming present obstacles to better lives for the urban poor calls for just this kind of expansion from local to wider metropolitan action, along with state and federal support for metropolitan approaches. Alleviation of urban poverty and its accompanying problems requires

[48] The Catholic church in Cleveland has developed a metropolitan-wide initiative of the kind envisioned here in its "Church in the City" program. Information on this initiative is available on the program's website at http://www.citc.org (downloaded July 12, 2001).
[49] Statement by Cardinal Roger Mahony, Chairman, United States Catholic Bishops Conference Domestic Policy Committee, "Faith-Based and Community Initiatives" (February 12, 2001). Available at http://www.nccbuscc.org/sdwp/mahony.htm (downloaded July 12, 2001).
[50] Pope Pius XI, *Quadragesimo Anno*, no. 79, in O'Brien and Shannon, eds., *Catholic Social Thought*, p. 60.

lowering the urban – suburban barriers that institutionally exclude the poor from sharing in a common good to which the middle class have ready access. Changing these structures will require political action by active citizens, both middle class and poor alike. Churches and other religious communities can make their greatest contributions to the common good by opening the minds of citizens on both sides of the urban – suburban walls to the possibility of a metropolitan community from which all will benefit. Such bridging could enhance the conscious level of solidarity that is the prerequisite of socially just institutions in metropolitan regions.

The proposals presented here are only illustrative of the directions that could be followed in seeking a metropolitan understanding of the common good. By themselves they suggest only the beginnings of the kind of solidarity that is needed for all to have better lives. The single greatest obstacle to such movement toward greater moral interdependence among the suburban middle class and the urban poor, however, is not the admitted sketchiness of these proposals. Rather it is the danger that many in the middle class will remain convinced that they have earned their good lives on their own and the urban poor are pretty much responsible for their own continuing poverty.

The cultural context of today's electronic and information-shaped society sets significant obstacles to the ethos of solidarity needed to support the metropolitan common good. A knowledge-based economy rewards those who can creatively negotiate the world of technology and information. Knowledge and technological creativity are resources that people possess in the inner domains of their consciousness. This easily leads to identifying the conditions of success with the "self" who possesses them. In earlier agricultural or industrial societies the resources needed for success, such as land or inherited money, were more easily distinguishable from the persons possessing them. Thus success was more readily seen as dependent on conditions and circumstances one did not create oneself. Today, however, people with greater knowledge and skill easily see themselves as earning greater rewards strictly on their own.[51] Well-educated members of the middle class come to regard

---

[51] For a provocative essay on the sense of entitlement among well-educated American youth, see David Brooks, "The Organization Kid," *Atlantic Monthly* 287, no. 4 (April, 2001), 40–54.

themselves as entitled to the kinds of lives they lead, while many of the urban poor are seen as undeserving.

Contrary to the cultural bias of our time, there is a long-standing Christian conviction, rooted in biblical, patristic, and medieval thought, that what one deserves can only be properly determined within a framework that takes the common good and the needs of the poor into account. Pope John Paul II has updated this traditional conviction in a way that addresses the realities of today's high-tech, knowledge-based economy. Entrepreneurial success is never a solo activity. It "requires the cooperation of many people working toward a common goal." Moreover, successful entrepreneurship depends on "the know-how, technology and skill" that has been handed on to those who become successful by many other people. Success is not generated by solitary creative acts.[52]

For example, the high-tech entrepreneurs who led the way in the creation of today's knowledge-based economy were dependent on the entire historical heritage of technological and scientific knowledge given them by others through education. The breakthroughs that generated the personal computer revolution came from the minds of very creative people, but these people did not act alone when they made their innovations. All the discoveries in physics, mathematics, and technology of previous history stood behind them and nourished them. Indeed, the elementary literacy and basic mathematical skills of these innovators was a gift that had been given them by their families, their teachers, and by the millennia-old intellectual and cultural traditions into which they were born. In this perspective, even the most creative individual initiatives leading to today's new economy were but tiny increments to the work of an extensive community of other persons stretching back through human history. Technological creativity and the development of new knowledge are impossible unless an innovative thinker has received vast intellectual resources he or she had no role in creating. The common good contained in the heritage of a community is thus a precondition for even the most innovative breakthroughs.

If this dependence on communal resources is true of the most creative innovators in the new high-tech world, it is even more

[52] Pope John Paul II, *Centesimus Annus*, no. 32, in O'Brien and Shannon, *Catholic Social Thought*, p. 462.

obviously true in the case of ordinary middle-class suburbanites. They have not created their successful lives on their own. John Paul II writes that the work and enterprise of every human being depends on two inheritances: "the inheritance of what is given to the whole of humanity in the resources of nature and the inheritance of what others have already developed on the basis of those resources." In productive activity persons never act independently. There is always a element of dependence: "dependence on the Giver of all the resources of creation and also on other human beings, those to whose work and initiative we owe the perfected and increased possibilities of our own work."[53] Successful middle-class suburbanites will significantly misunderstand themselves if they overlook all the ways the communities they live in have enabled them to become who they are. They will equally misunderstand the plight of the poor who live in the depressed neighborhoods in the nearby city. Only when present-day Americans come to recognize that all people are dependent on larger communities will the solidarity of a morally interdependent, socially just community become possible. In John Paul II's words, such recognition of mutual dependence is the moral precondition for the development of "ever more extensive working communities" bound together by "by a progressively expanding chain of solidarity."[54] Resources of knowledge and skill are not the purely private possession of anyone. They are meant to be at the service of others. They should be used to open up new avenues of participation and to lower the walls that divide the inner city from the world of the middle class.

Thus the development of a truly metropolitan community in which the walls between poor and middle class have been lowered calls for the recognition that the human capacity for intelligence can only be put to creative use when solidarity with others attains at least a rudimentary level. This is the principal cultural challenge that must be faced in the effort to address the plight of the poor in American cities. It is a challenge to which the tradition of the common good can make a distinctive and perhaps unique contribution. Indeed, the fact that the tradition of reflection on

---

[53] Pope John Paul II, *Laborem Exercens*, no. 13, in O'Brien and Shannon, *Catholic Social Thought*, p. 369.
[54] *Ibid.*, nos. 32 and 43, pp. 463, 472.

the common good is so closely connected with the religious communities in the American context today suggests that the main contribution of these communities to overcoming urban poverty will be by directly addressing this cultural challenge. The Roman Catholic church is certainly the single most significant bearer of the tradition of reflection on the common good, but it is certainly not the only place such ideas are present. We have argued above that the Catholic tradition itself seeks common ground with those from other traditions precisely because of its commitment to a good that is genuinely common. Such efforts to find common ground by engaged dialogue across religious traditions suggest a similar effort at engagement across the walls that divide metropolitan areas on class and caste lines.

America's cities, therefore, are called to a new awareness that all their citizens share one another's fates. This awareness can grow both from Christian theological roots and from a reasoned reflection on experience that is fully accessible to those who are not Christians. A public philosophy grounded on such an awareness will not answer every question that arises in efforts to address the problems of the urban poor in the United States today. It will not provide detailed guidance in every policy debate. But it could set the direction such efforts and policies must follow. This is the direction of greater solidarity and of active pursuit of the common good in a metropolitan community.

CHAPTER EIGHT

The global common good

The increased interactions among the peoples of diverse nations of the world today requires a revitalized understanding of the common good they share. It also calls for the expansion of more traditional conceptions of the common good beyond the borders of individual nation-states. In an interdependent world the idea of the common good must take on a more universal definition. At the same time the institutions that can help both define and pursue this global common good are notably underdeveloped. The tension between the need for a vision of globally shared goods and the lack of institutions to seek such goods sets the problem to be addressed in this final chapter. The question has three dimensions. First, some signs will be sketched of a growing awareness that attaining good human lives is a shared task that cuts across national boundaries. Building on what has already been said about this in chapter 2, the first part of this chapter will also note some of the factors that make visions of a universal community simultaneously necessary and difficult to attain. Second, a normative understanding of the common good and its implications for the just creation and distribution of goods that reach across the boundaries of particular communities such as nation-states and cultural groupings will be presented. Third, some more practical proposals will be advanced for how this normative understanding can provide bearings for social and political activities in an increasingly interdependent world. These proposals touch on the way citizens understand themselves and the communities they belong to. They also have implications for the development of institutions that will enable citizens to act upon the normative vision proposed. It is hoped that the vision of the global common good proposed might guide both thought and action in ways that lead to better lives for all the world's people today, especially for those who bear the heaviest burdens of suffering. The goal is not to set forward an ideal that solves all world-wide problems in some grand thought experiment. Rather it is to provide direction toward a significantly improved state of well-being for the earth's people in ethically challenging but feasible ways.[1] Movement in such a direction is itself a key part of the global common good in our moment in history.

THE BIRTHPANGS OF A TRANSNATIONAL COMMON GOOD

Emerging patterns of transnational interaction and interdependence call for reflection on the question "what kind of community makes the good life possible?" The term "globalization" has been much used in recent years to describe the changing contexts within which people seek good lives. It is rarely defined, however. Robert Keohane and Joseph Nye provide some useful precision by describing globalization as the increase in networks of interdependence among people at multicontinental distances.[2] This description highlights the fact that the phenomenon of globalization involves complex *networks* of interdependence, not single strands of interconnection such as increased trade or increased communication via new electronic media.[3] As was suggested in the discussion of American public opinion in chapter 2, evaluations of globalization are significantly influenced by which strand of the growing global network is at issue. Before proposing an explicitly normative approach to the transnational common good, therefore, it will be useful to distinguish some of the emergent elements in this network and to note some common evaluative responses to them.

[1] This objective is similar to what John Rawls has called a "realistic utopia," though the substance of what is proposed here is different from what Rawls thinks is needed and possible. See Rawls, *The Law of Peoples*, pp. 11–23.
[2] Robert O. Keohane and Joseph S. Nye, "Globalization: What's New? What's Not? (And So What?)" *Foreign Policy* (Spring, 2000), 104–119, at 105.
[3] For an in-depth analysis of the diverse dimensions of globalization, see David Held, Anthony McGrew, David Goldblatt, and Jonathan Perraton, *Global Transformations: Politics, Economics and Culture* (Stanford, CA: Stanford University Press, 1999). Similar though not identical dimensions of globalization are distinguished and analyzed in Joseph S. Nye and John D. Donahue, eds., *Governance in a Globalizing World* (Washington, D.C.: Brookings Institution Press, 2000), Part One, "Trends in Globalization."

First, there are economic aspects of globalization. International trade, the extraordinarily rapid movement of international capital, and the growth of transnational business corporations all have very large impacts on the lives of most people around the globe today. This impact leads many, especially those who are not in the economic elite, to conclude that they are losing control of their economic fate. There is little doubt that recent economic developments have been accompanied by both increased poverty and increased inequality in developing countries, especially in Africa. The number of people world-wide with incomes of less than $1 per day rose from 1,183 million in 1987 to 1,198 million in 1998.[4] In addition, the policies of international institutions like the World Trade Organization, the International Monetary Fund, and the World Bank continue to put constraints on the economic decisions of the governments of developing countries. They do this through the conditions they lay down concerning trade, loans, debt relief, and other forms of financial assistance. Thus at Seattle, Prague, and Genoa, highly visible critics charge these international institutions with contributing to inequality, poverty, and suffering in the developing world. These charges are justified, in my judgment, when directed at the Structural Adjustment Programs of the 1980s and early 1990s and at WTO trade norms that would restrict poor countries' access to drugs for the treatment or prevention of diseases such as AIDS and malaria. There are some hopeful signs, however, that such policies are beginning to change, particularly in the World Bank's efforts to formulate a Comprehensive Development Framework over the past several years and in its most recent World Development Report entitled "Attacking Poverty." In the view of economists Ravi Kanbur and Nora Lustig, the Report's principal authors, there are some notable signs that equality is reappearing on the development agenda.[5]

Critiques of globalization that identify it with a form of external control that has negative effects on many of the citizens of one's own country are in line with the classical "realist" analysis

[4] See The World Bank, *World Development Report 2000/2001*, Table 1.1, p. 23.
[5] See Ravi Kanbur and Nora Lustig, "Why Is Inequality Back on the Agenda?" Department of Agricultural, Resource, and Managerial Economics Working Paper 99-14 (Ithaca, NY: Cornell University Press, 1999). Kanbur and Lustig had oversight of the drafting of the World Bank's *World Development Report 2000/2001*.

of how people respond to international affairs. The realist model predicts that people will react in terms of their country's national self-interest. So those who see globalization as having a negative impact on some or all of the people of their country will resist it. This response is widespread in the developing world, where globalization is often simply identified with unjust exclusion of poor countries from influence on powerful economic forces. It should be noted, however, that this realist response is not confined to developing countries. In the United States, US labor unions are among the strongest critics of globalization. Union members see the rapid movement of capital as serious threats to their jobs and wages when US corporations move their plants to countries where wages are low. Perhaps ironically, this pursuit of self-interest has recently led US labor organizations to advocate higher wages, better working conditions, and stronger protection of the rights of workers in developing countries. Indeed AFL-CIO President John Sweeney sees an alliance emerging among "workers, environmentalists, religious leaders, and students." In Sweeney's reading, this alliance is based on new linkages among the interests of American workers, workers in poor countries, and environmental concerns. In his words, US labor is "not against globalization, but for a new internationalism" that advocates "workers' rights and human rights and consumer and environmental protections in the global economy."[6] This suggests that new intercontinental economic connections can lead to new solidarities across borders. If this prognosis is correct, some aspects of the new international economic linkages will call forth very different evaluative responses by those concerned with transnational solidarity than some of the policies proposed by the WTO or the Structural Adjustment Programs of the IMF in the recent past. This irony points to how crucial it is to be clear about the meaning of globalization before attempting to evaluate it.

A second dimension of globalization is environmental and health related. Environmental degradation is a serious transnational threat as well as a local and regional one. The environmental well-being of every country is linked with that of most or even all

---

[6] See the Remarks by AFL-CIO President John J. Sweeney, World Economic Forum, Davos, Switzerland (January 28, 2001). Available on the Internet at http://www.aflcio.org/publ/speech2001/sp0128.htm (downloaded April 16, 2001).

other countries to a significant degree. For example, CO_2 emissions from the burning of fossil fuels in developed or newly industrialized countries as well as the cutting of trees in the rain forests of tropical regions of developing countries both seriously threaten to change the climate of the entire globe. In a parallel way, the transmission of infectious diseases such as AIDS across national boundaries has also grown as economic integration has increased. A recent United Nations Development Program study has called both the protection of the environment and the protection of human health "global public goods."[7] The UNDP study uses a standard economic definition of a public good as one that free market exchanges will not generate on their own. These goods are both global and public in the sense that any one nation can enjoy them only when other nations also enjoy them in some proportional way. David Held has described this as the growth of "overlapping communities of fate."[8] The people of an individual nation share in a global public good precisely because their nation is part of a global network in which that good is present. In an analogous way, we can speak of global public bads. For example, climate change, the transmission of diseases, or the proliferation of weapons of mass destruction are negative realities that reach across multicontinental distances. Thus important goods and bads in the domains of the environment and health are increasingly global. A judgment on which aspects of globalization are either desirable or undesirable will depend on relative assessment of the possibilities of attaining these common goods, the threats posed by these common bads, and the way these goods and bads are interrelated with each other. In either case, normative judgments with important policy implications must be made on the basis of increasingly global information. This might itself be called the globalization of the task of ethical inquiry.

These environmental and health-related dimensions of globalization are challenging the adequacy of a state-centered model of the international order. They widen the definition of the community that is relevant to the well-being of the individuals we care about. This widening is necessary because the national interest as

---

[7] See Kaul, Grunberg, and Stern, eds., *Global Public Goods*, especially the essays on environment and health.
[8] Held, *et al.*, *Global Transformations*, p. 445.

understood in traditional realism does not correspond to the way the threats of environmental degradation, disease transmission, and weapons proliferation cut across national boundaries. Such issues evoke attitudes and normative stances that can be called cosmopolitan, in which the focus of concern is not limited to the well-being of fellow citizens of a nation-state. These *de facto* forms of interdependence expand the notion of interest beyond national borders.[9] To the degree this occurs, linking the terms "national" and "interest" becomes increasingly incongruous. The globalization of concern and response would be recognized as a precondition of the well-being of all. This gives the term "globalization" a considerably more positive ethical meaning than that heard in protests against IMF or World Trade Organization policies.

Third, there is an explicitly political dimension of globalization. Complex challenges to the sovereignty of nation-states are being raised by the idea of universal human rights, which has been playing an increasing role on the world stage since the Universal Declaration of Human Rights was proclaimed by the UN General Assembly in 1948. The Universal Declaration has become the charter document of an international human rights regime composed of overlapping global, regional, national, and non-governmental institutions. These range from the UN High Commissioner for Human Rights and the International Criminal Tribunals for Rwanda and Yugoslavia, to the European and Inter-American Courts of Human Rights, to the US State Department's Bureau of Democracy, Human Rights, and Labor, to NGOs such as Amnesty International and Human Rights Watch. These institutions, often working together, have raised increasingly strong challenges to the sovereignty of states by seeking to hold them accountable to norms that reach well beyond their national interests as traditionally understood. Such challenges were evident in the International Criminal Tribunal for Rwanda's first-ever genocide conviction in September 1998 and again when Slobodan Milosović was handed over to The Hague in 2001 to be tried for crimes against humanity

---

[9] For discussions of cosmopolitanism that hark back to both the Stoics and Kant, see Martha Nussbaum, *Cultivating Humanity*, chap. 2, "Citizens of the World;" Nussbaum, "Patriotism and Cosmopolitanism," in Joshua Cohen, ed., *For Love of Country: Debating the Limits of Patriotism* (Boston: Beacon Press, 1996), pp. 2–17; R. J. Vincent, *Human Rights and International Relations* (Cambridge: Cambridge University Press, 1986), pp. 118–123.

during the horrors that occurred in Bosnia. The efforts to establish a standing International Criminal Court seek to institutionalize such accountability for grave human rights abuses in a permanent international setting. The effectiveness of these and similar efforts to protect and enforce human rights, of course, falls short of the legal guarantees available within the state boundaries of constitutional democracies. Nevertheless, the evolving international human rights regime directly challenges state sovereignty as an absolute limit on political accountability. This challenge is a legal-political one. More important in the long run, though, is the way it stretches cultural understandings of the scope of moral responsibility.

The political aspects of globalization also include reconsideration of the legitimacy of humanitarian intervention to protect people threatened by genocide, ethnic cleansing, forced migration, internal displacement, or other grave human rights violations. Such proposals raise apprehension on two fronts. Less powerful nations fear that legitimizing intervention can open the door to new forms of hegemonic control of the weak by the strong.[10] Such concerns have been at the core of the Organization of African Unity's historically strong commitment to the preservation of the sacredness of national boundaries. This OAU commitment expresses legitimate suspicions by formerly colonized peoples about any intervention in the name of "civilization" or other putatively humanitarian concerns. On the other hand, some analysts in the developed world see support for humanitarian intervention as confusing foreign policy with "social work."[11] This argument exemplifies the classic realist view that national self-interest, not altruistic concern, should regulate international affairs.

Despite these objections, UN Secretary General Kofi Annan has argued for a new assessment of state sovereignty in light of new forms of interdependence across borders. In Annan's words:

State sovereignty, in its most basic sense, is being redefined – not least by the forces of globalization and international co-operation. States are now widely understood to be instruments at the service of their peoples, and not vice versa . . . When we read the [United Nations] charter today, we

---

[10] See J. Bryan Hehir, "Military Intervention and National Sovereignty: Recasting the Relationship," in Moore, ed., *Hard Choices*, pp. 29–54.
[11] Michael Mandelbaum, "Foreign Policy as Social Work," 17. See Stephen John Stedman, "The New Interventionists."

are more than ever conscious that its aim is to protect individual human beings, not to protect those who abuse them.[12]

This mode of thinking conceives of human beings as, first, members of the world-wide human community with rights that derive from their humanity as such, and second, as members of the communities of existing nation-states. This kind of argument is in effect an appeal for the globalization of citizenship – for granting membership in the human community a higher value than citizenship in a particular nation-state, at least in extreme situations where humanity itself is threatened. Again, we see that the moral significance of globalization depends on which dimension of the global network we focus upon.

These economic, environmental, and political matters are but three of the strands being woven into the emerging network of globalization. There are others, such as the technological links of the Internet and the increasing interactions on the level of culture. Cultural globalization itself has very different manifestations, such as the influence of popular music on youth world-wide and the increasingly visible influence of world religions on politics. As examples of this global impact of religion one need only point to the present role of Islam in world politics and to the influence of Pope John Paul II's travels in locations as diverse as the Middle East, the Philippines, Central Europe, and Latin America. Globalization is a many-dimensional reality; it cannot be reduced to a single line of analysis such as the economic without distorting it in ways that will lead to serious misunderstanding. This many-dimensioned reality raises a host of new questions about how we define the community within which good lives can be attained.

This is a formidable agenda. At its heart is the question of how diverse forms of human association will help make good lives possible for the human beings who have no choice but to live on the same earth together. Today, as never before, secession from an interconnected world is not a live option. The choices concern what kinds of global interdependence are worthy of commitment and how these should be related to those that exist within states and regions. Decisions must also be made about how global connections should be related to bonds that are not geographically defined, such

---

[12] Kofi A. Annan, "Two Concepts of Sovereignty," *The Economist* (September 18, 1999), 49.

as those formed by religion, ethnicity, economic interest, or commitment to normative values like human rights or environmental protection. To adapt Aristotle's language, to secure the good for an interdependent world is a nobler and more divine task than to do so for a single neighborhood, city, or nation-state. But within such a world there must be space for less extensive forms of community as well. How to envision the shape of such an overlapping set of communities and the overlapping goods they make possible is the challenge raised by the globalized world whose birthpangs we are living through today.

WHAT KIND OF GLOBALIZATION?

NORMATIVE CONSIDERATIONS

Trans-border interconnections in the economic, environmental, and political domains are forms of interdependence that exist *de facto*. Protests against them arise because they are judged inadequate from the standpoint of ethical standards such as justice, fairness, or equality. These normative standards lead to the conclusion that there is something wrong with the institutional arrangements currently governing global interactions and with policies that affect quality of life for so many people. Such objections are directed toward existing patterns of interdependence that are marked by inequality, lack of reciprocity, and the marginalization of those with less power. The birthpangs of globalization thus raise challenging questions about how these *de facto* patterns of interdependence can be transformed. In the words of Pope John Paul II, they point to "the need for a solidarity which will take up interdependence and transfer it to the moral plane."[13] The question then becomes what normative standards the many strands of the global web of interaction should be held to.

One possibility is a cosmopolitan ethical vision of the pure type. In this view only one community is ethically relevant to global interaction: the world-wide community of all human beings as such. The shared good that can be achieved in this world-wide community trumps the well-being that can be attained in smaller or lesser

---

[13] Pope John Paul II, *Sollicitudo Rei Socialis*, no. 26, in O'Brien and Shannon, eds., *Catholic Social Thought*, p. 411.

communities. In such a pure form of cosmopolitanism, national, ethnic, religious, or other differences among people are subordinated to the humanity they share. If, however, this vision is pressed to mean that these differences are "morally irrelevant" it risks excessive generality and abstractness.[14] Cosmopolitanism can neglect the moral significance of local and particular relationships. If one is not at home in some concrete, particular place or community one cannot be said to have a home at all. In seeking to expand the circle of affection and commitment to the earth as a whole, it risks making everyone homeless. This is surely a significant limitation of the pure form of the cosmopolitan moral vision. Nevertheless, to criticize cosmopolitanism on these grounds without further qualifications will reinforce the unequal and non-reciprocal patterns of globalization that are evident today.

Fortunately, there are alternatives to both an abstract cosmopolitanism and a *status quo* acceptance of existing boundaries. Kwame Anthony Appiah has called one such alternative "rooted cosmopolitanism."[15] It is "rooted" because it affirms the importance of concrete relationships embedded in communities with particular traditions and particular social strengths and needs. It accepts cultural, religious, and gender differences among people as well as their economic and political situations as relevant in the development of moral standards for a globalizing world.[16] At the same time it is cosmopolitan in affirming the importance of these communal and social particularities not only for oneself and one's people but for all others as well. Thus it affirms the moral relevance of

---

[14] Martha Nussbaum uses the phrase "morally irrelevant" to describe national, religious, and other differences in "Patriotism and Cosmopolitanism," p. 5. Nussbaum, however, does grant some lesser legitimacy to the claims of less extensive communities.

[15] Kwame Anthony Appiah, "Cosmopolitan Patriots," in Cohen, ed., *For Love of Country*, pp. 21–29.

[16] Appiah defends the liberal state as a key means to overcoming the divisive effects of the "imagined" constructions of race, ethnicity, or nationhood. Nevertheless his argument about the direction poor African societies should move continues to stress the importance of the economic and social plight of African societies. Thus I take it that Appiah would affirm rootedness in these economic and social conditions as key to a normative African response to the issues of globalization. See his *In My Father's House: Africa in the Philosophy of Culture* (New York/Oxford: Oxford University Press, 1992), esp. chaps. 1, 7, 8. For a parallel though different argument see Michael Walzer's discussion of "reiterative universalism" in "Nation and Universe," in Grethe B. Peterson, ed., *The Tanner Lectures on Human Values*, vol. XI (Salt Lake City: University of Utah Press, 1990), pp. 507–556.

the common humanity of all people while avoiding an abstract idea of universal community that submerges differences in a stifling homogeneity.

This rooted cosmopolitanism thus respects and, indeed, celebrates differences among communities and peoples, but with a proviso. Communal particularities and different ways of organizing public life through government are to be accepted as long as they respect basic human rights. In Appiah's words, "So long as these differences meet certain ethical constraints – so long, in particular, as political institutions respect basic human rights – we are happy to let them be."[17] Appiah here is doubtless presuming something like the list of human rights contained in the UN Universal Declaration. This begs some hard questions, however, in the face of disputes about which rights belong on a list that applies in all cultures and about whether the notion of rights is itself compatible with all moral traditions. In order to affirm that the demands of the Universal Declaration can be applied to all societies without being oppressive, we must presume that there is a commonality among all persons even in the midst of their differences of nationality, citizenship, religion, gender, ethnicity etc. As Martha Nussbaum puts it in response to the critics of her cosmopolitian proposal, "Whatever else we are bound by and pursue, we should recognize, at whatever personal or social cost, that each human being is human and counts as the moral equal of every other."[18]

The understanding of justice discussed in the previous chapter shows that the affirmation of equality and human rights need not be rooted in an individualistic understanding of the human person. This understanding of justice leads to a conception of human rights as the minimum requirements of participation in community. Universal human rights, therefore, presume the existence of a moral community to which all humans belong. At the minimum, being treated justly means being treated as a member of this community and in accord with the common human dignity shared by all people. This has important implications for all domains of the thickening global network. The most fundamental forms of injustice on the global stage are those that marginalize people, countries, or cultures from at least minimal levels of active participation in the

[17] Appiah, "Cosmopolitan Patriots," p. 26.
[18] Nussbaum, "Reply," in Cohen, ed., *For Love of Country*, p. 133.

common goods that come into existence in the larger surrounding wholes.

Such unjust exclusion can take many forms. There is marginalization based on communal identity: exclusion from participating in the positive benefits of *de facto* interdependence on the grounds of ethnicity, culture, or religion. The most extreme forms of such exclusion are evident in the forced migration of refugees, internal displacement, ethnic cleansing, and the abomination of genocide. Less dramatic but still deeply unjust examples are economic policies that sustain or increase poverty, lack of education, no access to basic health care, and unemployment. When the world possesses the resources to address these deprivations but fails to do so, those who suffer the continuing deprivation are effectively marginalized. We implicitly tell them: "Your kind of people" do not count as members of the human community. This is the ultimate injustice, for it contradicts the most fundamental demand of justice that every member of the human family be treated as such. Injecting this vision of justice into the current debates about globalization could lead to action and policy that enhance solidarity on the multiple levels where it is lacking today. This is one of the chief contributions of a normative understanding of the common good in a globalizing world today.

The injustice of economic marginalization occurs when poor nations, such as many of those in sub-Saharan Africa, are trapped in a cycle of poverty by their debts to international financial institutions. In 1998, the countries of Africa paid more than four times as much to foreign creditors than they spent on health and education, while fewer than half of their children went to school.[19] This cycle is reinforced by the meager agricultural exports from developing countries caused by heavy subsidies to the agricultural sector in developed countries. A poor country caught in this cycle will be fated to remain at best on the edge of the global market. To be sure, markets and trade can be engines of improved well-being for those who already have access to them. But as Pope John Paul II has said, "The fact is that many people, perhaps the majority today, do not have the means which would enable them to take their place in an

---

[19] See Administrative Board of the United States Catholic Conference, "A Jubilee Call for Debt Forgiveness" (April 1999), sec. I. Available on the United States Catholic Bishops' Conference website, at http://www.nccbuscc.org/sdwp/international/adminstm.htm (downloaded July 24, 2001). This statement presents an overview of a common-good based approach to the indebtedness of developing countries.

effective and humanly dignified way within a productive system in which work is truly central . . . Thus, if not actually exploited, they are to a great extent marginalized; economic development takes place over their heads."[20] This exclusion from access to finance and markets leads to a lack of education and basic health care, which in turn makes it less likely that the people in many African countries will be able to enter into the networks of global interdependence on terms that respect their dignity. Forms of globalization that lead to such exclusion should be challenged from a normative perspective that sees the protection of human dignity and the achievement of social participation as two sides of the same coin.

This understanding of justice also calls for the development of global political institutions that will enable poor countries and their citizens to have greater voice when decisions are being made about indebtedness, world trade, and other forms of economic interdependence. As Robert Keohane and Joseph Nye have pointed out, such forums presently look like clubs whose members are limited to political and economic elites. Trade ministers meet at the World Trade Organization, finance ministers at the International Monetary Fund, and heads of the most developed countries at G8 summit meetings. Though these organizations are formally accountable to the states that are their members, they represent only certain constituencies within those states, frequently conduct their business in closed sessions, and operate as distant bureaucracies. Votes in these international agencies are often distributed in proportion to the wealth or budgetary contributions of the member states and sometimes non-members are not officially represented at all. This has been called "globalization's democratic deficit."[21] Control over the decisions of these international organizations by the people whose well-being they affect is at best attenuated and at worst non-existent.[22] Overcoming both the perceived and real

[20] Pope John Paul II, *Centesimus Annus*, no. 33, in O'Brien and Shannonu, eds., *Catholic Social Thought*, pp. 463–464.
[21] Joseph S. Nye, Jr., "Globalization's Democratic Deficit: How to Make International Institutions More Accountable," *Foreign Affairs* 80, no. 4 (July/August, 2001), 2–6.
[22] Robert O. Keohane, "International Institutions: Can Interdependence Work?" *Foreign Policy* 110 (Spring, 1998), 92. Keohane and Joseph Nye develop the "club" characterization somewhat more fully in their "Introduction" to Nye and Donahue, eds., *Governance in a Globalizing World*, esp. pp. 26–36.

aspects of this deficit is essential if a backlash against globalization is to be avoided. It is even more essential from the normative standpoint of the common good. If large blocs of the world's people have no effective voice in shaping the global institutions that fundamentally affect their well-being, they are not being treated as genuine members of the human moral community. Lack of active participation in shaping global institutions and policies can effectively reduce the majority of the world's population to the status of supplicants seeking generosity from richer and more powerful neighbors. New avenues for voice and agency, therefore, must be opened up if very large numbers of people are to share in the potential political and economic benefits of globalization. A normative understanding of social justice as requiring at least minimal participation in the common good, therefore, calls for greater transparency, openness, accountability, and access than exists today.

The need for more just economic and political participation in the common goods that are achieved globally in no way denies the importance of smaller communities with different traditions or that organize their social and political interaction in distinctive ways. As a form of agency, such participation builds upon the fact that diverse political or cultural communities have distinctive capacities, needs, and perspectives that enable them to make distinct contributions to the shaping of global common goods. A participatory understanding of social justice on the global level, therefore, is not an abstract or rootless type of cosmopolitanism. The principle of subsidiarity, classically presented in Catholic discussions of the common good, has direct relevance here. It has been increasingly employed to address the democratic deficit that has been a source of considerable concern in the European Union. This principle presumes that social vitality comes from communities with which people have ties of tradition, locality, or other forms of experienced connection. Indeed, these connections are sources of empowerment that enable people to act together in shaping a common life. Without such local or particularistic connections, the forces of globalization would quickly isolate individuals and further reduce their power to share in goods being developed across borders. So an appeal for social justice rooted in a vision of the global common good must not lead to the destruction of smaller local or cultural communities. It does not call for the abolition of ethnic, patriotic, religious, or cultural loyalties.[23]

The normative understanding of justice does, however, relativize these loyalties. It sets limits on what can be done in the name of distinctive traditions or polities. Respect for local, regional, ethnic, and religious distinctiveness cannot justify denial of the fundamental human dignity of outsiders or their exclusion from goods essential to this dignity. Thus social justice requires abstention from actions that exclude groups from active participation in the transnational common good and that global institutions avoid such exclusion as well. This common good-based understanding of justice also calls for action that goes beyond exclusion to active support for inclusion. Global policies and institutions ought to make it possible for all human beings to live in dignity under the circumstances of *de facto* interdependence that actually prevail.[24] The fundamental dignity and worth of human beings will not be secured simply by leaving people or particularist communities alone. The preservation of human dignity requires positive action in support of those who are vulnerable to *de facto* conditions of unequal and non-reciprocal interdependence. The basic demands of social justice, therefore, call for the development of institutions that make interdependence in solidarity a realistic possibility.

In other words, in a globalizing world there are social goods essential to the well-being of all people that can only be secured within positive forms of interdependence that stretch across traditional communal and national boundaries. Global institutions have a direct effect on whether these goods are achieved or not. Human dignity depends on being able to contribute actively to the

[23] For a discussion of the relevance of the principle of subsidiarity on the global level, see Pope John XXIII, *Pacem in Terris*, nos. 140–141, in O'Brien and Shannon, eds., *Catholic Social Thought*, pp. 153–154; and Pope John Paul II, Address to the Fiftieth General Assembly of the United Nations, New York (October 5, 1995), nos. 7–9. The latter document is avaliable on the website of the Holy See, at
http://www.vatican.va/holy_father/john_paul_ii/speeches/1996/documents/hf_jp-ii_spe_05101995_address-to-uno_en.html (downloaded July 25, 2001).

[24] For a persuasive argument that the classic distinction between negative and positive rights is an inadequate way of describing the relation between duties to avoid actions that violate human dignity, duties to protect people from such violations, and duties to aid people to live in dignity, see Henry Shue, *Basic Rights: Subsistence, Affluence, and US Foreign Policy* (Princeton, NJ: Princeton University Press, 1996), esp. pp. 51–60. A key to Shue's argument is the need to create institutions that support human dignity.

creation of these goods and on sharing in their distribution once they exist. This vision of a world-wide moral community, therefore, makes moral demands on the shape of global institutions. Pope John Paul II referred to these demands when he stated that "In practice, this means making solidarity an integral part of the network of economic, political and social interdependence that the current process is tending to consolidate. These processes call for rethinking international cooperation in terms of a new culture of solidarity."[25]

Such solidarity begins with a respect for distinctive communities and traditions that is often called tolerance. But it moves on to positive initiatives that will enable all people and communities to participate with dignity in the growing web of global interactions. It calls, then, for transformation of the prevailing global patterns of economic, political, and cultural interaction, not simply for tolerance of difference within the *status quo* institutional framework. The degree to which such transformation enables greater participation by groups that are marginalized in the present global order is thus a benchmark for assessing how well the common good of humanity as a whole is being achieved.[26] This shared good makes demands of justice on states, on interstate organizations both global and regional, on transnational agents such as corporations and NGOs, and on cultural groupings such as religious and ethnic communities. It requires that they act in ways that secure the fundamental human rights of all, where human rights are understood as the "minimum conditions for life in the [global] human community."[27]

More specifically, this normative understanding of justice has implications for what it means to say that the distinctiveness of diverse cultures and polities should be respected provided they respect the human rights of outsiders. For this conception of justice has important implications for the meaning of the full range of human rights. In the days of the recently ended Cold War, the West was largely

[25] Pope John Paul II, Message for World Day of Peace (January 1, 2000), no. 17. Available online at http://www.vatican.va/holy_father/john_paul_ii/messages/peace/documents/hf_jp-ii_mes_08121999_xxxiii-world-day-for-peace_en.html (downloaded July 24, 2001).

[26] The idea of a "benchmark" for the attainment of the common good is borrowed from Michael Novak, *Free Persons and the Common Good* (Lanham, MD: Madison Books, 1989), pp. 111–113. It will be evident, however, that the overall account of the common good presented here departs significantly from much of Novak's account.

[27] See National Conference of Catholic Bishops, *Economic Justice for All*, no. 77, section heading. Also see the discussion of justice in chapter 7 of the present book.

inclined to think of human rights in individualistic terms and to give priority to the civil and political rights to free speech, due process of law, and political participation. In contrast to this emphasis, the Eastern bloc and many nations in the Southern hemisphere influenced by Marxism and socialism stressed social and economic rights, such as those to adequate food, education, basic health care, and other aspects of economic development. A commitment to intellectual solidarity not only suggests that each of these approaches ought to learn from the strengths of the other, but also that the opposition between individual freedoms on the one hand and mutual solidarity in society on the other is a false dichotomy. Persons can live in dignity only when they live in a community of freedom, a community in which both personal initiative and social solidarity are valued and embodied. The accountability, transparency, and representativeness of international institutions are political aspects of the linkage of personal initiative and social solidarity in the global setting today. International institutions that are open and accountable provide the political space that is a central concern of civil and political rights. The linkage between initiative and solidarity also has economic dimensions. It will be manifest only when persons have both the material and economic resources that make agency in community possible, namely social and economic rights. Thus both civil-political and social-economic rights raise challenges to the unequal and non-reciprocal patterns of participation in many international institutions today. This sets a large agenda before the key actors of our interdependent world. This agenda can give normative guidance for the direction in which global social, political, and economic institutions should move.[28]

From a pragmatic point of view, therefore, a human rights proviso to the celebration of difference is no small matter. Nor is it an

---

[28] For a thoughtful discussion of how human rights that cannot be immediately implemented still remain rights and provide normative guidance for the direction of institutional change, see Amartya Sen, *Development as Freedom*, pp. 228–231. Here Sen appeals to Kant's notion of "imperfect duties" to describe the obligation to develop institutions that will ultimately make it possible to secure rights that cannot be feasibly attained at present. This argument is further developed in United National Development Programme, *Human Development Report 2000: Human Rights and Human Development* (New York/Oxford: Oxford University Press, 2000), chap. 1, esp. pp. 24–26. Chapter 1 of this Report was written by Sen. It provides the conceptual framework for its treatment of the relation between rights and development (see p. v).

alternative to a normative vision of the common good. Universal human rights and the global common good are mutually implicating; you cannot have one without the other. The attainment of basic human rights, of course, is not the fullness of the shared good of which the human race is capable. That fullness would only be attained in the community Christians know as the communion of saints and the reign of God and the more secular thinkers call utopia. Securing human rights or even taking significant steps toward securing them, however, is a minimal requirement of respect for the dignity of all the members of the human moral community. Seeking to meet this normative requirement, therefore, will call for significant alterations in some, perhaps many, of the political, economic, and cultural interactions that are in fact shaping the global network of our world today.

The shape the global system will ultimately take is very much up-for-grabs today. One possible future is a new hegemony by the powerful over the weak, in which the economic and military power of the few controls and dominates the many. This, of course, is what many of the critics of globalization fear is actually occurring. At the same time, it is highly unlikely that efforts simply to withdraw from the global web will secure a decent life for those who are presently on the weaker side of the power equation. Thus we need practical ways to pursue forms of global interdependence that embody the normative conception of justice advocated here. Such a strategic agenda is necessary if we are to avoid relegating the idea of the global common good to the status of an excessively abstract ideal. To be sure, normative considerations do not provide a map for policy or a blueprint for institutions. But some further considerations about the dynamics of global change today show the relevance of the norms of justice, participation, and solidarity for the direction in which things could move.

A NETWORK OF CRISSCROSSING COMMUNITIES

One possible response to the new patterns of interdependence linking people together across the borders of nation-states today would be the establishment of something analogous to world government to oversee the pursuit of the common good globally. Such a response

presumes that international government is needed to secure the
common good globally, just as national governments are needed
to secure the shared good of people within a geographic territory.
Following this line of argument, in 1963 Pope John XXIII suggested that an international system composed of nation-states was
no longer adequate to secure well-being in an increasingly interconnected world. In his words, "Under the present circumstances
of human society both the structure and form of governments as
well as the power which public authority wields in all the nations of
the world, must be considered inadequate to promote the universal
common good." To remedy this inadequacy, John XXIII proposed
the establishment of a "public authority, having worldwide power
and endowed with the proper means for the efficacious pursuit of
its objective," namely, the world-wide common good. Therefore he
asserted that normative moral considerations require that a world-
wide "public authority" be established. John XXIII's proposal was
carefully qualified by his insistence that this authority be freely
agreed to by the peoples of the world. He also asserted that this
global authority be regulated by the principle of subsidiarity; the
role of nation-states and other communities and associations of less-
than-global scope must not be abolished or repressed.[29] John XXIII
gave particular endorsement to the founding of the United Nations,
with its goals of promoting peace among nations based on mutual
respect and of protecting the human rights of all persons and the
legitimate right of all nations.[30]

John XXIII notably anticipated some of the possibilities that
have been emerging in recent years about the restructuring of the
international system in light of the new linkages of interdependence we have been considering. Considerably more needs to be
said, however, about how to pursue normative concerns about the
common good and global social justice. John XXIII's almost exclusive focus on a possible international "public authority" suggests
that something like a world government, with all his qualifications
concerning subsidiarity presumed, can be the main institutional
vehicle that carries us toward a fuller achievement of shared well-
being under conditions of globalization. The issue is more complex

---

[29] Pope John XXIII, *Pacem in Terris*, nos. 135–145.   [30] *Ibid.*, nos. 135–138.

than this. Pursuit of the shared good under conditions of interdependence will make normative demands on nearly all people and communities. These range from intimate relationships and families, through local, national, and regional communities that are geographically defined, to historically rooted religious and cultural communities that cut across borders, to the growing number of new transnational associations that include both corporations and NGOs. The behavior of all these communities will have an impact on whether interdependence leads to common goods or common bads. Sometimes these impacts will be indirect and remote; sometimes they will be direct and proximate. But in either case, a normative perspective that takes the common good seriously will be relevant to these communities' self-understanding and decisions. An exclusive focus on global political institutions or authorities like the UN thus runs the risk of overlooking some of the important normative implications of a common good ethic under conditions of interdependence. Here we will indicate some of these implications, though certainly not all of them.

One of the principal reasons that the notion of the common good has new relevance on the global level is the declining autonomy and independence of states. In this regard Pope John XXIII's analysis of the situation was remarkably prescient about political and economic tendencies that were only beginning to appear in the early 1960s. Today, however, economic and other forms of interdependence increasingly highlight the fact that the borders of existing nation-states provide an inadequate frame of reference for thinking about the good life. The ability of the communities defined by national borders to secure the well-being of their citizens through independently determined policies is declining. Interdependence thus blurs a central feature of the map of social existence that is the legacy of modern history, namely the independence and autonomy of the peoples of territorial nation-states. One could argue, of course, that the new patterns of globalization should not be allowed to disrupt the political, economic, and cultural patterns to which people have grown accustomed on the basis of their experience of the history of modern states. An ethos that grants central value to the autonomy of both individuals and well-established political or cultural communities will be inclined in this direction. But it is far from clear that such a "don't tread on me" stance will in fact lead to better lives for those inclined to advocate it.

The pressures of interdependence are thus leading many governments to pursue the traditional task of seeking the good of their own people by "pooling" or sharing their sovereignty with other nation-states. The prime example of this phenomenon is, of course, the European Union, which is neither a single superstate nor simply a concert of entirely independent states bound together by *ad hoc* treaty. This phenomenon of pooled sovereignty is present, though considerably less developed, in other regions of the world. It is often restricted to a specific domain of interdependence, such as free trade in the case of the North American Free Trade Agreement, or human rights in the case of the Inter-American Commission and Court on Human Rights. But there are noteworthy signs, however, that other regions are recognizing the potential benefits to their own people of relinquishing claims to absolute national independence. For example, African countries have recently begun efforts to transform the very weak Organization for African Unity into an African Union based on the European model.[31] Realizing this goal will be highly problematic at best. Nevertheless, it is significant that the pressures of globalization have precipitated greater political movement toward pan-Africanism than did the cultural and ideological commitments of the fathers of African independence such as Kwame Nkruma and Leopold Senghor. Such pressures suggest that the good of self-determination can be sought more effectively as a joint undertaking with other countries than through sovereign independence or state autonomy. Such a suggestion is very much in line with the republican idea that the freedom of self-governance is a joint undertaking with others, not a solo performance. That key aspects of the human good of freedom can only be attained in a community of freedom is becoming more evident under conditions of interdependence than in the midst of seventeenth-century religious wars in Europe or in the anti-colonial struggles of the mid-twentieth century. This suggests that the transnational common

---

[31] See the documents approved at the 37th OAU Assembly of Heads of State and Government, Lusaka, Zambia (July 2–11, 2001). Available on the OAU Internet site at: http://www.oau-oua.org/Lusaka/Documents.htm (downloaded July 27, 2001).

good not only has renewed normative force today but also political salience and practical relevance.

Factual interdependence raises a direct challenge to the effectiveness of the government of nation-states acting on their own, rather than to the legal standing of these governments under international law.[32] There is little doubt that nation-states will remain central actors on the global stage. The legal sovereignty of national governments continues to be an important tenet of international law and can be expected to remain so. In fact, international organizations such as the United Nations and its regional counterparts such as the Organization of American States depend on sovereign states for their existence. These international organizations are constituted and controlled by states. The same is true of international agencies and conventions governing finance, trade, the environment, the movement of refugees, and many other domains of activity that cross national borders.

Nevertheless, national governments acting autonomously are less able to produce the conditions of the good life for their citizens than in the past. For example, sustaining global public goods such as an intact environment, prevention of the spread of HIV/AIDS, and limiting the deployment of nuclear, biological, and chemical weapons as well as small arms and landmines clearly require cooperation across state borders. Thus states are sometimes willing to cede some aspects of their formal sovereignty and independence of action in the interest of effectiveness. In Keohane's words, "Governments find they must enter into international agreements limiting their own legal freedom of action, in order to obtain the desired action from their partners."[33] The creation of a common European currency is a powerful example of how much the nations of Western Europe think they have to gain from exchanging some of their independence for expected benefits of economic cooperation. The extent and subject of this cooperation, however, remain very much open questions, as is clear in the controversies over the

[32] Robert O. Keohane, "Sovereignty, Interdependence, and International Institutions," in Linda B. Miller and Michael Joseph Smith, eds., *Ideas and Ideals: Essays on Politics in Honor of Stanley Hoffmann* (Boulder, CO: Westview Press, 1993), pp. 91–107, at p. 93.
[33] *Ibid.*, p. 94.

Kyoto protocol on climate protection and over WTO rules affecting intellectual property rights to drugs for the treatment of AIDS in Africa.[34] It is no accident that such controversies are most likely to arise when the benefits and costs of cooperation will be unequally distributed in the short or medium terms.

A strategic question, then, is how to make the international organizations and regimes of cooperation supportive of the well-being of the people within the cooperating states and of people of the world more generally. Negatively put, this is the issue of the democratic deficit of international agencies discussed above. Although international institutions seek to protect and generate transnationally shared goods that individual states cannot secure on their own, there is a danger that these institutions will become agents of the well-being of some people but not others. The most likely distortion, of course, is that they will become agents of those with the power and the money. To counter this danger, international organizations and regimes must be made more accountable to the people whose well-being they affect. Otherwise transnational cooperation could lead to a net loss for the good of democratic self-governance despite such institutions' potential for enhancing self-governance. Such accountability can be increased by giving those affected more direct political representation in their decisions. For example, input into the decisions of the WTO and IMF could come not only from trade and finance ministries but also from governmental agencies concerned with labor and environmental matters. Countries with fewer resources but greater stakes should have some say regarding policy outcomes that seriously affect them. Given both the potentially high benefits of global economic integration for some, and its potentially great harms for others, some type of formal representation in the process of decision-making seems one of the conditions of legitimacy for emerging international institutions.

Indeed, the political economist Dani Rodrik has placed a hesitant bet that efforts to make an increasingly integrated world economy responsive to the well-being of those it affects will lead to the development of federal structures of global governance in the future. He argues that increasing the legitimacy of international

---

[34] Scott Barrett, "Montreal versus Kyoto: International Cooperation and the Global Environment," and Lincoln C. Chen, Tim G. Evans, and Richard A. Cash, "Health as a Global Public Good," in I. Kaul, *et. al.*, *Global Public Goods*, pp. 192–219, 284–304.

institutions would itself benefit both those who see themselves as the current losers in the global economy, such as labor and environmental groups, and those who are the current winners, like exporters, transnational businesses, and financial interests. Without such legitimacy, economic integration is likely to produce a backlash in the name of both the economic interests of those who suffer its pain and of the citizenship rights of representation and self-government that are increasingly valued throughout the world.[35] Rodrik acknowledges, however, that such participatory, federal governance of international institutions is a possible direction over the long term and that more "realistic" solutions are needed in the short run. These include strengthening the multilateral institutions themselves, more consistent reliance on international standards, and providing "escape clauses" to these standards when countries or groups within them are disproportionately harmed.[36]

Such formal democratization of the governance of global institutions is, however, only one of the ways that their legitimacy as vehicles of a genuinely global common good ought to be pursued. As Keohane and Nye point out, domestic democratic politics within countries does not occur only at focused points of decision such as formal legislative votes or popular elections. It also occurs in the long intervals between elections through media attention, the formation of public opinion in public debate, lobbying, interest-group agitation, and even protests.[37] There are significant analogues to all of these manifestations of democratic self-governance in the transnational arena, even though their influence is considerably less direct than in the domestic politics of democratic countries. Developing forms of governance that will serve the common good of those affected by globalization will require strengthening the capacity of these less formal modes of influence. It will also mean deepening the commitment of those who exert this less formal influence to the well-being of a broadened range of global stakeholders. If public opinion and the agitation that it leads to remain narrowly focused, there is risk of simply transferring interest group politics

---

[35] Dani Rodrik, "How Far Will International Economic Integration Go?" *Journal of Economic Perspectives* 14, no. 1 (Winter, 2000), 177–186, at 185.
[36] Rodrik, "Governance of Economic Globalization," in Nye and Donahue, eds., *Governance in a Globalizing World*, pp. 347–365, at p. 364.
[37] Keohane and Nye, "Introduction" to Nye and Donahue, eds., *Governance in a Globalizing World*, pp. 32–36.

to the global level. On the other hand, if awareness of the mutual
vulnerability and potential mutual benefits of reciprocal interdependence can be increased among larger segments of the world's
people, these less formal channels of democratic politics can be
crucial to pursuing the global common good. Pursuit of the intellectual solidarity discussed above will, therefore, have important
practical consequences in the political and economic domains of
globalization. The dynamics of culture, politics, and economics all
occur on the same planet and constantly interact with each other.
Thus the development of cultural orientations in which solidarity
has a higher value will be crucial to generating forms of global
politics and economics that are socially just. If cultural identities
can evolve in ways that grant increased value to solidarity, significant positive political and economic consequences for the global
common good will become more likely.[38]

Incipient movement of public opinion toward a stronger sense of
responsibility across international borders is evident on a variety of
fronts. Instantaneous communication makes the territorial borders
between nation-states almost entirely porous to the transmission of
information about what is going on in the larger world. Governments have little control over the flow of politically relevant information. This information explosion opens extensive new possibilities for action by non-governmental organizations with grass-roots
constituencies. These NGOs press both national governments and
international organizations for action on numerous issues. Jessica
Mathews maintains that the computer and telecommunications
revolution is having a major impact on the loci of power in international affairs: "In every sphere of activity, instantaneous access
to information and the ability to put it to use multiplies the number of players who matter and reduces the number who command
great authority. The effect on the loudest voice – which has been
government's – has been the greatest."[39]

---

[38] The so-called "constructivist" school of international relations theory stresses the potential for such cultural influence on the political and economic aspects of international
affairs. See Stephen M. Walt, "International Relations: One World, Many Theories,"
Foreign Policy (Spring, 1998), 29–46; Alexander Wendt, "Anarchy Is What States Make of
It: The Social Construction of Power Politics," *International Organization* 46, no. 2 (Spring,
1992), 391–425.
[39] Mathews, "Power Shift," 51.

This information revolution and the resulting growth of the role of NGOs are already having significant effects on the exercise of international responsibility, both for good and for ill. The role of human rights NGOs is a prime example of this positive effect. But NGOs, like all other social agents, are subject to the tunnel vision of seeing the world only in light of the specific issues that concern them.[40] The instantaneous transmission of television images of human suffering can also have both positive and negative influences on the public sense of solidarity and moral responsibility. Michael Ignatieff has pointed out how it can lead to a greater public compassion and can stimulate movement toward a global order in which human rights play a normative role in foreign policy. On the other hand, repeated exposure to images of violence and starvation can give rise to public moral disgust, leading to a haughty sense of superiority, a deepened perception of the divisions between the civilized "us" and the savage "them."[41] Such disgust leads either to disengagement or to a righteous quest for hegemony in the name of civilization.

For example, the case of American intervention in Somalia showed how public opinion can swing abruptly from compassion to disgust. Public compassion led to US intervention on behalf of starving children whose bloated bellies had been seen on television screens in American living rooms. When a dead American soldier was dragged through the streets of Mogadishu by a Somali warlord and his clan, however, the resulting disgust led to total American disengagement. This withdrawal set the stage for American passivity in the face of the Rwandan genocide that slaughtered 800,000 persons and displaced two and a half million more. As former United Nations Undersecretary General Brian Urquhart has pointed out, these gyrations of opinion and policy were bad for the people of Somalia, disastrous for the victims in Rwanda, destabilizing for much of Africa, and harmful to the credibility of the United Nations.[42]

---

[40] *Ibid.*, 64.

[41] Michael Ignatieff, *The Warrior's Honor: Ethnic War and the Modern Conscience* (New York: Henry Holt, 1997), pp. 10 and 72–108.

[42] Brian Urquhart, "Looking for the Sheriff," *New York Review of Books* 45, no. 12 (July 16, 1998), 50–51.

On balance, though, the effect of the globalization of politically relevant information on a sense of responsibility seems solidly positive. Over the past several decades there has been a dramatic increase in the number of transnational organizations rooted in the non-governmental public sphere of civil society (NGOs).[43] They include transnational advocacy networks concerned with human rights, poverty reduction, justice for women, asylum for refugees, protection of the environment, combating AIDS, banning of landmines, establishment of an International Criminal Court, and many other important issues. Many of these are working to move public opinion, national governments, and international institutions to adopt norms of action that reflect greater solidarity with those who are vulnerable and marginalized in the present global order. They provide information that will help frame the issues that will be decided by governments and international institutions in ways that highlight their normative significance. They promote the implementation of these norms by exerting leverage on the relevant bodies and by monitoring outcomes so decision-makers can be held accountable.[44]

Many of these transnational movements working for global justice are somewhat paradoxically focused on concerns for particular groups of people – women, the poor, specific ethnic and cultural minorities. This poses the most challenging question raised by the phenomenon of globalization – how to achieve effective and universal respect for the common humanity of all people even in the midst of their differences.[45] Neither a commitment to universality alone nor to cultural differences alone will provide an adequate moral stance toward a globalizing world. Effective respect for both

---

[43] The number of international NGOs rose from just over 1,000 to more than 5,000 over the second half of the twentieth century. See Held *et al.*, *Global Transformations*, p. 54, Figure 1.1.
[44] Margaret E. Keck and Kathryn Sikkink, *Activists Beyond Borders: Advocacy Networks in International Politics* (Ithaca, NY: Cornell University Press, 1998), pp. 2–3, 16–25. For a similar breakdown of the roles played by transnational NGOs see L. David Brown, Sanjeev Khagram, Mark H. Moore, and Peter Frumkin, "Globalization, NGOs, and Multisectoral Relations," in Nye and Donahue, eds., *Governance in a Globalizing World*, pp. 271–296, at 283.
[45] See Held, *et al.*, *Global Transformations*, p. 369, and Roland Robertson, *Globalization: Social Theory and Global Culture* (London: Sage Publications, 1992), esp. pp. 177–181.

the universal dignity of all people and for the cultural and religious differences among them are both needed. How to combine these two kinds of commitments is the central moral and cultural problem of our time.

A reconstructed and developed understanding of the tradition of the common good can help address this challenge. A normative vision of the common good in its full global reach involves commitment to a community that is both universal in scope and that takes the differences among peoples and cultures with the full seriousness they deserve. Authentic universality can only be achieved by an inclusive community that does not project its own vision of the good life on others in an imperialistic fashion. But authentic universality calls for more that simply leaving others who are different alone. In a globalizing world we are fated to interact across the cultural and religious boundaries that have for so long divided the world into different camps. Today the question is not whether there will be such interaction, but whether it will be peaceful or violent, mutual or hegemonic. If it is to be peaceful and mutual, it will call for interaction that requires both listening and speaking in a genuine conversation across the many kinds of boundaries that have divided the world in the past and that continue to divide it today. This is intellectual solidarity. It will also call for a form of social justice that enables diverse peoples to participate actively in contributing to and benefiting from the emergent patterns of global interdependence that affect them. This is social solidarity.

Whether today's radical shifts in the patterns of international interaction turn out to be good or bad, therefore, is both an intellectual, cultural question and a social, institutional question. In Stanley Hoffmann's view, a positive outcome will require that the liberal tradition with its stress on tolerance "be thoroughly reconstructed – and that task has not proceeded very far, either in its domestic or international dimensions."[46] This is the intellectual challenge that is addressed to cultural and religious communities whose norms will exert either positive or negative influence on international decisions and institutions. Reflection on the common good can

---

[46] Stanley Hoffmann, "The Crisis of Liberal Internationalism," *Foreign Policy* 98 (1995), 159–177, at 177.

make an indispensable contribution to a normative framework oriented toward the inclusive well-being of the people affected by globalization. Whether such a normative vision emerges will, in turn, help decide whether the requisite institutional and governmental innovations occur.[47] Such social innovation in transnational finance, trade, and governance is needed to bring a minimal level of well-being to the majority of the world's people today.

The complexity of these intellectual and social challenges is indeed daunting. Is it really possible to envision normative and social innovations occurring on such a wide geographical scale and on levels ranging from the local, to the national, to the international and transnational? The task might be made a bit less overwhelming by an appeal to historical memory. A number of scholars have recently suggested that there are significant analogies between the structure of medieval European society and the future we now face. For example, the distinguished scholar of international politics Hedley Bull has asked whether we may be witnessing the emergence of a "a modern and secular equivalent of the kind of universal political organization that existed in Western Christendom in the Middle Ages."[48] In the medieval system, rulers and nation-states were not sovereign. Rather, authority was diffused among multiple agents of government, including barons and dukes, princes, the Holy Roman emperors, bishops, and the pope. There was no one supreme authority over a given segment of the population, so the loyalties of these populations were multiple. Medieval politics was not a politics of the nation-state and of nationalism. The nation-state that has structured public life in Europe since the sixteenth century and that has spread throughout the world since the mid-twentieth century had not yet been invented. Politics was structured in a quite different way than we have come to take for granted over the past few centuries.

Bull did not himself think that the emergence of a "neomedieval" way of organizing the world was likely or probably even desirable. His reflections on this matter were written a quarter of a century ago, before the issues of globalization had become as salient as they have in our day. Others who have more recently

47 Mathews, "Power Shift," 66.
48 Hedley Bull, *The Anarchical Society* (London: Macmillan, 1977), p. 254.

studied the phenomenon of globalization and the new influence of transnational actors have been returning to Bull's thinking to propose that an accountable global system might in fact bear some significant similarities to the European medieval order.[49] This does not mean, of course, that our globalizing world is evolving into a kind of neo-Christendom or that the European *ancien régime* can or should be reestablished. The world is far too religiously and culturally pluralistic to revive Christendom, and suggestions that Europe serve as a model for the rest of the world have surely had their day. The medieval analogy, however, does suggest a fruitful way of thinking about the structural and political organization of the emerging international system. This analogy is based on certain similarities in the way the structures of the world today generate multiple and overlapping loyalties, as was true in premodern Europe. Political and communal loyalties today are becoming simultaneously more local and more transnational than the focused loyalty that patriots and nationalists of the modern era had to their state or nation.

An accountable form of governance in our world will have to be multilayered, including formal governmental bodies on local, national, regional, and international levels, but also comprised of intergovernmental regimes in which civil society-based NGOs play a key role.[50] Citizens in this world will have commitments to more than one community, including patriotic loyalties to a nation-state, but also likely including loyalties to a cultural or ethnic community, a profession, and one or more advocacy communities such as a labor union or a normatively committed group such as Amnesty International.[51] For many, these loyalties will include commitment to a religious community whose values transcend all other loyalties but that advocate a form of universal solidarity among all persons as fellow creatures of the transcendent God.

In the Europe of the medieval epoch, of course, the notion of the common good played a very important role in serious thinking about the direction of government, economics, and culture in a

[49] See Held, *et al.*, *Global Transformations*, p. 85, and Keck and Sikkink, *Activists Beyond Borders*, esp. pp. 209–217.

[50] The term "multilayered governance" is from Held, *et al.*, *Global Transformations*, pp. 62–77.

[51] For provocative discussions of these plural loyalties see Onora O'Neill, *Bounds of Justice* (Cambridge University Press, 2000), esp. chaps. 9 and 10; Amartya Sen, "Global Justice: Beyond International Equity," in Kaul, *et al.*, *Global Public Goods*, pp. 116–125.

world where nation-states did not exist. It also exerted practical influence, though as usual its promise was sometimes more evident in the breach than in the keeping. Is it too far-fetched to suggest that the idea of the common good could play an analogous role today? To go one step further, is it implausible that, in an era marked by unprecedented influence by NGOs, we might learn something from the largest NGO on the globe today that has also been the principal bearer of the common good tradition, namely the Catholic church? NGO influence today, of course, will have to be very different than was that of the church in medieval Europe, especially in taking religious and cultural pluralism with much greater seriousness. Such influence must also be accountable to norms of justice and to the people whose lives are affected, not only to insiders. Nonetheless, it may be fruitful to ask whether the Catholic community remembers something from its medieval history that could make a distinctive and perhaps even indispensable contribution to a globalizing world. This contribution could be a vision of social solidarity and justice based on the equal dignity of every member of the human family.

The religious and theological roots of such a just solidarity are entirely relevant to the complex task of responding to today's pressures of globalization. The easy but wrong way out when faced with these pressures is to seek the good life in some clearly bounded community. This is the source of the rise of enclaves, ethnonationalisms, and fundamentalisms so much in evidence today. These are destructive responses to the psychic, cultural, political, and economic weight of interdependence. If one is convinced however, that the ultimate good, the universal common good, is finally and authentically divine, one will be less tempted to absolutize any of the lesser solidarities that can be attained within history. As argued above, a Christian ethic can insist that none of the partial realizations of this ultimate common good should be confused with the real thing. Throughout the modern period of the supremacy of the nation-state system, faithful Christians have insisted that though patriotism is a virtue no state is authentically sovereign; only God is.[52] Today the Christian community can contribute a similar

---

[52] For a telling critique of the modern Western notion of sovereignty as applied to states and rulers, see Jacques Maritain, *Man and the State*, chap. 2, "The Concept of Sovereignty."

insight in a very different context. No solidarity that could be achieved by giving absolute loyalty to country, or ethnic group, or class, or movement, or even to some proposed world government, would finally be trustworthy. Indeed, unquestioned loyalty to any such community because of the shared good it can putatively provide would be a form of idolatry. Not only Christianity but all of the major religious traditions of the world have long known that idolatry is finally destructive; it never delivers what its gods promise. A Christian ethic and theology can therefore set people on guard against some of the most dangerous temptations of a newly globalizing world.

A Christian ethic and theology can also set people and communities free to build those solidarities and to work for those this-worldly aspects of the common good that can build up better forms of globalization. The common good that can be achieved in history is a pluralistic ensemble of goods. All of these goods can really, though imperfectly, reflect the ultimate good of the communion of all persons with God and each other in the reign of God and the communion of saints. Fidelity to this ultimate, transhistorical vision of the common good is not, therefore, a distraction from building up the forms of community and solidarity that are in fact achievable in history. Such fidelity is rather an empowerment for the work that we face today if we are to live well. Such work by Christians, of course, should go forward in partnership and dialogue with those holding other religious convictions and with non-believers as well. This work, though, calls for Christians to speak forth what they believe and hope about where the full common good lies. If they do so with the right combination of courage and humility, this will help bring the full common good closer for all.

The idea of the common good is an idea whose time has once again come. This book has tried to show that we need both a renewed understanding of the common good and a revitalized social commitment to it. This is evident in the kind of problems that must be faced in grappling with poverty in core American cities and in the dilemmas of an interdependent globe. Inner-city poverty highlights the negative consequences of sharp economic and class barriers between urban and suburban communities. Its presses us to pay greater attention to the mutual connections among people across the urban – suburban divide. Global interdependence points to the fact that these interconnections do not stop at national boundaries. In both of these domains we need to undertake the demanding task of developing persuasive, defensible, and usable ideas of the goods we can share in common. The alternative is to risk enduring common harms together. The choice today is not between freedom and community, but between a society based on reciprocal respect and solidarity and a society that leaves many people behind. This choice will have a powerful effect on the well-being of us all.

Bibliography

Electronic resources are separately listed below.

An-Na'im, Abdullahi Ahmed, *Toward an Islamic Reformation: Civil Liberties, Human Rights, and International Law*, Syracuse, NY: Syracuse University Press, 1990.

Annan, Kofi A., "Two Concepts of Sovereignty," *The Economist* (US edition), (September 18, 1999), 49.

Appiah, Kwame Anthony, *In My Father's House: Africa in the Philosophy of Culture*, New York/Oxford: Oxford University Press, 1992.

Appiah, Kwame Anthony and Gutmann, Amy, *Color Conscious: The Political Morality of Race*, Princeton, NJ: Princeton University Press, 1996.

Appleby, R. Scott, *The Ambivalence of the Sacred: Religion, Violence and Reconciliation*, Lanham, MD: Rowman and Littlefield, 1999.

Archibugi, Daniele, Held, David, and Köhler, Martin, eds., *Re-imagining Political Community: Studies in Cosmopolitan Democracy*, Stanford, CA: Stanford University Press, 1998.

Arendt, Hannah, *The Human Condition: A Study of the Central Dilemmas Facing Modern Man*, Garden City, NY: Doubleday Anchor, 1959.

Aristotle, *Nichomachean Ethics*, trans. Martin Ostwald, Indianapolis, IN: Bobbs-Merrill,1962.

Politics, trans. Benjamin Jowett, in *The Basic Works of Aristotle*, ed. Richard McKeon, New York: Random House, 1941, pp. 1127–1316.

Audi, Robert, "The Separation of Church and State and the Obligations of Citizenship," *Philosophy and Public Affairs* 18 (1989), 259–296.

Augustine, *Enarrationes in Psalmos*, Corpus Christianorum, Series Latina, vol. XXXIX, Turnhout, Belgium: Brepols, 1956.

De Doctrina Christiana (On Christian Doctrine), trans. D. W. Robertson, Indianapolis, IN: Bobbs-Merrill, 1958.

The City of God, trans. Henry Bettenson, London/New York: Penguin Books, 1972.

Bane, Mary Jo, "Poverty, Welfare, and the Role of the Churches," *America*, (December 4, 1999) 8–11.

Bane, Mary Jo, Coffin, Brent, and Thiemann, Ronald, eds., *Who Will Provide? The Changing Role of Religion in American Social Welfare*, Boulder, CO: Westview Press, 2000.

Barber, Benjamin, *Strong Democracy: Participatory Politics for a New Age*, Berkeley: University of California Press, 1984.

Bartlett, John, *Familiar Quotations*, revised and enlarged edition, ed. Emily Morrison Beck, Boston: Little, Brown, 1980.

Baxter, Michael J., "Review Essay: The Non-Catholic Character of the 'Public Church,'" *Modern Theology* 11, no. 2 (April, 1995), 243–258.

Bellah, Robert, Madsen, Richard, Sullivan, William M., Swidler, Ann, and Tipton, Steven M.,*Habits of the Heart: Individualism and Commitment in American Life*, Berkeley, CA: University of California Press, 1985.

Benhabib, Seyla, *Situating the Self: Gender, Community and Postmodernism in Contemporary Ethics*, New York: Routledge, 1992.

Berger, Peter, *An Invitation to Sociology: A Humanistic Perspective*, New York: Doubleday Anchor, 1963.

"Secularism in Retreat," *The National Interest* 46 (Winter, 1996/1997), 3–12.

Berger, Peter, and Luckmann, Thomas, *The Social Construction of Reality: A Treatise in the Sociology of Knowledge*, New York: Doubleday Anchor, 1967.

Billingsley, Andrew, *Mighty Like a River: The Black Church and Social Reform*, New York: Oxford University Press, 1999.

Blair, Erica, "Towards a Civil Society: Hopes for Polish Democracy," interview with Adam Michnik, *Times Literary Supplement* (February 19–25, 1988), 199.

Brackley, Dean, "Salvation and the Social Good in the Thought of Jacques Maritain and Gustavo Gutierrez," Ph.D. Dissertation, University of Chicago, 1980.

Brooks, David, "The Organization Kid," *Atlantic Monthly* 287, no. 4 (April, 2001), 40–54.

Brown, P. R. L., "St. Augustine's Attitude to Religious Coercion," *Journal of Roman Studies* 54 (1964), 107–116.

Bryk, Anthony S., Lee, Valerie E., and Holland, Peter B., *Catholic Schools and the Common Good*, Cambridge, MA: Harvard University Press, 1993.

Buber, Martin, *I and Thou*, second ed., New York: Charles Scribner's Sons, 1958.

Buckley, Michael J., *At the Origins of Modern Atheism*, New Haven, CT: Yale University Press, 1987.

Bull, Hedley, *The Anarchical Society*, London: Macmillan, 1977.

Callahan, Daniel, *What Kind of Life: The Limits of Medical Progress*, New York: Simon and Schuster, 1990.

"Bioethics: Private Choice and the Common Good," *Hastings Center Report*, (May/June, 1994), 28–31

False Hopes: Why America's Quest for Perfect Health is a Recipe for Failure, New York: Simon and Schuster, 1998.

Casanova, José, *Public Religions in the Modern World*, Chicago: University of Chicago Press, 1994.

Chicago Council on Foreign Relations, "American Public Opinion and US Foreign Policy 1999," ed. John E. Reiley, Chicago: Chicago Council on Foreign Relations, 1999.

Christiansen, Drew, "The Common Good and the Politics of Self-Interest: A Catholic Contribution to the Practice of Citizenship," in Donald Gelpi, ed., *Beyond Individualism: Toward a Retrieval of Moral Discourse in America*, Notre Dame, IN:University of Notre Dame Press, 1989.

Cicero, *De Re Publica*, trans. C. W. Keyes, Loeb Classical Library, Cambridge, MA: Harvard University Press, 1966.

Cohen, Joshua, ed., *For Love of Country: Debating the Limits of Patriotism*, Boston: Beacon Press, 1996.

Coleman, James, *Foundations of Social Theory*, Cambridge, MA: Harvard University Press, 1990.

Cox, Harvey, "The Transcendent Dimension: To Purge the Public Square of Religion is to Cut the Values that Nourish Us," *Nation* (January 1, 1996), 20–23.

Dallaire, Romeo A., "The End of Innocence: Rwanda, 1994," in Jonathan Moore, ed., *Hard Choices: Moral Dilemmas in Humanitarian Intervention*, Lanham, MD: Rowman and Littlefield, 1998, pp. 71–86.

Danziger, Sheldon and Gottschalk, Peter, *America Unequal*, Cambridge, MA: Harvard University Press, 1995.

DeKoninck, Charles, *De la primauté du bien commun contre les personnalistes. Le principe de l'ordre nouveau*, Québec/Montréal: Editions de l'Université Laval/Editions Fides, 1943.

Dewey, John, *The Public and Its Problems*, Athens, OH: Swallow Press/Ohio University Press, 1994; orig.: Henry Holt, 1927.

DiIulio, John, "The Lord's Work: The Church and the 'Civil Society Sector,'" *Brookings Review* (Fall, 1997), 27–35.

Dougherty, James, *The Fivesquare City: The City in Religious Imagination*, South Bend, IN: University of Notre Dame Press, 1980.

Douglass, R. Bruce and Hollenbach, David, eds., *Catholicism and Liberalism: Contributions to American Public Philosophy*, Cambridge: Cambridge University Press, 1994.

Downs, Anthony, *Neighborhoods and Urban Development*, Washington, D.C.: Brookings Institution, 1981.

"Cities, Suburbs, and the Common Good," *A Woodstock Occasional Paper*, Washington, D.C.: Woodstock Theological Center, 1991.

Dworkin, Ronald, *A Matter of Principle*, Cambridge, MA: Harvard University Press, 1985.

Eck, Diana L., *A New Religious America: How a "Christian Country" Has Become the World's Most Religiously Diverse Nation*, New York: HarperSanFrancisco, 2001.

Eck, Diana L. and the Pluralism Project at Harvard University, *On Common Ground: World Religions in America*, interactive multimedia, computer optical disc, New York: Columbia University Press, 1997.

Elshtain, Jean Bethke, *Women and War*, New York: Basic Books, 1987.

"Citizenship and Armed Civic Virtue: Some Critical Questions on the Commitment to Public Life," in Charles H. Reynolds and Ralph V. Norman, eds., *Community in America: The Challenge of Habits of the Heart*, Berkeley: University of California Press, 1988, pp. 47–55.

Eschmann, I. Th., "In Defense of Jacques Maritain," *The Modern Schoolman* 22 (1945) 183–208.

Esposito, John L., *The Islamic Threat: Myth or Reality*, New York: Oxford University Press, 1992.

Evans, Joseph W. and Ward, Leo R., eds., *The Social and Political Philosophy of Jacques Maritain: Selected Readings*, New York: Scribner's, 1955.

Fiss, Owen, "What Should Be Done for Those Who Have Been Left Behind?" *Boston Review* (Summer, 2000), 4–9.

Franklin, Robert M., *Another Day's Journey: Black Churches Confronting the American Crisis*, Minneapolis, MN: Fortress Press, 1997.

Fukuyama, Francis, *The End of History and the Last Man*, New York: Free Press, 1992.

Galston, William A., *Liberal Purposes: Goods, Virtues, and Diversity in a Liberal State*, Cambridge: Cambridge University Press, 1991.

Gannon, Thomas M., ed., *The Catholic Challenge to the American Economy: Reflections on the US Bishops' Pastoral Letter on Catholic Social Teaching and the US Economy*, New York: Macmillan, 1987.

Garrow, David J., *Bearing the Cross: Martin Luther King, Jr., and the Southern Christian Leadership Conference*, New York: William Morrow, 1986.

Geremek, Bronislaw, "Civil Society and the Present Age," in Geremek, et al., *The Idea of Civil Society*, Research Triangle Park, NC: The National Humanities Center, 1992.

Gibellini, Rosino, ed., *Paths of African Theology*, Maryknoll, NY: Orbis Books, 1994.

Gilder, George, *Wealth and Poverty*, New York: Basic Books, 1981.

Glenn, Charles L., *Choice of Schools in Six Nations: France, Netherlands, Belgium, Britain, Canada, West Germany*, Washington, D.C.: US Department of Education, Office of Educational Research and Improvement, Programs for the Improvement of Practice, 1989.

Gorostiaga, Xabier, "Geocultural Development," paper presented to the conference on "Desafíos éticos para el siglo XXI," Santiago, Chile, 1995.

Gremillion, Joseph, ed., *Food/Energy and the Major Faiths*, Maryknoll, NY: Orbis Books, 1978.

Gutmann, Amy and Thompson, Dennis, *Democracy and Disagreement*, Cambridge, MA: Harvard University Press, 1996.

Gutmann, Amy, ed., *Work and Welfare*, Princeton, NJ: Princeton University Press, 1998.

Hadden, Jeffrey K., "Religious Broadcasting and the Mobilization of the New Christian Right," *Journal for the Scientific Study of Religion* 26 (1987), 1–24.

Hassner, Pierre, "Morally Objectionable, Politically Dangerous: Huntington's *Clash of Civilizations* I," *The National Interest* 46 (Winter, 1996/97), 63–39.

Hauerwas, Stanley, *A Community of Character: Toward a Constructive Christian Social Ethic*, Notre Dame, IN: University of Notre Dame Press, 1981.

Hefner, Robert W., *Civil Islam: Muslims and Democratization in Indonesia*, Princeton, NJ: Princeton University Press, 2000.

Hehir, J. Bryan, "Church-State and Church-World: The Ecclesiological Implications," in The Catholic Theological Society of America, *Proceedings of the Forty-First Annual Convention* (1986), 54–74.

Held, David, McGrew, Anthony, Goldblatt, David and Perraton, Jonathan, *Global Transformations: Politics, Economics and Culture*, Stanford, CA: Stanford University Press, 1999.

Himmelfarb, Gertrude, *One Nation, Two Cultures*, New York: Alfred A. Knopf, 1999.

Hoffmann, Stanley, "The Crisis of Liberal Internationalism," *Foreign Policy* 98 (1995), 159–177.

Hollenbach, David, *Claims in Conflict: Retrieving and Renewing the Catholic Human Rights Tradition*, New York: Paulist Press, 1979.

Justice, Peace, and Human Rights: American Catholic Social Ethics in a Pluralistic World, New York: Crossroad, 1988; second printing: 1990.

"The Common Good Revisited." *Theological Studies* 50 (1989), 70–94.

"Religion and Political Life" *Theological Studies* 52 (1991), 87–106.

"Christian Social Ethics after the Cold War," *Theological Studies* 53 (1992), 75–95.

"Virtue, the Common Good, and Democracy," in Amitai Etzioni, ed., *New Communitarian Thinking: Persons, Virtues, Institutions, and Communities*, Charlottesville: University of Virginia Press, 1994, pp. 143–153.

"Contexts of the Political Role of Religion: Civil Society and Culture," *San Diego Law Review* 30 (1994), 879–901.

"Public Reason/Private Religion? A Response to Paul J. Weithman," *Journal of Religious Ethics* 22, no. 1 (1994), 39–46.

"Common Good," in Judith A. Dwyer, ed., *The New Dictionary of Catholic Social Thought*, Collegeville, MN: Liturgical Press, 1994, pp. 192–197.

"Civil Society: Beyond the Public-Private Dichotomy," *Responsive Community* 5 (Winter, 1994–1995), 15–23.

"Freedom and Truth: Religious Liberty as Immunity and Empowerment," in J. Leon Hooper and Todd Whitmore, eds., *John Courtney Murray and the Growth of Tradition*, Kansas City, MO: Sheed and Ward, 1996, pp. 129–148.

"Tradition, Historicity, and Truth in Theological Ethics," in James M. Childress and Lisa Sowle Cahill, eds., *Christian Ethics: Problems and Prospects*, Cleveland, OH: Pilgrim Press, 1996, pp. 60–75.

"The Common Good in the Postmodern Epoch: What Role for Theology?" in James Donahue and M. Theresa Moser, eds., *Religion, Ethics, and the Common Good*, Annual Publication of the College Theology Society, vol. 41, Mystic, CT: Twenty-Third Publications, 1996, pp. 3–22.

"Politically Active Churches: Some Empirical Prolegomena To A Normative Approach," in Paul Weithman, ed., *Religion and Contemporary Liberalism*, Notre Dame, IN: University of Notre Dame Press, 1997, pp. 291–306.

"Is Tolerance Enough? The Catholic University and the Common Good," *Conversations on Jesuit Higher Education* 13 (Spring, 1998), 5–15.

"Solidarity, Development and Human Rights: The African Challenge," *The Journal of Religious Ethics* 26, no. 2 (1998), 305–317.

"The Common Good and Urban Poverty," *America* (June 5–12, 1999), 8–11.

"Civil Rights and the Common Good: Some Possible Contributions of Religious Communities," in Gary Orfield and Holly J. Lebowitz, eds., *Religion, Race, and Justice in a Changing America*, New York: Century Foundation Press, 1999, pp. 169–174.

Hollinger, Robert, ed., *Hermeneutics and Praxis*, Notre Dame, IN: University of Notre Dame Press, 1985.

Holm, Hans-Henrik and Sørensen, Georg, eds., *Whose World Order? Uneven Globalization and the End of the Cold War*, Boulder, CO: Westview Press, 1995.

Hooper, J. Leon, *The Ethics of Discourse: The Social Philosophy of John Courtney Murray*, Washington, D.C.: Georgetown University Press, 1986.

Hooper, J. Leon, ed., *Religious Liberty: Catholic Struggles with Pluralism*, Louisville, KY: Westminster/John Knox Press, 1993.

Bridging the Sacred and the Secular: Selected Writings of John Courtney Murray, S.J., Washington, D.C.: Georgetown University Press, 1994.

Hunter, James Davison, *Culture Wars: The Struggle to Define America*, New York: Basic Books, 1991.

Huntington, Samuel P., "Religion and the Third Wave," *The National Interest* 24 (Summer, 1991), 29–42.

The Third Wave: Democratization in the Late Twentieth Century, Norman: University of Oklahoma Press, 1991.

"The Clash of Civilizations?" *Foreign Affairs* 72 (Summer, 1993), 22–49.

The Clash of Civilizations and the Remaking of World Order, New York: Simon and Schuster, 1997.

"The Erosion of American National Interests," *Foreign Affairs* 76, no. 5 (September/October, 1997), 28–49.

Ignatieff, Michael, *The Warrior's Honor: Ethnic War and the Modern Conscience*, New York: Henry Holt, 1997.

Juergensmeyer, Mark, *Terror in the Mind of God: The Global Rise of Religious Violence*, Berkeley: University of California Press, 2000.

Kanbur, Ravi and Lustig, Nora, "Why Is Inequality Back on the Agenda?" Department of Agricultural, Resource, and Managerial Economics Working Paper 99-14, Ithaca, NY: Cornell University Press, 1999.

Kant, Immanuel, *The Foundations of the Metaphysics of Morals*, trans. Lewis White Beck, Indianapolis, IN: Bobbs-Merrill, 1959.

Katz, Bruce, "Enough of the Small Stuff: Toward a New Urban Agenda," *Brookings Review* 18, no. 3 (Summer, 2000), 4–9.

Katz, Bruce, ed., *Reflections on Regionalism*, Washington, D.C.: Brookings Institution, 2000.

Katz, Bruce and Bradley, Jennifer, "Divided We Sprawl," *Atlantic Monthly* 284, no. 6 (December, 1999), 26–30, 38–42.

Kaul, Inge, Grunberg, Isabelle, and Stern, Marc A., eds., *Global Public Goods: International Cooperation in the 21 st Century*, New York and Oxford: Oxford University Press, 1999.

Keck, Margaret E. and Sikkink, Kathryn, *Activists Beyond Borders: Advocacy Networks in International Politics*, Ithaca, NY: Cornell University Press, 1998.

Keohane, Robert O., "International Institutions: Can Interdependence Work?" *Foreign Policy* 110 (Spring, 1998), 82–96.

Keohane, Robert O. and Nye, Joseph S., "Globalization: What's New? What's Not? (And So What?)" *Foreign Policy*, (Spring, 2000), 104–119.

Kepel, Gilles, *The Revenge of God: The Resurgence of Islam, Christianity and Judaism in the Modern World*, trans. Alan Braley, University Park: Pennsylvania State University Press, 1994. (French original: *La Revanche de Dieu:Chrétiens, Juifs et Musulmans à la reconquête du monde*, Paris: Editions du Seuil, 1991.)

Klein, Joe, "In God They Trust," *New Yorker*, (June 16, 1997), 40–48.

Kuhn, Thomas S., *The Structure of Scientific Revolutions*, second edn., Chicago: University of Chicago Press, 1970.

Kull, Steven and Destler, I. M., *Misreading the Public: The Myth of a New Isolationism*, Washington, D.C.: Brookings Institution, 1999.

Küng, Hans, ed., *Yes to a Global Ethic*, trans. John Bowden, New York: Continuum, 1996.

Küng, Hans and Kuschel, Karl-Josef, eds., *A Global Ethic: The Declaration of the Parliament of the World's Religions*, trans. John Bowden, New York: Continuum, 1993.

LaCugna, Catherine M., "The Relational God: Aquinas and Beyond," *Theological Studies* 46 (1985), 647–663.

Landy, Thomas M., "Connecting Poverty and Sustainability," *Boston College Environmental Affairs Law Review* 21 (Winter, 1994), 277–289.

Lasch, Christopher, *The Revolt of the Elites and the Betrayal of Democracy*, New York: W. W. Norton, 1995.

Levine, Daniel H., ed., *Churches and Politics in Latin America*, Beverly Hills, CA: Sage Publications, 1979.

Lindbeck, George, *The Nature of Doctrine: Religion and Theology in a Postliberal Age*, Philadelphia, PA: Westminster Press, 1984.

Lovin, Robin, "Perry, Naturalism, and Religion in Public," *Tulane Law Review* 63 (1989), 1517–1539.

MacIntyre, Alasdair, *After Virtue: A Study in Moral Theory*, Notre Dame, IN: University of Notre Dame Press, 1981.

  Whose Justice? Which Rationality? Notre Dame, IN: University of Notre Dame Press, 1988.

  Three Rival Versions of Moral Enquiry: Encyclopaedia, Genealogy and Tradition, Notre Dame, IN: University of Notre Dame Press, 1990.

Mamdani, Mahmood, *Citizen and Subject: Contemporary Africa and the Legacy of Late Colonialism*, Princeton, NJ: Princeton University Press, 1996.

Mandelbaum, Michael, "Foreign Policy as Social Work," *Foreign Affairs* 75, no. 1 (January/February, 1996), 16–32.

Mann, Michael, "Has Globalization Ended the Rise and Rise of the Nation-State?" *Review of International Political Economy* 4, no. 3 (Autumn, 1997), 472–496.

Maritain, Jacques, *The Person and the Common Good*, trans. John Fitzgerald, Notre Dame, IN: University of Notre Dame Press, 1966, originally published in 1947.

  Man and the State, Chicago: University of Chicago Press, 1951.

Markus, R. A., *Saeculum: History and Society in the Theology of Saint Augustine*, Cambridge: Cambridge University Press, 1970.

Markus, R. A., ed., *Augustine: A Collection of Essays*, New York: Doubleday, 1972.

Marsh, Charles, *God's Long Summer: Stories of Faith and Civil Rights*, Princeton, NJ: Princeton University Press, 1997.

Marty, Martin E., *The One and the Many: America's Struggle for the Common Good*, Cambridge, MA: Harvard University Press, 1997.

Marty, Martin E. and Appleby, R. Scott, eds., *Fundamentalisms Comprehended, The Fundamentalism Project*, vol. v, Chicago: University of Chicago Press, 1995.

Mathews, Jessica T., "Power Shift," *Foreign Affairs* 76, no. 1 (January/February, 1997), 50–66.

May, William W., ed., *Vatican Authority and American Catholic Dissent*, New York: Crossroad, 1987.

McLaughlin, Terence H., O'Keefe, Joseph, and O'Keefe, Bernadette, eds., *The Contemporary Catholic School: Context, Identity, and Diversity*, London/Washington, D.C.: Falmer Press, 1996.

Mead, Lawrence, *Beyond Entitlement: The Social Obligations of Citizenship*, New York: Free Press, 1986.

Meilander, Gilbert, *The Limits of Love: Some Theological Explorations*, University Park: Pennsylvania State University Press, 1987.

Miller, Linda B. and Smith, Michael Joseph, eds., *Ideas and Ideals: Essays on Politics in Honor of Stanley Hoffmann*, Boulder, CO: Westview Press, 1993.

Moore, Jonathan, ed., *Hard Choices: Moral Dilemmas in Humanitarian Intervention*, Lanham, MD: Rowman and Littlefield, 1998.

Mouw, Richard J. and Griffioen, Sander, *Pluralisms and Horizons: An Essay in Christian Public Philosophy*, Grand Rapids, MI: Eerdmans, 1993.

Murdoch, Iris, *The Sovereignty of Good*, New York: Schocken Books, 1971.

Murray, Charles, *Losing Ground: American Social Policy 1950–1980*, New York: Basic Books, 1984.

Murray, John Courtney, "Intercreedal Co-operation: Its Theory and Its Organization," *Theological Studies* 4 (1943), 257–286.

 We Hold These Truths: Catholic Reflections on the American Proposition, New York: Sheed and Ward, 1960.

 "The Declaration on Religious Freedom: Its Deeper Significance," *America* 114 (April 23, 1966), 592–593.

Naím, Moisés, "Washington Consensus or Washington Confusion?" *Foreign Policy* 118 (Spring, 2000), 87–103.

Namwera, L., *et al.*, eds., *Towards African Christian Liberation*, Nairobi: St. Paul Publications-Africa, 1990.

National Conference of Catholic Bishops, *Economic Justice for All: Pastoral Letter on Catholic Social Teaching and the US Economy*, Washington, D.C.: United States Catholic Conference, 1986.

Neilsen, Neils, *Revolutions in Eastern Europe: The Religious Roots*, Maryknoll, NY: Orbis Books, 1991.

Neuhaus, Richard J., ed., *Augustine Today*, Grand Rapids, MI: Eerdmans, 1993.

Niebuhr, H. Richard, *Christ and Culture*, New York: Harper and Row, 1951.

Novak, Michael, *Free Persons and the Common Good*, Lanham, MD: Madison Books, 1989.

Nussbaum, Martha C. and Glover, Jonathan, eds., *Women, Culture, and Development: A Study of Human Capabilities*, Oxford/New York: Clarendon/Oxford University Press, 1995.

Nussbaum, Martha C., *Cultivating Humanity: A Classical Defense of Reform in Liberal Education*, Cambridge, MA: Harvard University Press, 1997.

Nye, Joseph S. and Donahue, John D., eds., *Governance in a Globalizing World*, Washington, D.C.: Brookings Institution Press, 2000.

Nye, Joseph S., "Globalization's Democratic Deficit: How to Make International Institutions More Accountable," *Foreign Affairs* 80, no. 4 (July/August, 2001), 2–6.

O'Brien, David J. and Shannon, Thomas A., eds., *Catholic Social Thought: The Documentary Heritage*, Maryknoll, NY: Orbis Books, 1992.

Ogletree, Thomas, *Hospitality to the Stranger: Dimensions of Moral Understanding*, Philadelphia, PA: Fortress Press, 1985.

Okun, Arthur, *Equality and Efficiency: The Big Tradeoff*, Washington, D.C.: Brookings Institution, 1975.

Olyan, Saul M. and Nussbaum, Martha C., eds., *Sexual Orientation and Human Rights in American Religious Discourse*, New York: Oxford University Press, 1998.

O'Malley, John W., "Reform, Historical Consciousness, and Vatican II's Aggiornamento," *Theological Studies* 32 (1971), 573–601.

"Developments, Reforms, and Two Great Reformations: Towards a Historical Assessment of Vatican II," *Theological Studies* 44 (1983), 373–406.

"To Travel to Any Part of the World: Jerónimo Nadal and the Jesuit Vocation," *Studies in the Spirituality of Jesuits* 16, no. 2 (1984).

The First Jesuits, Cambridge, MA: Harvard University Press, 1993.

O'Malley, John W., Bailey, Gauvin A., Harris, Steven, Kennedy, T. Frank, eds., *The Jesuits, Cultures, Sciences, and the Arts, 1540–1773* Toronto: University of Toronto Press, 1999.

O'Neill, Onora, *Bounds of Justice*, Cambridge: Cambridge University Press, 2000.

Panikhar, K. N., "Globalization and Culture," *Voices from the Third World* 20, no. 1 (1997), 49–58.

Paris, Peter J., *The Social Teaching of the Black Churches*, Philadelphia, PA: Fortress Press, 1985.

Parker, Geoffrey, *The Thirty Years' War*, London: Routledge and Kegan Paul, 1984.

Patterson, Orlando, *The Ordeal of Integration: Progress and Resentment in America's "Racial" Crisis*, Washington, D.C.: Civitas Counterpoint, 1997.

Peterson, Grethe B., ed., *The Tanner Lectures on Human Values*, vol. XI, Salt Lake City: University of Utah Press, 1990.

Pieper, Josef, *The Four Cardinal Virtues: Prudence, Justice, Fortitude, Temperance*, trans. Richard Winston, *et al.*, New York: Harcourt, Brace, and World, 1965.

Pranger, Robert J., *The Eclipse of Citizenship: Power and Participation in Contemporary Politics*, New York: Holt, Rinehart and Winston, 1968.

Przywara, Erich, ed., *An Augustine Synthesis*, New York: Sheed and Ward, 1936.

Putnam, Robert, "The Prosperous Community: Social Capital and Public Life," *The American Prospect* 13 (Spring, 1993), 35–42.

Making Democracy Work: Civic Traditions in Modern Italy, Princeton, NJ: Princeton University Press, 1993.

"Bowling Alone: America's Declining Social Capital," *Journal of Democracy* 6, no. 1 (January, 1995), 65–78.

"Tuning In, Tuning Out: The Strange Disappearance of Social Capital in America," *PS: Political Science and Politics* 28, no. 4 (December, 1995), 664–665.

Bowling Alone: The Collapse and Revival of American Community, New York: Simon and Schuster, 2000.

Queen, Christopher S. and King, Sallie B., eds., *Engaged Buddhism: Buddhist Liberation Movements in Asia*, Albany, NY: State University of New York Press, 1996.

Rahner, Karl "Theological Reflections on the Problem of Secularization," *Theological Investigations*, vol. X, New York: Herder and Herder (1973), pp. 318–348.

"Toward a Fundamental Theological Interpretation of Vatican II," *Theological Studies* 40 (December, 1979), 716–727.

Ratzinger, Cardinal Joseph, *Church, Ecumenism and Politics: New Essays in Ecclesiology*, New York: Crossroad, 1988.

Rawls, John, *A Theory of Justice*, Cambridge, MA: Harvard University Press, 1972.

"The Idea of an Overlapping Consensus," *Oxford Journal of Legal Studies* 7 (1987) 1–25.

Political Liberalism, New York: Columbia University Press, 1993.

"The Idea of Public Reason Revisited," *University of Chicago Law Review* 64 (1997), 765–807.

The Law of Peoples, Cambridge, MA: Harvard University Press, 1999.

Reiley, John E., ed., "American Public Opinion and US Foreign Policy 1999," Chicago: Chicago Council on Foreign Relations, 1999.

Rescher, Nicholas, *Pluralism: Against the Demand for Consensus*, Oxford: Clarendon Press, 1993.

Richman, Alvin, "American Support for International Involvement: General and Specific Components of Post-Cold War Changes," *Public Opinion Quarterly* 60 (Summer, 1996) 305–321.

Rigney, Daniel and Kearl, Michael, "A Nation of Gray Individualists: Moral Relativism in the United States," *Journal of Social Philosophy* 25, no. 1 (Spring, 1994), 20–45.

Riordan, Patrick, *A Politics of the Common Good*, Dublin: Institute of Public Management, 1996.

Robertson, Roland, *Globalization: Social Theory and Global Culture*, London: Sage Publications, 1992.

Robinson, Randall, *The Debt: What America Owes to Blacks*, New York: Dutton, 2000.

Rodrik, Dani, "How Far Will International Economic Integration Go?" *Journal of Economic Perspectives* 14, no. 1 (Winter, 2000), 177–186.

Rorty, Richard, "The Priority of Democracy to Philosophy," in Merrill D. Peterson and Robert Vaughan, eds., *The Virginia Statute for Religious Freedom: Its Evolution and Consequences in American History*, Cambridge and New York: Cambridge University Press, 1988), 257–282.

"Religion as Conversation-Stopper," *Common Knowledge* 3, no. 1 (1994), 1–6.

Ross, Andrew C., *A Vision Betrayed: The Jesuits in Japan and China, 1542–1742*, Maryknoll, NY: Orbis Books, 1994.

Ryan, John A., *A Living Wage*, revised and abridged edn., New York: Macmillan, 1920.

Sandel, Michael, *Liberalism and the Limits of Justice*, Cambridge: Cambridge University Press, 1982.

Democracy's Discontent: America in Search of a Public Philosophy, Cambridge, MA: Harvard University Press, 1996.

Santurri, Edmund N., "Rawlsian Liberalism, Moral Truth, and Augustinian Politics," *Journal for Peace and Justice Studies* 8, no. 2 (1997) 1–36.

Sen, Amartya, *Development as Freedom*, New York: Alfred A. Knopf, 1999.

Shklar, Judith N., *Ordinary Vices*, Cambridge, MA: Harvard University Press, 1984.

"The Liberalism of Fear," in Nancy Rosenblum, ed., *Liberalism and the Moral Life*, Cambridge, MA: Harvard University Press, 1989, pp. 21–38.

Shue, Henry, *Basic Rights: Subsistence, Affluence, and US Foreign Policy*, Princeton, NJ: Princeton University Press, 1996.

Sidorsky, David, ed., *Essays on Human Rights: Contemporary Issues and Jewish Perspectives*, Philadelphia, PA: Jewish Publication Society of America, 1979.

Simon, Yves R., *The Tradition of Natural Law: A Philosopher's Reflections*, ed. Vukan Kuic, New York: Fordham University Press, 1967.

Society of Jesus (Jesuits), *Constitutions of the Society of Jesus and their Complementary Norms, A Complete English Translation of the Official Latin Texts*, Saint Louis, MO: Institute of Jesuit Sources, 1996.

Spence, Jonathan D., *The Memory Palace of Matteo Ricci*, New York: Viking, 1984.

Stedman, Stephen John, "The New Interventionists," *Foreign Affairs* 72, no. 1 (1992–1993), 1–17.

Stout, Jeffrey, *Ethics after Babel: The Languages of Morals and Their Discontents*, Boston: Beacon Press, 1988.

Taylor, Charles, *Philosophy and the Human Sciences*, Cambridge: Cambridge University Press, 1985.

   Sources of the Self: The Making of the Modern Identity, Cambridge, MA: Harvard University Press, 1989.

   Philosophical Arguments, Cambridge, MA: Harvard University Press, 1995.

Teilhard de Chardin, Pierre, *The Phenomenon of Man*, New York: Harper and Row, 1965.

TeSelle, Eugene, "The Civic Vision in Augustine's *City of God*," *Thought* 62 (1987), 268–280.

   "Toward an Augustinian Politics," *Journal of Religious Ethics* 16, no. 1 (1988), 87–108.

Thernstrom, Stephen and Thernstrom, Abigail, *America in Black and White: One Nation, Indivisible*, New York: Simon and Schuster, 1997.

Thomas Aquinas, *Summa contra Gentiles*, selections in *Basic Writings of Saint Thomas Aquinas*, 2 vols., ed. Anton C. Pegis, New York: Random House, 1945.

   Summa Theologica, 5 vols., trans. Fathers of the English Dominican Province, Allen, TX: Christian Classics, 1948.

Times Mirror Center for People and the Press, *The Pulse of Europe: A Survey of Political and Social Values and Attitudes*, Washington, D.C.: Times Mirror Center, 1991.

Tracy, David, *Plurality and Ambiguity: Hermeneutics, Religion, Hope*, San Francisco: Harper and Row, 1987.

United National Development Programme, *Human Development Report 2000: Human Rights and Human Development*, New York/Oxford: Oxford University Press, 2000.

Urquhart, Brian, "Looking for the Sheriff," *New York Review of Books* 45, no. 12 (July 16, 1998), 50–51.

Vatican Council II, *The Documents of Vatican II*, Abbott, Walter M. and Gallagher, Joseph, eds., New York: America Press, 1966.

Vatican Council II, *Vatican Council II: Constitutions, Decrees, Declarations*, revised translation, ed. Austin Flannery, Northport, NY: Costello Publishing Co., 1996.

Verba, Sidney, Schlozman, Kay Lehman, and Brady, Henry, *Voice and Equality: Civic Voluntarism in American Politics*, Cambridge, MA: Harvard University Press, 1995.

Vincent, R. J., *Human Rights and International Relations*, Cambridge: Cambridge University Press, 1986.

Viteritti, Joseph P., *Choosing Equality: School Choice, the Constitution, and Civil Society*, Washington, D.C.: Brookings Institution Press, 1999.

Wallis, Jim, *The Soul of Politics: A Practical and Prophetic Vision for Change*, Maryknoll, NY: Orbis Books, 1994.

Who Speaks for God? An Alternative to the Religious Right – A New Politics of Compassion, Community, and Civility, New York: Delacorte, 1996.

Walt, Stephen M., "International Relations: One World, Many Theories," *Foreign Policy* (Spring, 1998), 29–46.

Walzer, Michael, *Spheres of Justice: A Defense of Pluralism and Equality*, New York: Basic Books, 1983.

Obligations: Essays on Disobedience, War, and Citizenship, Cambridge, MA: Harvard University Press, 1970.

"The Way We Live Now Poll" results published in *The New York Times Magazine* (May 7, 2000), throughout this issue of the Magazine, 18 ff.

Weithman, Paul J., "Toward an Augustinian Liberalism," *Faith and Philosophy* 8, no. 4 (1991), 461–480.

Weithman, Paul, ed., *Religion and Contemporary Liberalism*, Notre Dame, IN: University of Notre Dame Press, 1997.

Wendt, Alexander, "Anarchy Is What States Make of It: The Social Construction of Power Politics," *International Organization* 46, no. 2 (Spring, 1992), 391–425.

West, Cornel, *Race Matters*, Boston: Beacon Press, 1993.

Keeping Faith: Philosophy and Race in America, New York: Routledge, 1993.

Williamson, John, ed., *Latin American Adjustment: How Much Has Happened?*, Washington, D.C.: Institute for International Economics, 1990.

Wilson, Paul, ed., *Open Letters: Selected Writings 1965–1990*, New York: Vintage, 1992.

Wilson, William Julius, *The Declining Significance of Race: Blacks and Changing American Institutions*, 2nd edn., Chicago: University of Chicago Press, 1980.

The Truly Disadvantaged: The Inner City, the Underclass, and Public Policy, Chicago: University of Chicago Press, 1987.

"Race-Neutral Programs and the Democratic Coalition," *The American Prospect* 1 (Spring, 1990), 82–89.

When Work Disappears: The World of the New Urban Poor, New York: Knopf, 1996.

The Bridge over the Racial Divide: Rising Inequality and Coalition Politics, Berkeley: University of California Press, 1999.

Wolfe, Alan, *One Nation After All: What Middle-Class Americans Really Think About: God, Country, Family, Racism, Welfare, Immigration, Homosexuality, Work, the Right, the Left and Each Other*, New York: Viking, 1998.

"Couch Potato Politics," *New York Times* (March 15, 1998), 17.

Moral Freedom: The Search for Virtue in a World of Choice, New York: W. W. Norton, 2001.

World Bank, *World Development Report 1997: The State in a Changing World*, Oxford and New York: Oxford University Press, 1997.

World Development Report 2000/2001, Oxford and New York: Oxford University Press, 2000.

Wuthnow, Robert, *Acts of Compassion: Caring for Others and Helping Ourselves*, Princeton, NJ: Princeton University Press, 1991.

Yoder, John Howard, *For the Nations: Essays Public and Evangelical*, Grand Rapids, MI: Eerdmanns, 1997.

"The Way We Live Now Poll," conducted for the *New York Times* by Blum and Weprin Associates Inc., results reported and interpreted in *New York Times Magazine* (May 7, 2000), pp. 18 ff.

Electronic resources

Bush, President George W., "Remarks by the President to the World Bank" (July 17, 2001). Available on the White House website at http://www.whitehouse.gov/news/releases/2001/07/20010717-1.html (downloaded December 16, 2001).

Chicago Council on Foreign Relations, "American Public Opinion and US Foreign Policy" (1995). Available at http://www.ccfr.org/publications/opinion/opinion95.html (downloaded December 16, 2001).

Chicago Council on Foreign Relations, "American Public Opinion and US Foreign Policy" (1999). Available at http://www.ccfr.org/publications/opinion/AmPuOp99.pdf (downloaded December 16, 2001).

Cleveland "Church in the City" program website available at http://www.citc.org (downloaded July 12, 2001).

Clinton, President Bill, speech during visit to Rwanda (March 25, 1998). Available at http://usinfo.state.gov/regional/af/prestrip/w980325a.htm (downloaded June 28, 2001).

Inter-University Consortium for Political and Social Research, *General Social Survey* (1994). Available at http://www.icpsr.umich.edu/gss/ (downloaded August 3, 2001).

Loury, Glenn C., "Social Exclusion and Ethnic Groups: The Challenge to Economics," Annual World Bank Conference on Development Economics, Washington, D.C. (April 28–30, 1999). Available on the website of the World Bank at http://www.worldbank.org/research/abcde/washington_11 /pdfs/loury.pdf (downloaded June 2, 2000).

Mahony, Cardinal Roger, Chairman, United States Catholic Bishops Conference Domestic Policy Committee, "Faith-Based and Community Initiatives" (February 12, 2001). Available at http://www.nccbuscc.org/sdwp/mahony.htm (downloaded July 12, 2001).

Nader, Ralph, "In the Public Interest" (December 7, 1999). Available on the website of Issues 2000 at http://www.issues2000.org/Ralph_Nader_Free_Trade.htm (downloaded June 20, 2001; no longer available).

Organization for African Unity, 37th OAU Assembly of Heads of State and Government, Lusaka, Zambia (July 2–11, 2001). Available on the OAU website at http://www.oau-oau.org/Lusaka/Documents.htm (downloaded July 27, 2001).

Pope John Paul II, Address to the Fiftieth General Assembly of the United Nations, New York (October 5, 1995). Available on the website of the Holy See, at http://www.vatican.va/holy_father/john_paul_ii/speeches/1996/documents/hf_jp-ii_spe_05101995_address-to-uno_en.html (downloaded July 25, 2001).

Message for World Day of Peace (January 1, 2000). Available at http://www.vatican.va/holy_father/john_paul_ii/messages/peace/documents/hf_jpii_mes_08121999_xxxiii-world-day-for-peace_en.html (downloaded July 24, 2001).

Program on International Policy Attitudes, *Americans on Globalization: A Study of US Public Attitudes*, "Globalization in General" (March 28, 2000). Available at http://www.pipa.org/OnlineReports/Globalization/contents.html (downloaded June 19, 2001).

Americans on Foreign Aid and World Hunger: A Study of US Public Attitudes (February 2, 2001). Available at http://www.pipa.org/OnlineReports/BFW/toc.html (downloaded June 19, 2001).

Public Broadcasting System, *Frontline*, "The Two Nations of Black America" (February 10, 1998). Available at http://www.pbs.org/wgbh/pages/frontline/shows/race/ (downloaded July 27, 2001).

Rivlin, Alice, "The Challenge of Affluence," Adam Smith Award Lecture, National Association of Business Economists (September 11, 2000). Available on the website of the Brookings Institution at http://www.brook.edu/es/urban/speeches/challengesofaffluence.pdf (downloaded July 10, 2001).

Russell Sage Foundation, *Multi-City Study of Urban Inequality* (1992 –). Available at http://www.russellsage.org/special_interest/index.htm (downloaded May 26, 2000).

Sachs, Jeffrey, "A New Global Consensus on Helping the Poorest of the Poor," World Bank's Annual Bank Conference on Development Economics (April 18, 2000). Available at http://orion.forumone.com/ABCDE/files.fcgi/210_Sachs.pdf (downloaded July 16, 2001).

Sweeney, John J., remarks at World Economic Forum, Davos, Switzerland (January 28, 2001). Available at http://www.aflcio.org/publ/speech2001/spo128.htm (downloaded April 16, 2001).

United Auto Workers Action Alert, "No Fast Track for Bush Administration" (June 4, 2001). Available at http://www.uaw.org/action/060401fasttrack.html (downloaded July 16, 2001; no longer available).

United States Catholic Conference, Administrative Board, "A Jubilee Call for Debt Forgiveness," (April 1999). Available on the website of the United States Catholic Bishops' Conference at http://www.nccbuscc.org/sdwp/international/adminstm.htm (downloaded July 24, 2001).

United States Conference of Mayors, "A Status Report on Hunger and Homelessness in America's Cities" (December 2000). Available at http://www.usmayors.org/uscm/hungersurvey/hunger2001.pdf (downloaded December 16, 2001).

US Metro Economies: The Engines of America's Growth, A Decade of Prosperity (2001). Available at http://www.usmayors.org/citiesdrivetheeconomy/index3.html (downloaded July 11, 2001).

Williamson, John, "What Should the Bank Think about the Washington Consensus?" (July 1999). Available at http://www.iie.com/papers/williamson0799.htm (downloaded July 16, 2001).

Index

Lightning Source UK Ltd.
Milton Keynes UK
UKOW02f1811091215

264436UK00001B/43/P